£6-00

Charles,
This is the 194
Why must editors
make changes
unilaterally?
Hope you enjoy
this effort.

Les
13 July 2011

Red Army's Do-It-Yourself Nazi-Bashing Guerrilla Warfare Manual

The Red Army's Do-It-Yourself Nazi-Bashing Guerrilla Warfare Manual

The Partisan's Companion

Updated and Revised Edition

1942

Edited by
Lester Grau and Michael Gress

CASEMATE PUBLISHERS
Philadelphia & Newbury

Published in the United States of America
and Great Britain in 2011 by
CASEMATE PUBLISHERS
908 Darby Road, Havertown, PA 19083
and
17 Cheap Street, Newbury RG20 5DD

Copyright 2011 © Lester Grau and Michael Gress

ISBN 978-1-61200-009-1
Digital Edition: ISBN 978-1-61200-020-6

Cataloging-in-publication data is available
from the Library of Congress and the British Library.

All rights reserved. No part of this book may be reproduced or
transmitted in any form or by any means, electronic or mechanical
including photocopying, recording or by any information storage
and retrieval system, without permission from the Publisher in
writing.

10 9 8 7 6 5 4 3 2 1

Printed and bound in the United States of America.

For a complete list of Casemate titles please contact:
CASEMATE PUBLISHERS (US) Telephone (610) 853-9131,
Fax (610) 853-9146 E-mail: casemate@casematepublishing.com

CASEMATE PUBLISHERS (UK) Telephone (01635) 231091,
Fax (01635) 41619 E-mail: casemate-uk@casematepublishing.co.uk

CONTENTS

	Foreword *by David M. Glantz*	vii
	Preface	ix
	THE PARTISAN'S COMPANION	1
	XXV Anniversary of the Great October Socialist Revolution	2
	On Partisan Warfare *by M.I. Kalinin*	
	ORDER of the Peoples' Commission of Defense *by J. Stalin*	
Chapter I.	FUNDAMENTAL PARTISAN TACTICS	20
Chapter II.	HOW THE FASCISTS ATTEMPT TO FIGHT THE PARTISANS	38
Chapter III	EXPLOSIVES AND DEMOLITION	44
Chapter IV.	COMBAT WEAPONS	70
Chapter V.	REVOLVER AND PISTOL	105
Chapter VI.	BE ABLE TO USE THE ENEMY'S WEAPONS	116
Chapter VII.	RECONNAISSANCE	142
Chapter VIII.	CAMOUFLAGE	153
Chapter IX.	HOW TO FIGHT ENEMY AVIATION	166
Chapter X.	ANTI-CHEMICAL PROTECTION	172
Chapter XI.	HAND-TO-HAND COMBAT	186
Chapter XII.	RENDERING FIRST AID	193
Chapter XIII.	MARCH AND BIVOUAC	200
Chapter XIV.	HOW TO STORE FOOD	215
Chapter XV.	LIFE IN THE SNOW	220
	Chapter Notes	232

FOREWORD

The June 1941 German invasion of the Soviet Union caught the Soviet leadership unprepared. As the remnants of the Red Army staggered back toward Moscow, the German forces swept over the Soviet countryside, capturing thousands of square miles of Soviet countryside. There was little to stop them. The Soviet Union desperately threw half-trained soldiers in their path while they looked for other ways to slow the Fascist invader. One possible weapon was guerrilla forces. While the Soviet leadership espoused guerrilla war, they did not want the common people to rise against the Germans. Even in these perilous times, the Soviet government wanted control. The Soviet answer was not to employ locals. Rather they quickly formed army reservists, party activists and secret police into partisan detachments and sent them into the German-occupied areas. Unfamiliar with the local area, surrounded by the enemy, and short on food and equipment, these initial detachments accomplished little, and few survived.

In 1942, when the Soviet Union decided to expand partisan war to incorporate the local Soviet citizens now living under German occupation, they did so while also extending Soviet control over the guerrillas. Military officers were assigned to lead the guerrilla bands. Military discipline was extended over the bands, and they were reorganized into squads, platoons, companies and battalions. A central partisan staff provided command and control over the guerrillas from Moscow. The partisans were trained to a common standard. Communist Party organizations were reintroduced, and the secret police watched the Germans—and the partisans.

By 1943, it was obvious that Germany was losing the war. The partisan ranks swelled as did the training requirements for the partisan commanders. This 1943 edition of the *Partisan's Companion* helped train the new guerrillas to a common standard in a hurry. It is an interesting document that covers partisan tactics, German counter-guerrilla tactics, demolitions, German and Soviet weapons, scouting, camouflage, anti-tank warfare, anti-aircraft defense, defense against a chemical attack, hand-to-hand combat, first aid, field living and winter survival. It can be read by individual partisans, but is really designed for squad and platoon-level instruction. This handbook contains the Soviet lessons of two bitter years of war and provides a good look at the tactics and training of a mature partisan force. It is geared to the partisan detachment (battalion) and smaller units. The partisans already were men and women who were expected to be reasonably self-sufficient, capable of making simple repairs and constructing their own shelter, camp ware, skis, snowshoes, and sleds. Their units were supposed to move and live clandestinely, harass the enemy, and support the Red Army through reconnaissance and attacks on the German supply lines. They were also the agents of Soviet power and vengeance in the occupied regions.

Soviet historians credit the partisans with tying down ten percent of the German army and with killing almost a million enemy soldiers. They clearly frustrated German logistics and forced the Germans to periodically sideline divisions to hunt the partisans. They clearly were part of the eventual Soviet victory over Germany.

This Soviet concept of central control of guerrilla warfare did not end with World War II. Communist guerrillas in China, Korea, and Vietnam were also centrally controlled, trained, and directed. Later, this model was employed in various "wars of national liberation" and even by the Fedayeen in Iraq.

So, I invite you to sit back and learn the not-so-arcane skills of being a Nazi-hunting partisan while freezing in the Pripet Marshes.

David M. Glantz
Mark W. Clark Visiting Professor of history
The Citadel, Charleston, South Carolina

PREFACE

This book has been more influential than its size might indicate. It is the final edition of the Soviet manual used to train guerrillas to fight the Nazis. It has gone through two previous editions, so this is the battle-tested material that a partisan really needed to know. It provided instruction in Russian on partisan tactics, field craft, weapons and survival. It assumed that the reader had little or no military training. The value of the book did not pass with the end of the war. During the 1960s and 1970s, the Soviet Union provided instruction on guerrilla war to citizens of the Third World, many of them students at the Patrice Lumumba University in Moscow. This instruction was designed to support "wars of national liberation" in Africa, Latin America, the Middle East and Asia. The Partisan's Companion was a base document for the course material used to train the future guerrillas.

During the Great Patriotic War (the Soviet Union's fight with Germany during World War II), the Soviet Union fielded the largest partisan force in history. During the war, there were some 1,100,000 men and women served as partisans in some 6,000 detachments.[1] The Soviet Union had been in existence for just over two decades, but Russia had a lengthy experience in guerrilla warfare.

Russian history is liberally sprinkled with peasant rebellions, breakaway Cossack hosts, run-away serfs, unhappy minorities and religious dissenters. The vastness of Russia allowed dissatisfied subjects to evade Tsarist control—and sometimes to attack the Tsar's representatives.

When Napoleon invaded Russia in 1812, guerrilla bands sprang up to harass the lines of communication and rear area of the invading armies. The guerrillas were initially local militia or poorly-armed peasants who fought as part of a village band—or a band formed from several hamlets. These guerrillas functioned independently of government control and their actions were not coordinated with the military plan. The guerrillas harassed invaders and made supply difficult, but were outside government control. Frequently they were merely brigands and opportunists loosely disguised as patriots. In order to establish some order, responsiveness and cooperation with the partisans, General Mikhail Barclay de Tolly and Field Marshal Pyotr Bagration formed partisan detachments from their regular forces to support their armies. These partisan detachments were composed of Cossacks, cavalry, infantry and Jaeger (light-infantry) forces. They sometimes cooperated with the local partisan bands, but the detachments more often fought on their own. The partisan forces grew into partisan armies. The primary lesson the Russians drew was that partisans are a useful ally when the actions of the peasant bands are subordinated and integrated into the unified plan of action of the regular armed forces.[2]

As the Russian Empire expanded, the Russian Army gained considerable experience battling guerrilla forces of conquered and incorporated peoples. This was particularly true in the Caucasus, particularly in Dagestan and Chechnya where Imam Shamil conducted a long guerrilla struggle against Tsarist control. The Chechen/Dagestan campaign was finally won by the axe and the rifle. The Russians deforested the mountain redoubts where the guerrillas hid while systematically capturing their fortress villages.

During the Russian Civil War, following directly on the heels of World War I, guerrilla forces fought across the torn Russian empire. Some of these guerrilla bands were clearly allied with the Reds or the Whites or the various foreign interventionist forces. Others were freelancers who formed temporary alliances with either or both sides. Still others were bands of nationalists, anarchists and brigands that were beyond any governments' control. The guerrillas that were allied with one side or another were often of limited value as their actions were uncoordinated with those of the maneuver forces.

During the 1920s and 1930s, the Soviet Union had its next major experience with partisan forces. Islamic nationalists in the Fergana Valley of Soviet Central Asia rose in revolt against Soviet rule. After several fumbling starts, the Soviets conducted a coordinated military, economic, political and internal development campaign that shattered and disbursed the *Basmachi* [bandit] movement.

Partisan warfare was a key element of Soviet defense planning during the early 1930s. Ya. K Berzin, the head of the Red Army Intelligence Service and Iona Yakir, the commander of the Kiev Military District established partisan detachments, schools, bases and weapons depots in the Kiev, Belorussian and Leningrad Military Districts. These detachments even participated in formal maneuvers. Cadres who were members of the military, party or secret police prepared to lead partisans in the event of an invasion. The military printed partisan training manuals and prepared other materials. The NKVD (the forerunner of the KGB) formed its own professional partisan detachments. Many of the partisan instructor cadre would serve in the Spanish Civil War.[3]

But preparation for partisan war was threatened by a crucial debate over the optimum strategy to defend the Soviet Union. There were two camps. The first, led by Marshal Tukachevsky, advocated an offensive or annihilation strategy. If the Soviet Union was invaded, the Red Army would respond with an offensive that would immediately invade the territory of the attacker and defeat the enemy on his own territory, forcing the enemy to bear the destruction of his own infrastructure. The second camp, led by General-Major Svechin, advocated a defensive or attrition strategy. If the Soviet Union was attacked, the border troops and Red Army would fight a deliberate retreat, drawing the enemy deep into the Soviet Union where his lines of communication would be overextended, his logistics strained and his strength dissipated. Then the Red Army would mass forces and launch a powerful counteroffensive, destroying the enemy.[4] Partisan warfare was a major component of the defensive strategy.

Eventually, the annihilation school won the debate and Defense Commissar Kliment Voroshilov declared that Soviet territory was inviolable and that the Red Army could handle any threat. The advocates of partisan warfare were branded defeatists or traitors who were preparing to hand the forward areas and their military stores over to a putative enemy. The partisan cadre were disbursed and purged. Many were imprisoned or killed. The manuals were destroyed.[5]

During 1938, the Soviet Union invaded Finland. The Finnish Army fought the Red Army to a standstill in the snow-covered forest swamps of Karelia. The Finns did this with a combination of regular forces manning the fortified Mannerheim Line and small raiding groups hitting the flanks and rear areas of their enemy.

Germany and the Soviet Union agreed to divide Poland and when Germany invaded Poland, the Red Army followed suit. The Red Army was deployed in Poland, forward of its forward defense lines, when Germany invaded the Soviet Union on 22 June 1941. The Red Amy was overwhelmed and could not launch an immediate offensive into Germany. The attrition school was right. Large areas of the Soviet Union fell under German control. In some areas, the Germans were initially greeted as liberators, however German attitudes of Slavs as *untermenschen* muted this welcome. While some inhabitants openly collaborated and supported the Germans, others resisted their arrival. Most bided their time. The Red Army was reeling back from a major defeat. Thousands of soldiers were captured or killed. Others were now trapped behind German lines. They eventually became the basis for the first partisan resistance units. The trapped soldiers took their weapons into the forests to resist the Germans.

The Soviet Union was fighting for its very existence, so it used every weapon at its disposal. This included guerrilla war. On 3 July 1941, Stalin addressed the nation by radio:

> In areas occupied by the enemy, guerrilla units, mounted and on foot, must be formed, diversionist groups must be organized to combat the enemy troops, to foment guerrilla warfare everywhere, to blow up bridges and roads, damage telephone and telegraph wires, set fire to forests, stores, transports. In the occupied regions conditions must be made unbearable for the enemy and his accomplices. They must be hounded and annihilated at every step and their measures frustrated.[6]

However, guerrilla war was a two-edged sword, since the stability of the state was threatened by these very partisans. During the Civil War, Red partisan bands flaunted Communist political and military control and some even defected to the Whites. The area now under Nazi control had recently suffered under the famine induced by the Soviet forced collectivization of agriculture. The area had then experienced the wrenching experience of forced industrialization and the purges. The Baltic States of Estonia, Latvia and Lithuania as well as Eastern Poland had been recently forcibly incorporated in the Soviet Union and their loyalty was suspect at best. Local partisans operating behind enemy lines were beyond direct state control. Would they stay loyal and uncontaminated by exposure to foreign ideology and nationalist/separatist movements? Or would they be the center of an organized resistance to the reestablishment of Soviet power after the war? There had to be some way to organize and control the partisans.[7] Yet the trained partisan cadres and manuals were gone.

The Soviet Union hurriedly formed and trained partisan detachments to infiltrate into the enemy rear area. This was no haphazard selection of keen local volunteers sent back to fight in their own neighborhoods. These partisans were loyal communist party and Komsomol [young communist] members, civil war veterans, and NKVD [forerunner of the KGB] members and Red Army reservists. In October 1941, the Red Army's Main Political Administration authorized the reissue of an outdated Civil War manual as the first edition of the *Partisan's Companion*.[8]

The book was published in Moscow on 27 December 1941 with a press run of 50,000 copies. The few attempts to update it included a political speech by Stalin, a brief chapter on German weapons (one rifle, one pistol, one submachine gun and one grenade) and a chapter on fighting on skis from the Winter War with Finland. An NKVD official who read the book quipped "I attentively read this manual as advised and then I put it in my files where it remains as a historic document".[9]

Since the first partisan groups formed for infiltration were composed of party loyalists, they were primarily city dwellers. The Red Army was getting the healthiest and most fit men, so the partisan bands got the less-physically fit and older party loyalists. There was a shortage of weapons and radios everywhere, so the partisan detachments were under-equipped. The detachments were rushed through training and infiltrated behind enemy lines.

These initial detachments did not do well. They were not local and did not know the neighborhood. The locals did not flock to their standard. The Germans were hunting them. There was little or no support and logistics structure in place. Regional historians estimate that only seven percent of these initial partisans in the Ukraine and 17 percent of the Partisans around Leningrad survived until the spring of 1942. The underequipped partisans of 1941 did little damage to the enemy, but their ranks were thinned dramatically by the enemy, disease, starvation and the weather.[10]

Partisan fortunes improved in 1942. The Germans were stopped on the outskirts of Moscow, proving to the locals that the Germans could be stopped. The German treatment of the population in the occupied area was intolerable and many of the locals took to the forests to form guerrilla bands. They were joined by the Red Army soldiers who had been trapped behind enemy lines by the German rapid advance or who had escaped from German captivity. The soldiers brought military training and discipline to the partisans. Molodaya Gvardia [The Young Guard] Printing House published the 2nd Edition of the *Partisan's Companion*. It was much different book than the first edition. It incorporated the hard lessons of the current war—lessons that had been paid for in blood.

On 30 May 1942, the Soviet Government formed the Central Staff of the Partisan Movement (*Tsentralnyy shtab parmizanskogo dvizheniya*). Panteleimon K. Ponomarenko, the Belorussian Party First Secretary, was appointed head of the staff. The staff, and Ponomarenko, would remain in power until 13 July 1944.[11] Ponomarenko had little understanding of the logistics and tactics of partisan warfare, but he was a party bureaucrat that understood that the partisan war would be fought as a political, as well as a military, contest. He shared Stalin's concern that the partisans must remain under Soviet control.[12] The main staff departments were operations, intelligence and political. Pononmarenko was pulling the Red Army, NKVD and Party partisan detachments under Moscow's control. The operations department planned partisan missions, sent new detachments behind enemy lines, disbanded or combined detachments, provided tactical, technical and training material and coordinated the actions of subordinate partisan staffs. The operations department dispatched Red Army officers to command detachments and provide support to the Red Army. The intelligence department assigned reconnaissance missions, located newly formed or previously unknown partisan detachments and provided political and economic assessments of occupied territories. The political department conducted propaganda and agitation campaigns in the occupied territories, maintained contact with underground party organizations and publicized partisan actions in the Soviet media.[13]

In September 1942, Stalin issued the People's Commissariat on Defense Order 189, "On the Tasks of the Partisan Movement". The order gave state sanction and support to a popular mass partisan movement against Germany. The ordinary people were finally being brought into the guerrilla war. The partisans were to continue to attack German targets, disrupt German administration, prevent German seizure of grain and collect intelligence. They were also to conduct propaganda and agitation. The movement was expanded to include all Soviet nationalities that had German soldiers on their territory.[14]

The Central Staff of the Partisan Movement struggled to put the expanding bands of local partisans under central control. Military discipline was instilled in the bands by incorporation of Red Army soldiers and officers. Regular military organization and a command structure were imposed as detachments were organized into companies and platoons. Partisan detachments (battalions) were incorporated into Partisan divisions and Partisan armies. There was a concerted effort to get radios and radio operators to the Partisan detachments. In the summer of 1942, some 30% of the detachments had radio contact with external stations. By November 1943, almost 94% of the detachments had radio communications with the Central Staff. Party organizations were reestablished within the occupied regions.[15] The NKVD established surveillance of enemy activity, as well as detachment activity.

The partisan movement expanded dramatically in 1943. The victories at Stalingrad and Kursk showed that the German Army advance was stopped and that Germany was going to lose the war. For the fence sitters, this was the last opportunity to join the partisans and prove their loyalty to the Soviet Union and avoid later repercussions. The shortage of available German forces was accompanied by a German contraction of the territory they controlled. They had fewer forces to control their rear area and so they withdrew into the larger towns. This ceded large areas to the partisans and facilitated their recruitment efforts. The partisans recruited vigorously. Many locals joined the partisans to escape the German forced drafts and export of factory slave labor from the occupied regions.[16]

Logistic support to the partisans improved. During 1943, the Soviets used some 12,000 aviation sorties to deliver supplies behind enemy lines. They provided some 60,000 rifles, 34,300 submachine guns, 4,200 machine guns, 2,500 antitank rifles and 2,200 mortars along with ammunition and hand grenades.[17]

This 3rd Edition of the *Partisan's Companion* was published in May 1943 to support this growth in the number of partisans. It has 360 pages and was printed in 50,000 copies. It is a very different book from the first edition. There is no chapter on map reading. The partisans were local and they knew the territory. The Red Army officers assigned to the detachments could read maps to arrange supply drops and the like. There is no chapter on fighting on skis. The partisans frequently moved on skis, but rarely fought on them. The chapter on hand-to-hand combat remained mostly unchanged from the 1920s, while the chapter on German weapons was greatly expanded as was the chapter on Soviet weapons. The partisan tactics, German counter-guerrilla tactics, partisan air defense and chemical warfare chapters were completely new. The 3rd Edition was published in the Soviet Far East, reflecting the Soviet relocation of industry to the East.

In the end, the partisan movement was a success. It peaked in strength in July 1944 with some 280,000 partisans simultaneously under arms.[18] Russian historians credit it with killing, wounding or capturing a million enemy personnel. They further credit it with destroying some 4,000 armored vehicles, 58 armored trains, 10,000 railroad engines, 2,000 railroad bridges and 65,000 trucks and cars. They also credit it with tying down ten percent of the German armed forces. The Central Staff of the Partisan Movement was disbanded on 13 January 1944.[19] Most of the Soviet territory was liberated at that point and Moscow was eager to discover which partisan detachments were reluctant to stand down, turn in their weapons or support the return of Soviet power.

After the Germans were defeated, however, the Red Army had to defeat and root out partisan forces in the Ukraine and Baltic Republics. Stalin's fear of loss of control was justified, but by 1950, the major partisan units were defeated. The last partisans in the Baltic Republics surrendered in 1983.

This 3rd Edition of the *Partisan's Companion* did not become a mere curiosity and rarity on a library shelf. Guerrilla war was a prominent feature of the post-World War II world. European colonial powers were opposed by their subjects in the Middle East, Africa, Asia and the Pacific. Governments in Latin America were challenged and sometimes overthrown by local guerrilla groups. Mao Tse Tung came to power in China at the head of a guerrilla army. European empires contracted and disappeared as colony after colony gained independence following "wars of national liberation". During the Korean War, which had a significant guerrilla component, China and the Soviet Union cooperated closely to prop up North Korea and oppose the United Nations forces. However, the alliance between the two major communist powers eventually strained as both nations vied for leadership of the global communist movement. Both countries vied for influence in the uncommitted nations of the so-called "Third World". This influence included foreign and military aid as well as training for guerrilla warfare for disaffected citizens of countries that were friendly to the West. The 3rd Edition of the *Partisan's Companion* was a basic document for this training in the Soviet Union.

In October 1974, Panteleimon Ponomarenko was still deeply involved with guerrilla war. The grand old man of Soviet partisans was now a respected lecturer at the secret school for Arab "revolutionaries" at Novoe Nagoronoe in the Pushkin district some forty miles outside of Moscow (there were several such schools for different language groups in the Soviet Union). During one lecture to Palestinian guerrillas and Iraqi Baathists, Ponomarenko was speaking in detail about ways of hiding weapons in the forest. The leader of the Iraqi students gently reminded Pononmarenko that there were no forests in Iraq or Palestine. Without missing a beat, Ponomarenko merely substituted 'desert' for 'forest' in his lecture notes and continued to the edification of his students.[20]

This secret school prepared thousands of Arab "revolutionaries" over its twenty-year existence. Saddam Hussein, who admired Stalin, implemented Soviet methods of mass indoctrination, totalitarian control and party building. This extended to the Baathist party cellular organization and ubiquitous secret police.[21] The Baathist Fedayeen trained to become guerrillas to fight an invader. The US Army ended up fighting guerrillas whose training was based on the 3rd Edition of the *Partisan's Companion*.

Mike Gress grew up in Siberia where he and his friends used to play 'partisans and fascists" using stick 'guns' and pinecone 'hand grenades'. Everyone's father had served in the war. One of Mike's friends had his father's copy of the 3rd Edition of the *Partisan's Companion* and it served to sharpen their imaginations, the accuracy of their play and their survival skills. The book made a lasting impression on young Mike. Years later, Mike discussed the existence of this tactically important book while fishing with Les Grau, another Russian speaker. Les and Mike searched Russian libraries and archives for the book, but did not have a lot of luck. Finally, after almost a decade, a Russian researcher located a library copy and photocopied for them. The original book was not printed for the ages. The paper was poor quality and the photocopy did not improve the quality of the illustrations. Mike and Les went to work. The Russian was usually no problem, but the illustrations were. Fortunately, Mike's son Alex is a computer wizard. Alex found many of the illustrations in other Russian-language publications or on the Russian web. Alex enhanced or redid the other illustrations. Many of the illustrations are now sharper than those in the original.

We offer this English-language translation to the reader in the hope that it will provide not only a tactical appreciation for partisan combat but also an appreciation for the Spartan conditions and stoic realities of partisan life. It is a training manual, but in it, the reader can detect the hardiness and stubbornness of a people determined to defend their land.

Notes to Preface:

1 A. S. Knyaz'kov, "Partizanskoe dvizhennie v Belikoy Otechestvennoy Voyne 1941-1945 [The Partisan Movement During the Great Patriotic War 1941-1945], Voennaya Entsiklopediya [Military Encyclopedia]. Volume 6, Moscow: Voyenizdat-Military Publishing House of the Ministry of Defense of the Russian Federation, 2002, p. 273.

2 Yu. F. Sokolov, "Partizanskoe dvizhennie v Otechestvennoy Boyne 1812" [The Partisan Movement During the Patriotic War 1812], Voennaya Entsiklopediya [Military Encyclopedia]. Volume 6, Moscow: Voyenizdat-Military Publishing House of the Ministry of Defense of the Russian Federation, 2002, 280-281.

3 Kenneth Slepyan, *Stalin's Guerrillas: Soviet Partisans in World War II*, Lawrence: University Press of Kansas, 2006, 20-21.

4 Jacob W. Kipp, "Mass, Mobility, and the Red Army's Road to Operational Art", Ft. Leavenworth: Soviet Army Studies Office, 1988.

5 Slepyan, 21.

6 Slepyan, 15 citing *Pravda* of 3 July 1941, page 1 using translation from Joseph Stalin, *The Great Patriotic War of the Soviet Union*, New York: International Publishers, 1945, 15.

7 Slepyan, 2-3.

8 Slepyan, 30. An excellent translation of this first edition is available as *Partisan's Companion: Deadly Techniques of Soviet freedom Fighters During World War II*. Paul J. Schmitt is the translator and Paladin Press is the publisher. Some of the illustrations in this book are based on illustrations from the Schmitt translation.

9 Slepyan, citing page 191 of V. I. Boiarskii, *Partizany i Armiia; Istoriia uteriannykh vozmozhnostei* [Partisans and the Army: History of Misplaced Possibilities], Minsk: Kharvest, 2003.

10 Slepyan, 28, 32 and 33.

11 Knayaz'kov, 274.

12 Slepyan, 42-43,

13 Slepyan, 114.

14 Slepyan, 47-49.

15 V. N.l Andrianov, "Partizanskoe dvishenie v Velikoy Otechestbennoy voyne 1941-1945" [The Partisan movement in the Great Patriotic War 1941-1945], *Bol'shaya Sovetskaya Entsiklopediya* [The Great Soviet Encyclopedia], 1977.

16 Slepyan, 190.

17 Knyaz'kov, 275.

18 Andrianov.

19 Knyaz'kov, 275.

20 Evvgenii Novikov, "The De-Baathification of Iraq", *The Jamestown Foundation*

21 Novikov

СПУТНИК ПАРТИЗАНА

THE PARTISAN'S COMPANION

THE GUERRILLA FIGHTER'S HANDBOOK

3rd Edition (expanded)

OGIZ[1]
FAR EAST STATE PUBLISHING
1942

XXV ANNIVERSARY OF THE GREAT OCTOBER SOCIALIST REVOLUTION

The Report of the Chairman of the State Defense Committee Comrade J. V. Stalin to the mutual celebratory session of the Moscow Soviet Workers Deputies including Communist Party and social organizations of Moscow
November 6, 1942

Comrades!

Today we celebrate the 25th Anniversary of the victory of the Soviet revolution in our country. 25 years passed since we established the Soviet system. We are standing on the threshold of the 26th year of the existence of the Soviet system.

Customarily, at celebratory sessions dedicated to the October Soviet revolution we sum up results of work by state and party organizations during the past year. I am entrusted to present to you the summary report about those results in the last year – from November of the past year to November of this year.

During this period, our state and party organs' activities have been conducted in two directions: on the one direction, the peaceful development and organization of a strong rear area and logistics for our *Front*'s struggle – and on the other direction; organizing and conducting the Red Army's defensive and offensive operations.

1. Organizing Activity in the Rear Area.

During this period, the non-combat related activities of our leading organs was devoted to the relocation of our industry – military as well as civilian – to the eastern part of our country; to the evacuation and resettlement of our labor force and industrial equipment in the new places; to the expansion of the arable lands in the East and to enlarging the winter wheat crop there. And, finally – to the radical improvement of the work process at our enterprises, which work for the war *Front* and to the strengthening of work discipline in the rear areas – at factories and industrial plants as well as at the collective and state farms. It needs to be said that this was a most difficult and complex organizational task on a grand scale for all our Narkomats (ministries), including – the railroad. But we were able to overcome the difficulties. And today our plants and our collective and state farms, despite all the problems of war time are undisputedly working satisfactorily. Our military plants and related enterprises honestly and conscientiously supply the Red Army with cannons, mortars, aircraft, tanks, machine-guns, rifles and ammunition. Our collective and state farms also honestly and conscientiously deliver food to the population and the Red Army and raw materials to our industry. We shall admit that never before has our country had such a strong and well-organized rear area.

The result of all this complex organizational and creative work is seen not only in our country but in the people in the rear area. The people have become more organized, less negligent and more disciplined. They have learned to work under war time conditions, begun to understand their duty to the Motherland and to her protectors at the *Front* – the Red Army. In the rear area, there are fewer and fewer dimwits and slobs without a sense of civic duty. And there are more and more well organized and disciplined citizens.

But the past year was, as I have already stated, not only the year of civic development. It was at the same time the year of the Patriotic war against German invaders, who despicably and perfidiously invaded our peaceful country.

2. Military Actions on the Soviet-German *Front*

As to the military activity of our leading organs during the past year – it expressed itself in the development and support of the defensive and offensive operations of the Red Army against the German-Fascist troops. It is possible to divide the combat actions on the Soviet-German *Front* during the past year into two periods: the first period – predominantly a winter period, when the Red Army, after repulsing the German thrust on Moscow, went over to the initiative and began an offensive routing the German forces. In this four-month period, it advanced up to 400 kilometers in some areas. The second period was the summer when German-Fascist troops, emboldened by the absence of a Second *Front* in Europe, collected all their free reserves and broke through our *Front* on the South-western direction. They grabbed the initiative and in some areas advanced up to 500 kilometers during this five-month period.

Military actions during the first period, especially the successful actions of the Red Army in the Rostov, Tula, Kaluga regions, near Moscow, Tikhvin and Leningrad, revealed two significant facts. First, they have shown that the Red Army and its combat cadre have grown into a serious force which is capable of not only withstanding the thrust of the German-Fascist troops – they can defeat them in open battle and turn them back. Also, they have shown that the German troops, despite all their steadfastness, have some serious fundamental defects, which under specific favorable conditions can lead to their defeat by the Red Army. We cannot dismiss as an accident the fact that the German troops, which crossed all Europe in a triumphal march and smashed the first-class French army in one stroke, that these forces met real resistance only in our country. And not only resistance – they were forced to retreat from occupied positions by more than 400 kilometers, leaving behind colossal numbers of weapons, vehicles and ammunition. It cannot be explained only by the winter conditions.

The second period of military actions on the Soviet-German *Front* was characterized by the shifting the situation in favor of the Germans, who regained the initiative. They broke through our defense in the South-western direction, moved ahead and approached the Voronezh, Stalingrad, Novorossiysk, Pyatigorsk and Mozdok areas. Using to their advantage the absence of a Second *Front* in Europe, the Germans and their allies threw all their free reserves at the *Front*. They directed them on one axis – in the South-west – creating there a very significant superiority in forces and thus achieving considerable tactical success.

Obviously, the Germans are not that powerful at the moment that they can conduct offensives on three axes – South, North and Center, as happened during the first months of the German summertime offensive last year. But they are still powerful enough to organize serious offensive actions on one select axis.

What major objective did the German strategists pursue when they started their summer campaign on our *Front*? If we judge this from the commentaries of the foreign press, including German, the impression would be that the major goal was the capture of the oil-rich regions of Grozny and Baku. But the facts disprove such an assumption. The facts tell us that their advance on the oil-rich regions of the USSR is not the main, but a supporting goal.

What then was the main goal of the German offensive? It was to encircle Moscow on the eastern side, to cut her off from the Volga and Ural logistics bases and after that to attack Moscow directly. The movement of German troops' on the southern axis toward the oil-rich regions had a supporting goal: it was not only and not so much to capture those regions but to divert our main reserves to the South and weaken our Moscow *Front*, thus making their direct attack on Moscow more successful. It explains why the main grouping of the German forces is now not in the South but in the Orel and Stalingrad areas.

Recently, our people captured an officer of the German General Staff. He had with him a map that showed the plan of the advance with its 1941 timetable. The document stated that the Germans planned to capture Borisoglebsk by July 10, Stalingrad – July 25, Saratov – August 10, Kuibyshev – August 15, Arzamas – September 10 and Baku – September 25.

The document clearly supports our information that the main goal of the German summer campaign was to encircle Moscow from the East and after that to attack her directly, at the same time moving on the southern axis to divert our reserves far from Moscow and weaken the Moscow *Front* to make it easier to attack Moscow.

In short, the main goal of the German summer campaign was to encircle Moscow and finish the war that year.

Last November the Germans intended to capture Moscow with a direct attack, force the Red Army to capitulate and thus finish the war in the East. They fed their soldiers with these illusions. But they miscalculated, as we know. They were burned in their direct attack on Moscow and intention to capture Moscow by an encircling maneuver and finish the war here. They again are feeding their befuddled soldiers with those illusions. As is known their calculations proved wrong again. As a result of chasing two hares – the oil and the Moscow encirclement-the German-Fascist strategists found themselves in a difficult position.[2]

In this way, the tactical success of the German summer offensive displayed the obvious unreality of their strategic planning.

3. The Matter of the Second *Front* in Europe

Who can explain the fact that the Germans were, after all, able to retake the military initiative and achieve some serious tactical successes on our *Front*?

It explained by the fact that the Germans and their allies were able to assemble their uncommitted reserves and send them to the Eastern *Front* creating a major superiority in forces on one axis. There is no doubt that without such measures, the Germans would not be able to have any success on our *Front*.

But how did it happen that they could take the reserves and send them to the Eastern *Front*? There is a reason – the absence of the Second *Front* in Europe gave them that opportunity to conduct such an operation without risk to themselves.

Thus the major reason for their tactical success on our *Front* this year is the absence of a Second *Front* in Europe. This gave them the opportunity to throw all their uncommitted reserves to our *Front* and build a major superiority in forces on the South-Western axis.

Let us make an assumption that the Second *Front* existed in Europe – the same as it existed during World War I. Let's say that *Front* would divert 60 German divisions and 20 divisions of their allies. What situation would that create for the Germans at our *Front*? It is not difficult to grasp that their situation would be pathetic. Even more, it could be the beginning of the end of the German-Fascist troops because the Red Army would not be fighting where they are now but would be fighting near Pskov, Minsk, Zhitomir, and Odessa. And that means the German-Fascist army would face a catastrophe. Since that has not happened, it is due to the absence of the Second *Front* in Europe.

Let us to look at the Second *Front* question from a historical perspective.

During World War I Germany was forced to fight on two *Fronts*: in the West – mainly against England and France and in the East – against Russian troops. Thus the Second *Front* against Germany did exist. Out of 220 divisions which Germany had at the time, they positioned no more than 85 German divisions on the Russian *Front*. If we add the Germans' allies forces, namely 37 Austro-Hungarian divisions, two Bulgarian and three Turkish divisions, there was a total of 127 divisions fighting against Russian forces. The rest of the German and their allies divisions held the *Front* primarily against English and French troops. And a part of German forces were tied up in garrison duty in the occupied part of Europe.

That is how things stood during World War I.

How do things stand now, during World War II, let's say in September of the current year?

By confirmed data, without any doubt, out of the 256 divisions which Germany has today, no less than 179 are stationed at our *Front*. If we add other divisions: 22 Romanian, 14 Finnish, 10 Italian, 13 Hungarian, one Slovak and one Spanish, then we would have 240 divisions fighting at our *Front*. The rest of the German and their allies divisions are garrisoning the occupied countries (France, Belgium, Norway, Holland, Poland, Czechoslovakia, etc.). Part of these troops is fighting in Libya and Egypt against England, but the Libyan *Front* only diverts four German and 11 Italian divisions.

Instead of the 127 divisions that we faced during World War I, we now face no less than 240 divisions. Instead of 85 German divisions, 179 German divisions are now fighting the Red Army.

And that is the main and fundamental reason for the tactical successes of the German-Fascist forces on our *Front* during the summer of this year.

Quite often, the German invasion of our country is compared to Napoleon's invasion of Russia. But this comparison does not hold up to examination. Out of 600 thousand troops that invaded Russia, Napoleon had only 130-140 thousand troops near Borodino. That was all he could spare to the fight for Moscow. And yet the Red Army faces more than three million troops armed with the most modern weapons. How can one make any type of comparison?

Sometimes the German invasion of our country is compared to the invasion of Russia by Germany during World War I. But this comparison also does not hold up. First, during World War I there was a second *Front* in Europe which sharply hampered German activities. In this war there is no second *Front* in Europe. Second, in this war there are twice as many troops fighting against us then in World War I. It is clear that there is no comparison.

Now you can imagine how serious and extraordinary are the difficulties that confront the Red Army and how great is the heroism that the Red Army displays while fighting a war of liberation against the German-Fascist occupiers.

I think that no other country and no other army could withstand such a thrust by the ferocious bands of German-Fascist brigands and their allies. Only our Soviet country and the only our Red Army are capable of bearing such the onslaught (**Tumultuous applause**). And not only to bear it, but to overcome it.

Quite often the question is asked: Will there be a Second *Front* in Europe? Yes, there will, sooner or later. And it will be not just because we need it, but because our allies need it to no less a degree than we do. Our allies certainly understand that, after the fall of France, the absence of a Second *Front* could bring a bad end to all freedom-loving countries, including their own.

4. The War-time Alliance of the USSR, England and USA against Hitler's Germany and her Allies in Europe.

Today we can count as an undisputed fact that, in the course of the war imposed by Fascist Germany upon the worlds' people, a fundamental separation of forces has occurred. Two opposing camps have been created: the Italian-German coalition camp and the British-Soviet-American coalition camp.

It is also indisputable also that these two opposing coalitions are guided by two opposing programs of action.

The program of the Italian-German coalition could be described by the following points: racial hatred; domination of the "selected" nations; subjugation of other nations and seizure of their territories; economic slavery of the subjugated peoples and theft of their national property; destruction of their democratic freedom; and universal establishment of the Hitlerite regime.

The program of the British-Soviet-American coalition includes: liquidation of racial exclusivity; equality of the nations and inviolability of their territories; liberation of the enslaved nations and restoration of their sovereign rights; establishing the right of self determination for each and every nation; assistance to suffering nations and assistance in building their economic well-being; restoration of democratic freedom; and the destruction of the Hitlerite regime.

The Italian-German coalition's program created the situation where all occupied European countries – Norway, Denmark, Belgium, the Netherlands, France, Poland, Czechoslovakia, Yugoslavia, Greece and occupied regions of the USSR – feel a flaming hatred toward Italian-German tyranny, they harm the Germans and their allies as much as they can and wait for the appropriate moment to take vengeance on their oppressors for all the indignities and violence that the enslavers have brought on them.

Connected to this, the present time is characterized by the growing isolation of the Italian-German coalition as its moral and political reserves in Europe are running out and its weakness and decay are increasing.

The British-Soviet-American coalition's program has resulted in the fact that all the occupied countries in Europe are in full sympathy with the members of this coalition and are ready to give them any kind of support they need to the fullest extent of their abilities.

In connection with this, there is another specific characteristic of the present time-the moral and political reserves of this coalition are growing daily in Europe – but not only in Europe – and the coalition progressively attracts millions of sympathizers who are ready to fight together against the tyranny of Hitler.

If we look at the correlation of forces between those coalitions from a standpoint of human and material resources we can conclude that there is undisputable superiority on the side of British-Soviet-American coalition.

But there is a question: Is that advantage enough to win? There are quite a few occasions when there were plenty of resources, but they were distributed so ineffectively that the advantages were diminished to zero. Clearly, besides having the resources, there is a need for the ability to mobilize these resources and use them correctly. Do we have any basis to doubt that the British-Soviet-American coalition have that ability? There are some people who doubt this. But what is the basis of their doubts? We know that the people of the coalition in their own time have shown the abilities and skills to mobilize their countries' resources for economic, cultural and political developments. One can ask – what is the basis for the doubts that the people who were able to use the resources for economic, cultural and political developments can also use them for military purposes. I think these doubts are baseless.

There is an opinion that the British-Soviet-American coalition has all the chances for victory. And it would be victorious if it were not for one inherent shortcoming which may weaken and dissolve it. In their opinion the problem lies in the fact that the coalition consists of heterogeneous elements which have different ideologies – and that is the factor which would not let them organize joint actions against their mutual enemy.

I think this opinion is wrong.

It would be laughable to deny differences in the ideology and social systems of countries which belong to the British-Soviet-American coalition. But does this fact rule out the possibility and expediency of mutual actions against a common enemy who threatens them with enslavement? Undoubtedly – not. Even more – the present threat peremptorily dictates to the members of the coalition the necessity of mutual actions with the goal of saving mankind from a return to savagery and medieval atrocities. Is not the program of the British-Soviet-American coalition enough to be the basis of a mutual struggle against Hitler's tyranny to overcome it? I think it is more than enough.

These people's assumptions are also wrong because they have been disproved by the events of the past year. Actually, if these people were right we would see evidence of progressive alienation among members of the British-Soviet-American coalition. But not only do we not see such a development, quite the opposite, we have facts and events which tell us about a progressive rapprochement among the coalition's members and their unification into a single and indivisible military alliance. The past year's events give us the most direct evidence of that. In July 1941 – a few weeks after the German invasion of our country – Great Britain signed a treaty with us "About mutual actions in the war against Germany" [Anglo-Soviet Treaty of Mutual Assistance, 12 July 1941]. However, we did not have any agreement on the matter with the United States at that time. Ten months after that, on May 26, 1942, during Comrade Molotov's visit to Great Britain, we concluded the "Treaty of the Union in the War against Hitler's Germany and its Allies in Europe and of the Assistance and Mutual Help after the War" [The Twenty-Year Mutual Assistance Agreement Between the United Kingdom and the Union of Soviet Socialist Republics, 26 May 1942]. This treaty will be effective for 20 years. It signifies, by itself, a historic turn in the relations between our country and Great Britain. In July 1942, during Comrade Molotov's visit to the United States, the USA signed "An Agreement in Principle Concerning Mutual Assistance in the Conduct of War against Aggression" – an agreement which takes a very serious step forward in the relations of the USSR and USA. And finally, we have to note such an important fact as the Prime Minister of Great Britain, Mr. Churchill's visit to Moscow, which established complete understanding between the leaders of the two countries. There should not be any doubts that all those facts tell us about progressive rapprochement between the USSR, Great Britain and the USA and about their unification into a military alliance against the Italian-German coalition.

It turns out that the logic of these facts prevails against any other logic.

There is only one conclusion: the British-Soviet-American coalition has all the chances to defeat the Italian-German coalition and it will win without any doubt.

5. Our Missions

The war has ripped off all the covers and revealed all relations. The situation has become so clear that there is nothing easier than to determine our missions in the war.

In his conversation with the Turkish general Erkilet which had been published in the Turkish newspaper Jumkhuriet, the cannibal Hitler said:

"We will destroy Russia in order that it will never be able to rise again." It seems pretty clear, though slightly stupid. (**Laughter**). We do not have such a mission – to destroy Germany, because it is impossible to do so as it is impossible to destroy Russia. But to destroy Hitler's state – it is possible and necessary. (**Tumultuous applause**).

Then our first mission is exactly that – to destroy the Hitlerite state and its founders. (**Tumultuous applause**).

During the same conversation with the same general, the cannibal Hitler continued: "We will continue the war until there is no longer any organized military force in Russia." Again, it seems clear, though ignorant. (**Laughter**). We do not have such a mission to destroy any kind of organized military force in Germany because any intelligent person knows that it is not only impossible to do such to Germany – as it is also impossible to do the same to Russia – but it is pointless from the standpoint of a victorious side. But to destroy the Hitlerite army – it is possible and necessary. (**Tumultuous applause**).

Our second mission is exactly that – to destroy the Hitlerite army and its leaders. (**Tumultuous applause**).

Hitler's blackguards undertook as a right the torture of Soviet prisoners of war, killing them by the hundreds, putting thousands of them to death by starvation. They rape and kill civilians in the occupied regions of our country – men and women, children and the elderly – our brothers and sisters. They have set the goal of enslaving or destroying the population of the Ukraine, Byelorussia, the Baltic, Moldavia, the Crimea, and the Caucuses. Only the lowest type of people and scoundrels with no honor – those who have lowered themselves to become beasts – can commit such atrocities against innocent unarmed people. But that is not all. They have covered Europe with gallows and concentration camps. They have introduced an ignoble "system of hostages". They shoot and hang completely innocent people just because some German animals had been interrupted while raping women or robbing peaceful residents. They have turned Europe into a prison of nations. And they call it – "the New Order in Europe". We know the perpetrators of these atrocities – these builders of "the New Order in Europe", all those newly-baked governor-generals and governors, commandants and sub-commandants. Their names are known to thousands of tormented people. Let these executioners and torturers know that they cannot escape being brought to account for their crimes and avoiding the punishment of the tormented people.

Our third mission is to destroy the hated "New Order in Europe" and punish its creators.

Those are our missions (**Tumultuous applause**).

Comrades! We are in the great liberation war. We conduct it not by ourselves only, but with our allies. The war is bringing us the victory over the ignoble enemy of the humankind – over the German-Fascist imperialists. On war banners we can read:

Long live the victory of the British-Soviet-American alliance! (**Applause**).

Long live the liberation of the European nations from the Hitlerite tyranny! (**Applause**).

Long live the freedom and independence of our glorious Motherland! (**Applause**).

Damnation and death to the German-Fascist occupiers, their states, armies and "the New Order in Europe"! (**Applause**).

Glory to our Red Army! (**Tumultuous applause**).

Glory to our Navy! (**Tumultuous applause**).

Glory to our partisans – men and women! (**Long tumultuous applause. All rise. Ovation**).

ORDER
of the Peoples' Commissioner of Defense
November 07, 1942

#345

Moscow

Comrade Red Army warriors, commanders and political officers, partisans – men and women! Workers of the Soviet Union!

On behalf of the Soviet government and our Bolshevik party, I greet you and congratulate you on this the 25th anniversary of the victory of the Great October Socialist Revolution.

A quarter of century ago, the workers and peasants under leadership of the Bolshevik's party and the great Lenin established the rule of the Soviets in our country. The peoples of the Soviet Union have advanced on a glorious path during this time. In 25 years our country has become a mighty industrialized and collectivized agricultural state. The nations of the Soviet Union, who won their freedom and independence, have united into an unbreakable brotherly commonwealth. The Soviet people have liberated themselves from any kind of repression and through their persistent labor have ensured a prosperous and culturally-enriched life.

Today, our people celebrate the 25th anniversary of the Great October Revolution at the peak of the brutal fight against the German-Fascist occupiers and their allies in Europe.

At the beginning of the year, during the winter, the Red Army inflicted severe blows on the German-Fascist troops. After repulsing the German attacks on Moscow, it seized the initiative, went on the offensive and pushed the German forces back toward the West. It liberated a number of our country's regions from German slavery. Thus the Red Army demonstrated that under favorable conditions it can overcome the German-Fascist troops.

But, during the summer, the situation at the *Front* worsened. The Germans, taking advantage of the absence of the Second *Front* in Europe, massed all their reserves, moved them to our Ukrainian *Front* and broke through it. Paying enormous price in losses, the German-Fascists were able to advance in the South and create a threat to Stalingrad, the Black Sea shore, Grozny and the approaches to the Transcaucasus area.

Due to the steadfastness and bravery of the Red Army, the German plans to encircle and strike our capital from the rear were frustrated. The enemy has been stopped near Stalingrad. But despite being stopped near

Stalingrad and already losing tens of thousands of dead officers and soldiers, the enemy is throwing more and more new divisions into the battle and straining itself to the limit. The fight at the Soviet-German *Front* is becoming more and more intense. And the fate of our Soviet state, the freedom and independence of our Motherland depends on the outcome of that struggle.

Our Soviet people withstood all the severe trials that came their way with honor and they are filled with an unshakable faith in our victory. The war has become a rigorous test of the power and stability of the Soviet social system. All the hopes of the German imperialists that our Soviet state would disintegrate proved totally false. Socialist industry, collective farms, the friendship of the nations of our country and the Soviet government have all shown their strength and indestructibility. Our workers and peasants, all our intelligentsia, and all the peoples of our rear areas are honestly and selflessly working to supply our *Front* with everything it needs.

The Red Army bears the brunt of the war against Hitler's Germany and its satellites. With its selfless struggle against fascist armies, the Red Army won the love and respect of all freedom-loving people in the world. The soldiers and commanders of the Red Army, who lacked previous combat experience, have now learned how to beat the enemy, to destroy his manpower and machinery, to thwart the enemy's plans and stand steadfast in the defense of our cities and villages. Heroes, defending Moscow and Tula, Odessa and Sevastopol, Leningrad and Stalingrad, have proven the model of selfless bravery, iron discipline, steadfastness and skilled victory. These heroes are the benchmark for all the Red Army. The enemy has already experienced the Red Army's ability to resist. And it will certainly experience the might of the crushing blows of the Red Army.

There should be no doubt that the German occupiers will be thrown into new risky ventures. But the enemy's power is already undermined and is at its limits. During the war the Red Army has knocked out of action more than eight million enemy officers and soldiers. Today, the German army, diluted with Italians, Romanians, Hungarians and Finns, is much weaker than it was in the summer and fall of 1941.

Comrade Red Army warriors, commanders and political officers, partisans – men and women!

A defeat of the German-Fascist army and a cleansing of our Soviet land from Hitler's occupiers depend on your determination and steadfastness, your ability and readiness to carry out your responsibility to our Motherland.

We can and we must cleanse the Soviet land from Hitler's scum!

To do that we need to:

1) Firmly and resolutely defend the frontline, not permitting the enemy to advance, using all possible means to wear the enemy down, to destroy his manpower and machinery;

2) Use all means to tighten our iron discipline, strict order and unity of command in our army, to refine our troops' combat training – and to prepare for, with all our determination and perseverance, a crushing blow of the enemy;

3) To fan up the flames of the partisan movement in the enemy's rear, to destroy the enemy logistic areas, and to destroy the German-Fascist scoundrels.

Comrades!

The enemy already felt the striking power of the Red Army near Rostov, near Moscow, and near Tikhvin. The day is close when it will experience the power of the new blows of the Red Army. There will be a celebration on our streets [Будет праздник на нашей улице].

Long live the 25th anniversary of the Great October Socialist revolution!
Long live our Red Army!
Long live our Navy!
Long live our glorious partisans – men and women!
Death to the German-Fascist occupiers!

People's Commissioner of Defense

J. Stalin

ON PARTISAN WARFARE

M.I. Kalinin[3]

Comrade Stalin's call to the peoples of the Soviet territories occupied by Germans to develop the partisan struggle has fallen on fertile ground. Now it is obvious to everyone that the partisan movement deepens and widens more and more like a spring flood. The criminal rampage of the German-Fascist army, its bestial brutality toward the population of the captured territories – a brutality so savage that even stones cry out for vengeance – drives even the most peaceful people to the selfless struggle against Hitler's brigands.

But all the violence and brutality that the German occupiers inflict on the peaceful population are just a supplemental factor in the partisan struggle's development. The main sources that amply feed the partisan movement lie much deeper. They are in the heart the people itself. The basis of it was founded and then tirelessly developed for almost a quarter of a century on the strength of Lenin's and Stalin's policy. And now at this most difficult time for our country, the seeds planted in the people's souls have come to bear fruit.

Comrade Stalin's call to the population of the occupied territories is not a declaration – it is a directive to act. What kind of confidence in the people and what kind of conviction in the power of the call would it take to make the directive effective! Comrade Stalin's words have shown the population of the temporarily occupied territories a real outlet for their indignation and hatred toward their enslavers, the outlet for merciless vengeance on them.

The Soviet people are accustomed to addresses to them from the party and the government. Just look at twenty-five years of Soviet history and you will see that the Soviet people have been enlisted to carry out serious tasks. And what could be more serious then defense of our own country from foreign aggression?

The German fascists – that is the brigand band supported by a tiny but influential group of the big capitalist monopolies. For that close-knitted gang, national interests are alien if they are not about their enrichment. Their ideology, as it is delivered to the public, serves to delude the masses of the people. And, as a rule, deceit and falsification to the masses of the people is considered a kind of a valor within the fascist party.

The fascist ringleaders are totally indifferent to even their own soldiers' suffering.

The fascist clique looks at soldiers and even field-grade officers as the tool of realization of their predatory missions and after they are used – they are thrown away as useless scrap. All know that the fascists poison their own severely wounded and return their wounded who have not yet recovered to front line. The fascist ringleaders think that the fewer soldiers that return home from the *Front* – the less there will be to hassle the fascist 'bonzes' with their fretful demands and irritability and the more comfortable it would be for the reigning Hitler and his clique.

That is the enemy which our partisans are fighting. It is savage not only to the local population, but it is also brutal to its own who it does not need anymore, let alone those who the fascists do not trust and consider dangerous to the regime. Innumerable facts of the enemy's actions shows us that the fascists not only murder, torture, mock and rob the population under their yoke, but they also are sending young able-bodied men and women to Germany into slavery. We can say with certainty that 90% of those slaves will die from slow starvation and hard labor while making artillery rounds and cartridges that the Germans will use against the slaves' relatives.

Such an enemy needs to be beaten hard and long – to teach them, to bring them to understand that the partisans are the noblest citizens of the country suffering from their aggression.

The partisans have lived through a hard winter. And they spent that winter not in a passive fashion but by continuously striking severely at the German violators. Even the fascists themselves were forced to acknowledge the might of those blows. This should be an additional incentive for partisan combat during the summer period.

The help provided by partisans to the Red Army in its struggle against Germans is enormous and the strikes of the partisan detachments at the fascists take on more and more significance in the war's strategy. Undoubtedly, these results give a moral satisfaction to the partisans. Partisans not only increase their blows at the enemy in close cooperation with the army but also undertake broader and tactically complex operations – they drive away whole German garrisons from regional centers and villages, they liberate vast territories from the occupiers and they restore the power of the Soviets in the enemy's rear. Their power is not a peacetime power – it bristles with all the available arms for the fight with the sworn enemy.

It was for a good reason that People's Commissioner of Defense Comrade Stalin, in the First of May Order, included combat missions for the male and female partisans women along with directives to regular units of the Red Army.

In our present Patriotic War, the partisan movement is much more significant than during past wars. It has greater impact than its predecessors; the population joins the partisan movement in larger numbers – including women who show a miraculous selfless heroism. And we should keep in mind that during the present war, the partisans face the enemy equipped with first-class equipment. That means that the level of the partisan struggle should be high enough to strike the enemy successfully and use complex weapons end equipment captured from the enemy. No matter how hard the fascists try to disparage intellectual level of our farmers and city dwellers – these facts of the partisan movement refute that slander completely and entirely.

Farmers, workers and intelligentsia who fight in the partisan detachments show very high skills in using all means on hands and all methods while conducting battles. The German command is not happy about this. The Germans themselves acknowledge this fact. The Soviet population possesses not only high moral standards but also a high intellectual level. Considering this, who can believe the lies of the fascist fiends who commit atrocities in the East while they brazenly announce to the West that they are saving Europe from oriental barbarians?

Soviet partisans beat and will continue to beat these German dog-knights harder and harder – not only by their bravery and the boldness of their attacks but also by their skills and Russian native wit.

The partisan movement belongs to the people and its political ties join all the workers of the Soviet Union. It grows from a simple comparison of the fascist regime and the Soviet social system where a Soviet citizen felt and still feels like an owner. How can any free person – man or woman – submit to fascist slavery without a fierce fight to the death?! This submission has never happened in Russ before and is even less likely to happen in our free Soviet country.

The partisans – the avengers of the Soviet people – will pay back hundred-fold to the fascists for each and every atrocity committed. This is the only way to force the fascist gang to respect the rights of the other people.

The hatred toward fascists is growing and growing along with it is the partisan movement which has only one thought and only one aspiration toward one goal. It can be expressed by the words: "Death to the fascist occupiers!"

In that lies the might of Soviet patriotism and its love for the Motherland. In that lies the hatred of the fascist blackguards. In that lies the power of the broad partisan movement and it will help the Red Army to sweep away the fascist locust infestation from our land.

I.

FUNDAMENTAL PARTISAN TACTICS

CROSSING THE FRONT LINE

Crossing the front line into the enemy's rear takes very meticulous preparation. Communications with a Red Army commander is one of the main conditions to make it successful.

Tirelessly observe the enemy and conduct systematic reconnaissance. Collect information about the enemy, his force's location, his flanks, the boundaries between units, the deployment of his weapons systems, the location of his engineer obstacles, etc.

Also learn about the region where your detachment is going to operate. Studying a map and talking to the locals will give you a chance to orient yourself even on a totally unfamiliar terrain. Find the location of forests, open and broken terrain, populated areas, gullies, rivers and bridges. It is a good idea to find knowledgeable guides who are thoroughly familiar with the terrain and have connections among the local population. All of that will let you choose the most appropriate place to cross the front line.

The enemy should not be able to detect your crossing. Before starting, it is necessary to check weapons and equipment and adjust them well so nothing will be loose and make noise or shine.

To protect military secrets, do not take your documents, personal letters and photos with you.

The best weather for front line crossing is during fog, rain, strong wind (coming from the enemy's side), snow, and blizzard. The best time to cross is during the dark of night.

While crossing the front line, the partisans must avoid skirmishes with the enemy's units. Do not stop unless it is an emergency – go through the tactical depth of the *Front* in one single spurt. Try to mass the forces in the planned operational area as soon as possible and start surprise partisan actions in the enemy's rear area.

If there are some unoccupied sectors of the enemy's defense, a group of partisans can move into the enemy's rear area comparatively easily if they cross at night using reconnaissance and security measures.

But quite often the situation is more difficult. Then the group of partisans infiltrates the area by crawling from one concealed area to another. At the same time, send some fighters to the flanks. They can divert the enemy's attention away from the real direction of the group's movement.

If the front line is heavily saturated with enemy forces then the partisan detachment will infiltrate in small groups and, sometimes, by individual combatants. In such a situation, it is very important to designate a gathering point behind the front line.

While crossing the front line, the partisans could run into enemy's firing positions in the depth, as well as enemy reserves, patrols and security forces. It is better to be prepared for such encounters in advance and always be on your guard and ready to fight. Reconnaissance and security measures are your precautions against the unexpected.

It is imperative to observe all measures of concealment: no smoking, chatting with comrades or coughing. Move with light careful steps. Avoid moving on roads – they are used by the enemy for reconnaissance and patrols. The enemy puts mines on them and on trails and sets ambushes near them. When moving with a compass or with a guide during the night – do not forget to use your hearing. Try to move at night through the areas that are most saturated with the enemy and move through the concealed and safe areas at dawn.

While moving through the forest, avoid emerging onto meadows, roads and forest cuttings. Pay special attention to buildings that stand alone – they require meticulous reconnaissance. When you are sure that there is no enemy – move forward fast.

Keep in mind that it is possible to run into the fascist's submachine-gun ambush. They could be concealed in the folds of the terrain, shell holes, houses and in the trees in the forest. The submachine-gunners can let a partisan group pass and then open up with intensive fire from the rear to create panic. Remember: the fascist submachine-gunners' fire is mostly for the moral effect. Usually, the losses that it inflicts on troops are insignificant. When a partisan group suddenly runs into an ambush, the partisans should drop to the ground. Previously designated fighters – submachine-gun hunters – should kill them. While a submachine-gunner is shooting, the fighters identify the direction of fire and close in on him by quick bounds, gradually surrounding him. If the shooting suddenly stops – the shooter is looking for a target. It is necessary to lie down and conceal yourself. As soon as he opens fire again – continue to move closer to him.

In all cases of sudden encounters with the enemy – try to determine his strength. And after that – either fight to destroy the enemy or leave quickly changing your direction. After the partisans lose the enemy, they can resume moving in the original direction toward the planned objective.

If partisans, who are moving in the enemy's rear, meet a local inhabitant, they must take precautionary measures. If the local has been intercepted by a reconnaissance patrol and has not seen the main body of the partisan detachment, he must be led away so that he can not see all the partisans and determine their strength and direction of movement. After waiting for the main partisan group to pass undetected, the patrol interrogates and releases the detained local.

If the local has seen the partisan detachment's main group, then he must be detained and thoroughly searched and interrogated to determine that he does not belong to the fascist police or the local administration that the Hitlerites install in the captive regions. It is also desirable to get information about the enemy from him. In order to hide the true direction from the local, the detachment must change it. The detained local should accompany the detachment for several kilometers. After that, leave him under guard of at least two partisans while the detachment vanishes from view and moves for a sufficient distance. After that the detained local may be released. The detachment will again change the direction and go to the designated area.

On the return journey, when crossing the front line from the enemy's rear area into the area controlled by Red Army units, use the same rules as described before. Do not forget about meticulous camouflage [маскировка]. Carefully study the route and the crossing sector. Let the Red Army units know about your impending crossing. It would be the best to concentrate initially in one of the concealed areas 10 to 12 kilometers from the front line – behind the enemy's forward combat formations. In that area, the partisans rest and prepare themselves for the crossing. After that, they should make the last bound to friendly forces.

While crossing the front line – do not forget about conducting reconnaissance for the Red Army. Remember: you are bringing out the most current information about the enemy.

RECONNAISSANCE

Every partisan, while operating in the enemy's rear area, always and everywhere conducts reconnaissance. The success of all partisan combat actions depends first and foremost on continual and meticulous reconnaissance.

The reconnaissance should be done covertly while thoroughly camouflaged in order not to disclose the location and size of your detachment.

Remember: a partisan carries on reconnaissance not only for his detachment's interests but also for the interests of Red Army units. You must help the Red Army to learn about the enemy, find out its might, discover unit locations, minefields, firepower, logistics bases, etc. Also, let the Red Army know about enemy combat preparations and troop regroupings. Always try to get the most accurate and concrete information about the enemy.

Partisans should not limit themselves to combat reconnaissance—by observation or combat. They should collect information from reliable tested comrades, Soviet patriots from within the local population. Do not hesitate to enter the localities occupied by the enemy. Dress yourself as a local inhabitant and behave accordingly.

It is helpful to capture a "tongue" – an enemy prisoner. You can get necessary information from him. Try to transfer the prisoner to military command.

Every scout should acquire the necessary skills in map reading, moving on an azimuth, knowing how to camouflage himself and how to get ones bearings in unfamiliar terrain.

It is necessary to develop your skills of observation in order to ensure that you do not miss any details. A scout will have to climb trees, cross rivers and marshes, stay out in the rain and mud for a long time and endure other difficult conditions. You must toughen yourself and develop the necessary qualities of a scout – self-control and persistence.

The scout should try, if possible, to avoid taking notes about collected information. Develop your memory. Try to remember all relevant things in detail.

Read the "RECONNAISSANCE" chapter for the rules of how to conduct reconnaissance against different targets.

FIELD LOCATION

Partisans establish a field location to recuperate after difficult marches and combat, to provide help to wounded and to sick comrades.

A large forest is the best and most reliable shelter during any season. This is the place to build camouflaged dug-outs and lean-tos (look into the "March and Bivouac" chapter for how to do this). Fascists avoid going into the forests.

Partisans should camouflage their base thoroughly. It is necessary to hide not only the base location but also the tracks that could betray the detachment (especially in the wintertime). These are the principle methods of masking these tracks: 1) Try to enter and leave the forest during rain or snow – then the tracks will be washed away or covered with snow; 2) Select hard and stony paths where there will be no tracks; 3) Step carefully into your comrades' tracks.

A camp-fire is necessary for cooking and drying clothing. To learn how to make and hide the camp-fires – look into the "March and Bivouac" chapter.

The resting detachment must organize reliable security. The partisans' patrols should be located at a distance that would not let the enemy make a sudden attack on the detachment's main forces. The distance and position of the patrols depends on the terrain and other conditions. There should not be any fixed pattern. If the detachment is located on broken ground with thick vegetation, then you might be need two or more lines of security instead of one.

In addition to the immediate security posted when staying in a forest, you should post separate observers at the forest edge and on the approaches where the enemy would most probably come from. During daytime, these observers may climb trees to obtain good observation sectors.

It is necessary to develop a signal system to warn the detachment of an enemy threat. These signals must be passed quickly and reliably.

When living in dug-outs, make two exits instead of just one – exiting in opposite directions. If there is enough time, connect the dug-outs with underground passageways. Near the dug-outs, construct foxholes with overhead cover. Place simple obstacles against enemy tanks and infantry on the camp's approaches. Land mines should be placed on the main approaches. The mine's explosion will not only kill the fascists, but will also serve a signal to the partisans.

As a rule, partisans should avoid staying in inhabited areas. It is possible to do so only in those areas free of enemy troops and where it would take a significant amount of time for the enemy to come. In any case, it must be done only after very painstaking reconnaissance.

It is a must to establish reinforced security both in the inhabited area and on its approaches. The houses and streets must be guarded by sentries, patrols and observers. The local inhabitants should not be permitted to leave and all newcomers should be detained and sent to the command detachment. In order to prepare against an enemy unexpected attack, the inhabited area must be fitted out for a defense. Signals, the area for assembly upon alarm, withdrawal routes, should be determined. The duty sub-unit must be selected and put on guard. The vigilance of the security elements must be checked as often as possible.

While resting in any place – keep your weapons close and ready. When leaving the rest area or halt – remove all traces of your partisans presence. Do not leave any noticeable signs behind.

DESTROYING ENEMY TARGETS

Every partisan is obliged to find and destroy the enemy. While exterminating the fascists also destroy and disrupt his logistics areas which feed the Hitlerites. Know those targets in the enemy's rear area whose destruction will cause the most damage and weaken his forces:

a) **Enemy Lines of Communications**: railroads, highways, dirt and country roads (cart-tracks) used to move enemy forces and supplies; bridges; railroad structures – water towers, railroad switches, stations, depots, turntables, signal systems; filling stations on highways.

b) **Communications Means**: telegraph and telephone lines and stations, stationary and mobile radio stations, couriers carrying military correspondence.

c) **Transportation Means**: automobiles, tanker trucks, tractors, trailers, steam engines, railroad cars, airplanes and any wheeled transport.

d) **Airfields**: landing strips, aircraft hangars, fuel and ammunition storage.

e) **Artillery Parks**: cannon, artillery rounds, propellant charges storage sites and also other types of armament – rifles, machine-guns, mortars. Destroy only those weapons that you cannot take with you, bury or hide them.

f) **Depots**: weapons, ammunition, fuel, food, forage, clothing and personal equipment.

g) **Plants and Shops** used by the enemy to repair combat equipment and machinery.

To learn how to destroy enemy targets by the simplest means – see the "Explosives and Demolition" chapter.

Also find and destroy the fascists' chemical weapons – chemical depots, barrels, large cans and cylinders filled with toxic agents; chemical artillery shells; bombs; mortar shells; and various transport used to carry toxic agents. To know how to recognize the chemical objects hidden by the fascists and how to destroy them – see the "Protection from the Chemical Attack" chapter.

Success in any operation in the enemy rear area depends, in the first place, on the partisans' meticulous preparation. Even if there is no enemy presence in the immediate proximity – prepare yourself for an unexpected encounter with them. Conduct continuous and thorough reconnaissance of the targeted objective. The reconnaissance will give you the ability to discover the most vulnerable spot of the objective, the forces and means required for its destruction, the composition of the enemy guard and the most convenient and covert approaches.

When preparing to the operation – you must know:

a) Which vital element of the target is it necessary to destroy first and what means you will use – weapons fire, demolition or burning. Depending on this – prepare all the necessary means.

b) Time of the attack – day, night or dawn.

c) Signals for the beginning and end of the assault.

d) The withdrawal routes and the assembly area after the operation.

The element of surprise is the main requirement for the partisans' assault on any enemy objective. All preparation should be done with the strictest secrecy. Follow all the rules of covertness and camouflage. Immediately before the assault – cut off the communications between the objective and the inhabited areas and nearby enemy garrisons.

If a sizable force of partisans is sent to destroy the objective, then the group can act in approximately the following fashion. The main force uses a surprise attack to remove the guards and initiate combat – this is the assault and cover group. Under their protection, the demolition group destroys the target by an explosion or by setting it on fire. In addition to these groups, the partisan reserve protects the combat actions of both groups from a surprise enemy reinforcing attack should they unexpectedly arrive. The reserve covers the withdrawal of all the force after the operation.

If the partisans operate in small groups (three-four people) then there is no reason to start a fight. In such a case the partisans should quietly and covertly move close to the target. One or two partisans will prepare and carry out the target's destruction. At the same time, the remaining comrades secure and cover the demolition group from an enemy surprise attack. After the target is destroyed, everyone quickly withdraws.

When conducting a raid – act decisively, aggressively and quickly. The assigned mission must be carried out completely.

Remember: the enemy usually prepares firing data to engage probable targets should partisans attack nearby locations. Therefore, do not allow a large concentration of partisan forces without a real need. Massing may put the partisans under artillery, mortar or machine-gun fire quickly.

The reserve that covers the withdrawal must have enough automatic weapons to delay the enemy trying to pursue the partisans. It would be a good idea to have some land mines on hand – to toss behind them on the withdrawal routes. That would slow down the enemy and let the main partisan force break away and move to their base. It is advisable to withdraw by circuitous routes.

AMBUSH ON A RAILROAD

Defiantly derail the enemy's trains, destroy all his fascist manpower, all his cargo, burn his transport. The most advantageous place to derail a train is over a deep cutting when the train is going downhill. Then the steam engine would jump the tracks and strike the slope while the railroad cars continued to push down on each other creating a big jam. The rolling stock is destroyed and movement on that part of the railroad is stopped until the enemy is able to remove the twisted wreckage of metal and wood. The derailment of a train carrying a cargo of fuel also results in a fire.

Also it is advantageous to organize a fire assault along a deep railroad cutting. The fascists cannot disperse quickly to the sides. It is easy to destroy them with machinegun and submachine gun fire from the top rim of the cutting. A cutting also provides the ability to fire along all of the train.

Ambushes can also be set along the high railway embankments and turns – to make more railroad cars jump the tracks.

The place for the attack must be chosen away from railway stations and junctions where the fascists' garrisons are located, usually with armored trains and armored trolleys. Do not forget to cut communication lines with the nearby stations before making the assault, to make it difficult for the fascists to call for help. If time and numbers permit – place reserve groups of partisans several hundred meters from the place of the assault on both sides of the railroad. They should be ready to repulse by fire any attempt by the enemy's reinforcements to break through to the main ambush.

Before setting an ambush – do a thorough reconnaissance: determine the place of the ambush and the suitable approaches to it. One should study the traffic and security on the chosen segment of the railroad: when and what kind of trains pass through, when do the track inspectors and patrols make their rounds to check the tracks, does the enemy illuminate the tracks and surrounding area and are the trains guarded by trailing armored trolleys? It is also important to find out where the fascists' garrisons are located that could provide reinforcements to the derailment site.

Every partisan should know his personal part in the operation: to pick off an enemy sentinel, to dismantle or demolish railroad tracks, to cover comrades by fire, etc.

When attacking an enemy troop train, the partisans usually arrange their positions so that they can quickly surround the enemy. The main force of the ambush should be closer to the middle and end of the train, since, during a derailment, the leading railroad cars experience the heaviest impact and damage.

The part of the partisan group that is armed with machineguns and submachine guns should be located at the end of the train on both sides of the tracks. This puts them in a good position to fire down the length of the cars at the fleeing fascists. The partisans must open fire and cease fire at the order or special signal of the partisan commander; otherwise there is a chance that the comrades who are attacking the train will get hurt.

While in ambush, observe all the rules and requirements of camouflage. The signal for the attack on the train is the explosion under the tracks and the train's crash. Open rapid fire with rifles, machineguns and submachine guns on the railroad cars, throw hand grenades – evoke panic among the fascists, do not let them come to their senses and destroy them with bold and decisive actions.

If circumstances permit – try to find anything that could replenish your supplies – weapons, ammunition, food, clothing and medicine—within the enemy's cargo. After that – destroy everything that you cannot take with you

Look into the "Demolition" chapter for specific techniques for the blasting or damaging railroad tracks.

AMBUSH ON HIGHWAYS

Highways and dirt roads play an important role. The fascists use them to deliver personnel and supplies to the frontline. Disrupting supply, destroying enemy cargo and transport means that you disrupt his logistics system, hamper enemy plans for pending operations and provide enormous help to the Red Army units that fight the enemy at the frontline.

The fascists secure their transport with a heavy guard, they escort them with motorcycle patrols, set up systematic patrol routes, establish garrisons of covering forces on the most important roads, post sentries and establish secret observation points. During nighttime, they illuminate the roads with rocket flares. You should remember that when setting up ambushes on the highways and dirt roads.

The partisans' actions in such ambushes have much in common with ambushes on railroads. But there are some peculiarities. Highways and dirt roads have more of the narrow spaces that are suitable for setting up ambushes. It is possible to emplace land mines, dig a ditch across the road, construct a barrier, and destroy small wooden bridges and other river and swamp crossings. The most suitable places for ambushes would be: a cutting cleared in the thick forest, a log road across the marshes, a high and steep levee. It is the best to put land mines at those places. After the first explosion a traffic jam builds up because there is no exit from the road for the leading vehicles, and the following vehicles cannot turn around due to the narrow space. And that makes destruction of enemy personnel, transport and cargo much easier.

The most advantageous place to set an ambush would be a narrow segment with a turn. In this case the partisans can see and fire at the head and end of the column. Thus they should destroy the leading vehicle and the last one with explosives and hand grenades. That leaves the rest of the vehicles in the column bottled up, and makes the assault easier. Put landmines in the area of attack on the shoulders and sides of the road to prevent vehicles from leaving them.

It is very advantageous to use mobile ambushes. To create them – install land mines on the road in several places. This is an especially good ambush where there are two parallel roads not far away from each other. After inflicting losses on one transport column, the partisans quickly move to another sector or to the second road and assault the enemy there. The enemy gets the impression that there are several groups of partisan, not just one. The enemy troops sent to pursue the partisans have to decide where they are supposed to go. This makes the partisans' withdrawal easier after the mission is accomplished.

After destroying the enemy transport column, carefully check vehicles, wagons and enemy corpses. Collect all documents, papers, and letters. Take as much as possible of the military supplies with you and destroy the rest.

Partisans in an ambush are divided into separate groups: one of them conducts reconnaissance, another conducts the ambush itself and the third provides the covering force. The leader of the group defines the mission of each member. All partisans must know the signals for attack, withdrawal, etc. Reconnaissance must be conducted throughout the operation to prevent an unexpected attack by the reinforcing enemy units. Remember: a roadside ambush is the easiest way to capture a "tongue". The prisoner should be taken from the battlefield immediately.

ASSAULT ON AN INHABITED AREA

This type of operations is the most complex. There are various kinds of enemy objectives. For example, if there is a fascist headquarters in an inhabited area, then the partisans must destroy not only the headquarters itself but also the services: the communications center, the field power generator, supply dumps and repair shops, motor pools and fuel storage. In such an assault, the partisans would fight headquarters security troops and also specialized units – reconnaissance (including air reconnaissance), signal, etc.

All inhabited areas where the fascists are located are prepared for defense to some extent. They build various obstacles, foxholes and fire positions on the approaches and outskirts. They prepare separate buildings for defense so that the enemy is able to cover streets and internal squares with fire. Also, they prepare firing data in advance for artillery, mortar and machine-guns from neighboring points is in case the inhabited area is captured by the Soviet partisans or airborne troops.

The fascists' garrisons usually have wire and radio communications with neighboring garrisons and can get reinforcement fairly quickly.

All of that obliges the partisan to prepare the assault of the inhabited area with particular thoroughness in order to maintain surprise and the initiative in his actions. One must study the object of assault and conduct reconnaissance day to day.

It is necessary to know the inhabited area's layout, the location of its streets, squares and separate buildings. Every partisan should have a good orientation of the area. Make a detailed plan of the area. Put all the enemy targets which need to be destroyed on it. It is useful to look at them in person. Find out if they are built of stone or wood and which services are located in them. Learn the shortest ways between different objectives.

Also scout out where the fascist's garrison is located in the inhabited area: what is the total strength; how are the forces divided among guarded objects; what are the types of armament; when do the patrols, watch and guards change schedule? Learn which buildings house officers, headquarters staff and leaders of the fascist administration.

Determine the nature of the fascists' defense in the inhabited area: where are the obstacles; where are the firing points; how are the individual buildings prepared for defense – are there window covers, basements, shelters and cellars which could be used by the fascists for resistance? Check out if there are barricades and trenches on the streets and squares.

Carefully study the approaches to the inhabited area. Find out which approaches to the enemy's objectives you can use with minimal time and losses. For that you need to know: which sectors are heavily covered by obstacles, which firing points cover the approaches and thus need to be destroyed first, and where are the mine fields located, and is there is a way to around them? If a river or a marsh is near the inhabited area, then look into the possibility of using it for a covert approach to the targeted objects.

Reconnaissance must be conducted constantly. Always check and confirm all obtained information. Go to the Soviet patriots and close relatives and friends of the partisans, if they live in that town or village. Always maintain contact with them. Interrogation of captured fascists can help you to obtain some missing information.

Always remember the main conditions for the success of an attack on an inhabited area is surprise and initiative in actions. Sneak up on the enemy covertly, but after getting into contact – act boldly and decisively. Strike at the least expected spots. Try to catch the enemy off guard.

The best time for an assault is at night. Also you can assault the enemy during bad weather – during heavy fog or snow. But the night time is the best – since it lets you fully use the factor of surprise. But actions in the dark require careful preparation. Every partisan must know his mission precisely: which group he is a part of, what are his targets and how is he is supposed to destroy them. The partisans of the same group must know each other by sight. To recognize friend from foe, you can wear white bandages around the head or around an arm. Every partisan must know the challenge and password and the recognition signs. Every partisan must know the signals (light and sound) which are set for the attack and withdrawal. It is important that those signals are significantly different from the signals used by the enemy. Everyone must know the assembly area following withdrawal.

A successful assault may be achieved by a simultaneous attack from different directions. The partisans concurrently attack the enemy troops located in different parts of the inhabited area and at the most important objectives. If there is not enough force for such attack – destroy the enemy's troops first. After that – destroy the targeted objectives. Kill the fascist troops where they are located, do not let them unite, cut off their withdrawal routes and destroy them piece by piece.

The assault on an inhabited area occupied by the enemy and prepared for defense could be done in following way: the lead groups of the partisans silently remove the sentries or slip by them and launch a surprise attack on the enemy's firing positions, bunkers and fox-holes. They crush the enemy manpower at the outskirts of the inhabited area, destroy its weapons and destroy the telephone lines.

Their actions facilitate the operations of the follow-on groups. The follow-on groups quickly move to the most important objectives, destroy the enemy's manpower, suppress the objectives' security, capture prisoners and weapons, documents, correspondence, etc. It is important to attack several objectives simultaneously. The actions there must be rapid and bold. Use all weapons to the maximum extent. The enemy will get the impression that the attacking partisan force is much larger that it is. Try to surround the target and do not let the pressure subside until its complete destruction.

The groups that attack the objectives might encounter strong enemy resistance and even a counterattack from inside the inhabited area. For that eventuality, the partisans allocate a reserve that can quickly come to the aid of their comrades.

The partisan establish strong combat security simultaneously with their movement to the forming-up area for the attack on the inhabited area. The security is necessary to prevent the fascists from running away from the village and to repulse the enemy's assault from a neighboring area. The partisan covering forces should be located on the most-probable counterattack approaches and they should send pairs of sentries forward and to the sides of the approach at a distance that allows communication by sight. During the operation, isolate the inhabited area from the rest of the world. The covering forces also detain all inhabitants who are trying to leave the area.

The communications between separate groups of partisans and the commander of the entire operation is of utmost importance. Technical means of communications are difficult to use during such an assault, because the entire operation happens very rapidly. To provide communications, each partisan group allocates several couriers to deliver orders and reports.

The enemy may try to conduct a street battle. Small groups (two-three fighters) from the leading group must immediately occupy all the enemy's barricades and fighting positions inside the inhabited area. Their task is to prevent the fascists from using them for a street fight.

If a street battle ensues, the reserve is the first to get into it while the rest of the partisans assault the enemy objectives. The partisans, who are free from the mission after destroying the enemy's secondary targets – depots, auxiliary services, transport, etc. – join the reserve. If worst comes to worst, then part of the communicators may join the street fight. The reserve is reinforced by the partisans' tank destroyers and machinegunners. Some of the machineguns should be placed to cover streets and squares with fire. The reserve must prepare incendiary devices and explosives to destroy those buildings from which the enemy offers stiff resistance.

Remember the basic rules of street combat:

The enemy mostly takes shelter in houses that are prepared for defense: the basements, the rooms, the upper floors, the attic space near dormer windows and the area behind chimneys are converted into strong points. Corner houses are modified to cover intersections. Enemy's fire points are also located inside of yards, gardens and orchards.

Avoid moving and setting up on squares and wide streets. Hug the walls; cover yourself using building projections, doorways and columns. Fire at the buildings which are occupied by the enemy with machine-guns, throw fragmentation and anti-tank grenades into the rooms, set fire to wooden houses and buildings. Fascist garrisons in stone buildings must be destroyed with explosives. The light machineguns and submachine guns are advantageous in street combat. Street combat requires bravery, quick actions and cleverness.

Reconnaissance must be conducted throughout the operation to warn the detachment's command about approaching enemy troops.

If the mission of the partisan detachment is to capture and hold the inhabited point, then it can be done as follows. The combat security forces stay where they are and fortify the positions with trenches, foxholes, etc. The reserve group occupies the enemy's fortifications on the outskirts and prepares them for combat. The rest of the partisan groups capture what remains of the fascists garrison and administration; collect captured weapons, ammunition and equipment; and extinguish fires. The partisan scouts report on enemy's activities in the neighboring areas.

WITHDRAWAL FROM COMBAT

Surprise attacks and high mobility are basic to all partisans' actions. Protracted combat in the same place is disadvantageous for partisans: the enemy may use that time to bring up fresh forces. Try to avoid protracted combat if not specifically ordered to conduct it.

It sometimes happens that the enemy forces combat upon the partisans. As examples: the partisans have attacked the enemy's supply column, but the enemy security unit, that closely followed the column from behind, encircles the partisans and forces a fight; or partisans have derailed a train and started destroying the fascists who survived the wreck when German forces mounted on automobiles arrive from the neighboring station and surround the partisans on three sides; or a partisan detachment camped in the forest is surprised by a German punitive detachment. In cases like these, partisans are forced to accept combat.

If the force ratio and general situation do not allow the partisans to defeat the fascists by bold and decisive actions, then the partisans must quickly withdraw from the battle and shake off a pursuit.

The enemy may completely encircle the partisans. Then the partisans must fight to break through the weakest point of the encirclement. The mission of reconnaissance is to find where that point is. While the main forces conduct the breakthrough, part of the partisans cover them by fire to prevent the fascists from retightening the ring of encirclement. When the breakthrough is complete, those partisans armed with heavy weapons move to the breakthrough gap flanks – from there they help the rest of their comrades to escape from the encirclement. After that, they quickly occupy advantageous terrain and cover the withdrawal of the entire detachment with their fire. Then, they break contact with the enemy and move along circuitous routes to unite with their detachment.

When the encirclement is not complete and there is an exit, the partisans should withdraw in stages to bring out all weapons, ammunition, necessary rations and wounded comrades. To support this mission, groups of the most experienced and steadfast partisans are sent to the flanks of the area that has not yet been occupied by the enemy. They must hold back the enemy until the last possible minute. Those groups should be armed with automatic weapons and land mines. Another group of partisans provides fire support around the detachment perimeter to prevent the enemy from conducting a hasty attack. Land mines should be laid on the near approaches, where enemy's attacks are most probable. Part of the machineguns should be attached to the cover groups, and the other part should be used to fire from the depth of the detachment's location and to repulse enemy attacks from new directions.

Conduct reinforced reconnaissance during the entire period of withdrawal from encirclement and movement to a new location. Reconnaissance must determine: the enemy's strength and any grouping for an attack, if new enemy forces are approaching and is the withdrawal route clear of enemy.

Withdrawal from combat is a tense time. Very strict order and discipline among the partisans are decisive factors during this maneuver. There should not be any panic, confusion and unnecessary scurrying about! These should be decisively nipped in the bud. Everything must be done according to the commander's orders and directives.

Withdraw the group that is in the most difficult situation first: the enemy has concentrated superior forces against it and the terrain is not favorable for a successful defense. Evacuate the wounded and the sick with that group. Also evacuate armaments, spare ammunition and rations with that group.

After leaving the enemy's location, the group quickly reorganizes and prepares a defensive line to support the rest of the partisans by fire. Simultaneously, it prepares itself to attack the enemy rear area should circumstances require such an action. At the same time, they send the sick and wounded to the assembly area along with the weapons, ammunition and rations.

All the partisans covering their comrades' withdrawal stay at their initial positions and do not diminish their fire, rather they do the opposite. They increase their intensity of fire in order to deceive the enemy about the withdrawal. After the main force of the partisans withdraw through the enemy's combat line, the covering force begins a quick withdrawal on order of the commander. If the enemy's fire is heavy, then the partisans move by bounds from one line to another. The groups that protected the flanks join the covering force for withdrawal.

Over time, the partisans' main forces, which have withdrawn in parts, concentrate in the assembly area. There, the detachment reorganizes and, after posting reconnaissance and security, moves to the new area designated by the commander.

The partisan group that left first continues to hold its defensive line and covers the detachment's withdrawal by fire, preventing the enemy from conducting an organized pursuit. When the detachment has had time to move two-three kilometers, this group quickly moves in a direction that is different from the detachment's movement and draws the enemy along behind it on a false trail. Then the group boldly breaks away from the enemy and dissolves into small groups or even individuals. Later, they gather at the detachment's new location.

★ ★ ★

In this chapter we only discussed the main methods of the partisan tactics. Our partisans have amassed considerable combat experience in the fierce fight against the fascist fiends. The rules and advice collected in this book are based on this experience. But those are not recipes that cover every situation- they are just a general guide for action. Everything depends on many factors: the local environment; the general political and military situation; and the partisan detachments commanders' initiative. Always invent new methods to destroy the enemy, his machinery and his logistics. Remember that the main, fundamental commandment is to attack, to attack and to attack. If you act sluggishly and stay in the same place for long time – you just waste your strength and betray yourself to the enemy. Decisiveness, boldness, active offensive actions – those are the keys to success in the partisan fight.

II.

HOW THE FASCISTS ATTEMPT TO FIGHT THE PARTISANS

Partisans force the German occupiers always to be on their guard. They do not let the Hitlerite scoundrels rest by day or night, by creating an unbearable environment for them. Constant fear of the partisans' attack follows the Germans in all the temporarily occupied areas. The German command is forced to establish security and develop punitive measures against the partisans.

You must know how the fascists attempt to battle the partisan detachments. It will help you to avoid danger, better deceive the enemy and destroy him.

★ ★ ★

The Germans divide the occupied territory into separate areas which are a division's responsibility. The divisions have specially designated reserves to move immediately against the partisans.

The partisans must know the borders of the areas of the divisions' responsibility, and also the specific methods used by each division in their anti-partisan actions. It is necessary to know the locations and strength of their special reserves and take this into account in their own actions.

★ ★ ★

The German occupiers pay special attention to security of their lines of communication – highways and railroads. In the combat zones, that security is especially heavy: a battalion is assigned to each 100 kilometers of a road. Of course, depending on the number of artificial structures along the road and the terrain conditions, the strength of the force could be changed. The battalion assigns two soldiers as guards on each kilometer of the road. The remaining manpower constitutes patrols and reserves.

Separate companies have their own security zones. The companies establish field security posts with 10-12 soldiers each.

The battalion and company commanders usually stay with reserve units in the middle of their security zones.

The field posts and the reserve units build fortified strong points surrounded by barbed wire obstacles and usually located on cleared terrain that can be covered with fire. They move reserves from one place to another using automobiles, various motorized transport and trains with railroad cars that are adapted for conducting fire from them.

They secure individual sites with guard posts. The number of soldiers in the posts depends on the size and importance of the site. During nighttime, they usually double the size of the posts and put sentries not only under the bridges but also on the bridges piles. They also double the size of posts on terrain that is difficult to cover by fire.

The enemy patrols moves along the roads, often on motorcycles. During daytime, they patrol wide areas, sometimes extending several kilometers on both sides of the road. If there is a sizable enemy force, their area could reach up to 20 kilometers wide. The Germans also check all inhabited sites in this area. During nighttime, they only patrol on the road itself.

The Germans often burn down farmsteads near the railroad in order to improve sectors of fire and deprive the partisans of shelter.

The partisans must know the locations and strength of the German troops guarding the road sectors and also the transportation at their disposal. While preparing for the operation, calculate the time that it would take the German reserve units to arrive at one place or another. It is also necessary to decide where the best place is to cut the telephone lines between German units, how to track down enemy patrols and sentries and how to set up ambushes to liquidate them quietly.

The Germans send special units from one region to another to fight the partisans. German garrisons are stationed in the most inhabited areas in company strength and larger.

The Germans try to discover the location of a partisan detachment through their clandestine spies. Sometimes those are soldiers dressed in civilian clothes. Then the Germans select sites for ambushes. These ambush sites are usually occupied by forward detachments during nighttime. The main forces of the punitive expedition move to the line of ambush during daytime. While moving, the Germans scout inhabited areas and individual buildings and farms.

The heavy saturation of an area with German troops should be a warning sign for the partisans that the Germans are preparing an operation against them. And while the enemy troops study the terrain and population, the partisans could leave the area for a period of time.

If the situation and the force ratio permit the partisan to accept combat, it is necessary to prepare positions for a short duration resistance and after that move to counterattack and destroy the fascists. In such a case, the partisans set up ambushes along the enemy routes to destroy them with flanking fire. In any case the withdrawal routes, signals for withdrawal, and assembly areas after withdrawal must be defined in advance.

When the Germans prepare a punitive expedition, they usually do not conduct combat reconnaissance and especially reconnaissance in force because they think that it would warn the partisans about the operation that they are preparing. In these operations, the Germans only establish immediate march security.

To avoid a surprise encounter with the main enemy forces, the partisan detachment must take precautionary measures: send scouts far forward and reinforce immediate security.

To discover who are the German spies and soldiers disguised as civilians, the partisans must interrogate all people that they meet along the way.

★ ★ ★

The following are elements of the German tactics. They try to encircle the partisan detachment and attack it during the last hours of night or at dawn. If the detachment is located, for some reason, in an inhabited area, then the Germans open surprise fire with incendiary ammunition or signal flares at straw roofs to start a fire. Afterward usually they open up with mortar fire. Following this, the German assault forces attack from all directions. The Germans always constitute a reserve and all-round security. Separate German detachments communicate with each other by telephone and signal flares. They lay their telephone line as they advance.

Sometimes the Germans conduct a surprise attack on an inhabited area with motorized and cavalry units. When doing so, the motorized unit breaks through the inhabited area from one side and penetrates all the way through to the opposite outskirts. The cavalry subunits completely encircle the populated area. The cavalry usually conducts the check of all the population.

Partisans should take all of this in account when they set up in inhabited areas. They should particularly reinforce reconnaissance and security; also they should not let the locals leave – since there could be informants among them. Set ambushes along the roads that lead to the inhabited area and, if there is a chance, lay minefields on the most important approaches. Determine the best withdrawal routes and the assembly area in advance in case the enemy attacks. Each partisan of the detachment must know these.

★ ★ ★

The most common Fascist combat units to fight the partisans are companies or platoons. They are armed with heavy machine-guns and grenade launchers. They mostly move on bicycles, motorcycles and automobiles.

When the partisans are located on islands in the marshes that have difficult approaches to them, the Germans extensively use grenade launchers. Small units have tracking dogs with them.

Taking this into account, the partisans should build earthworks and, if possible – earth and timber fortifications to shelter themselves from grenade fire in their field locations. Further, the partisans must sprinkle their tracks with some special mixtures to hamper the search using tracking dogs. In forested terrain, the partisans should have ground observers as well as observers up in the trees.

★ ★ ★

In operations against partisans, the Germans recognize only one type of action – the offensive. They regard transitioning to the defense as extremely undesirable. If the offensive proves unsuccessful – they break contact and withdraw.

Therefore, the partisans must always vigorously impose their initiative on the enemy. But if a short assault does not produce desirable results – then the partisans should quickly break contact with the enemy and withdraw—if possible in a direction that the enemy does not know.

After withdrawal from battle, the partisans should reorganize and temporarily move to another area. To do so, they should have some emergency supplies of food stored in different places. Those supplies must be sufficient to support the partisans during the move to another area. Every partisan detachment should maintain communications with other partisan detachments in order to receive the help and food necessary during their movement to a different region.

★ ★ ★

The Germans also mount large expeditions to clear the partisans from particular regions. In such cases, they use a unit no smaller than a battalion to conduct a punitive march. The battalion usually has a zone of up to 20 kilometers on both sides of the road. A day's march of the unit is about 15 kilometers. They do not conduct reconnaissance so that they do not alert the partisans to the operation, but they always have local security. On the move, their troops check the inhabited areas and search individual buildings.

If there is enough time, the fascists stay two-three days in every large village to "work with the population". The fascists try to get information about the partisans using all brutal means, intimidation and, sometimes, bribery. While the main force stops or establishes a bivouac, mobile detachments return to the villages that they passed through earlier to determine the reaction of the partisans and the locals on the measures taken by the Germans.

Even while sending whole battalions on punitive expeditions, the Germans consider it impossible to sweep large forest tracts because it requires a very large force and is very dangerous. The fascists are afraid of large forest tracts.

If the partisans conduct systematic, thorough reconnaissance, they can easily discover these operations and have enough time to take countermeasures. If the partisans have sufficient force, they attack separate German units and destroy them. In this case, they should prepare their ambushes in advance. If the partisan strength is inadequate, they make the other possible decision – to withdraw from that area temporarily.

★ ★ ★

The Germans use aviation to find the partisan detachments. Their airplanes fly slow and at low altitude over the terrain and carefully look for movements on the roads, bonfires, smoke, etc.

The partisans must thoroughly hide their movements, using natural terrain features, vegetation and nighttime. They should not use open fires, but use hearths dug into the ground. They should try to produce as little smoke as possible. To deceive the Germans, they should light bonfires away from the detachment's location.

Each partisan must strictly observe all the rules of camouflage from air reconnaissance (see chapter "Camouflage") and be capable of destroying the fascists' aircraft with machinegun and rifle fire (see chapter "How to fight the enemy's aviation").

★ ★ ★

Here we have given only some general rules that the fascists use to fight the partisan detachments. But some German divisions may have their own specific methods and techniques for conducting security. The partisans should carefully study them to decipher the enemy's new tactics – to destroy Hitler's fiends more efficiently.

III

EXPLOSIVES AND DEMOLITION

EXPLOSIVES

In the enemy rear area, blow up bridges, railroad tracks, highways, dams, warehouses and repair shops. Use booby traps wherever possible. Place them on roads, near river crossings and inside buildings that the enemy could use for headquarters or living quarters.

Blow up enemy automobiles, tanks, cannon, fuel tanks, etc. Try to destroy as many enemy personnel or as much machinery as possible with a single explosion.

The following are the most frequent types of explosives you will deal with:

TNT (Trinitrotoluene). It comes in three types: 1) Crystalline powder of light yellow color; 2) Compressed into block charges of yellow color; 3) Melted – pieces and charges of yellowish-brown color.

Charges of compressed or melted TNT are made in a rectangular shape (200 or 400 grams each) or in a cylindrical shape (75 grams – drilling charges). The TNT charges are tapped for blasting caps (Figure 1).

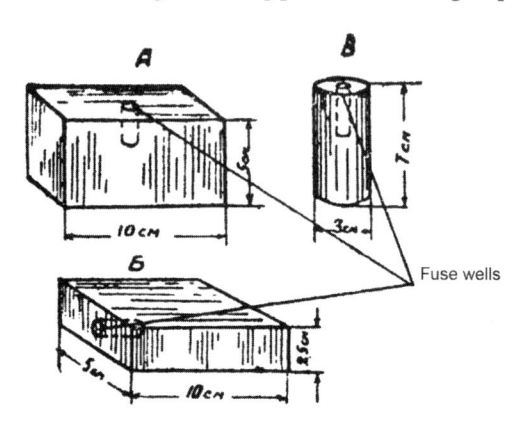

Figure 1. TNT Charges.

The charges are usually wrapped in waxed paper. The location of the fuse well is marked with a black dot. The TNT is fairly safe to work with.

Melinite (picric acid). It comes in three types: 1) A yellow-colored powder; 2) Compressed light-yellow-colored blocks; 3) Melted light-yellow chunks and discs.

If struck by a bullet, the melted melinite may burn, while the powder may explode. Prolonged contact of melinite with metals (except aluminum, tin and brass) will produce unstable compounds. Those compounds can easily explode as a result of a blow, friction or fire. You must be careful when storing melinite.

Melinite is detonated using the same methods as TNT.

Ammonal. Ammonal is safe to work with. It's shortcoming is that is easily becomes damp.

Boxes of explosives must be handled carefully and not bumped when moving them to avoid accidents. Do not smoke while working with explosives. Keep fire at least 50 meters from explosive storage. Explosives must be protected from the effects of sun, rain, snow and frost. Blasting caps, electric blasting caps and slow-burning fuses must be stored and transported separately from the explosives.

METHODS OF BLOWING UP OBJECTS

A **blasting cap** is used to produce an explosion. It is a small metal (copper or aluminum) tube. When it explodes from fire or an electric ignition, it detonates the main explosive charge. Be very careful while storing and working with the blasting caps and electric blasting caps. Protect them from impact, fire and moisture. To remove foreign objects from the tube of a blasting cap or electric fuse – tap lightly on its bottom or blow gently into it.

Bickford fuse (slow-burning fuse) has a gunpowder core that is wrapped in black hemp or brown gutta-percha. The fuse burns at a speed of one centimeter per second. Once ignited in the open air, it continues to burn under water (up to a depth of two meters).

Wick for igniting the Bickford fuse is made with a cord of threads which are infused with saltpeter brine.

A slow-burning fuse/blasting cap combination is used to detonate explosive charges safely. To make it – cut a piece of the Bickford fuse at a right angle. Push it lightly into the blasting cap until it is in contact with the explosive inside the cap. To prevent the fuse from falling out of the cap –

wrap the fuse with insulation tape and crimp the end of the cap with pliers (Figure 2).

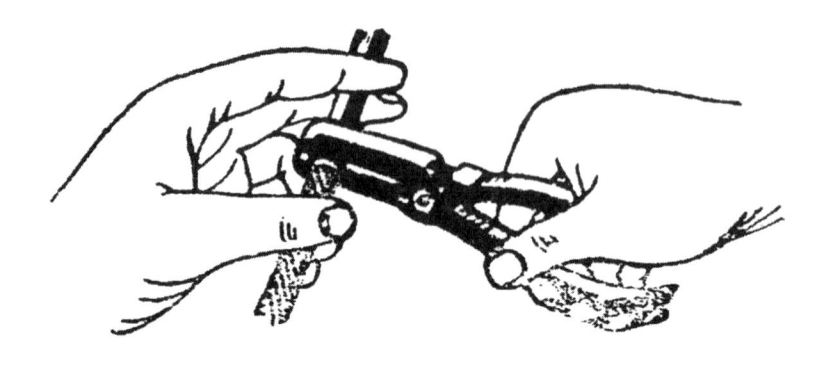

Figure 2. Crimping the Bickford fuse into a blasting cap.

The slow-burning fuse/blasting cap combination should be connected to the explosive charge only after the charge is fixed onto the target. To ignite the Bickford fuse – cut its end at an angle to uncover more surface of the gunpowder core. A piece of the fuse that is 60 centimeters long will burn for one minute. That time allows you to run away from the place of explosion. If you use shorter pieces of the Bickford fuse (10-20 centimeters) – be sure to calculate the explosion time precisely.

Detonating cord is used to produce several explosions simultaneously for example when demolishing a bridge, railroad tracks, etc. The cord consists of a blasting explosive wrapped in hemp impregnated with waterproof mastic. The detonating cord is red or blue. The detonating speed of the cord is about 7000 meters per second. It is easily distinguished from the Bickford safety fuse – the detonating cord's wrap has a red thread in it. When ignited, the detonating cord burns in separate sharp spurts, sometimes exploding. Never use the detonating cord in place of the slow-burning fuse and do not ignite it with matches. The detonating cord should be detonated only with a blasting cap or by an explosive charge. When setting a demolition network, you can tie the detonating cord in any knot but it must be tied tight.

A diagram of the connection of several charges with detonating cord is shown in Figure 3.

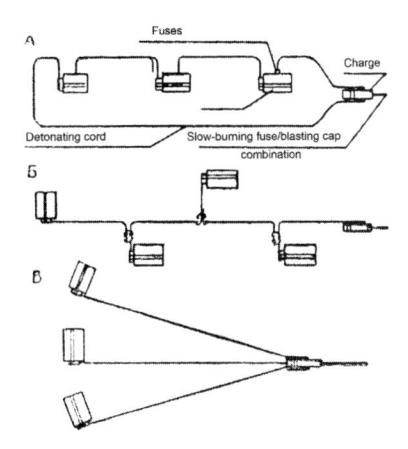

Figure 3. Diagram showing the connection of several explosive charges using detonating cord.

Detonating cord explodes under water – providing it has not been submerged longer than 12 hours.

Every demolition preparation in the enemy's rear area must succeed. Therefore, it is important that all preparations for demolition and destruction of important enemy target are done with the greatest care and following all the established rules:

1. Before setting out, insure that the ends of the Bickford fuse, the detonating cords and the blasting caps are protected from moisture (put some wax or mastic on them).

2. If the detonation will be underwater or in a damp place, – thoroughly insulate the connections of the Bickford fuse and blasting caps with rubberized tape.

3. After igniting the Bickford fuse, do not leave until you make sure that it is burning well.

4. Always count number of explosions.

5. Always wait at least 15 minutes before approaching an unexploded charge. In case the failed charge is set with detonating cord – wait at least two hours before you approach it.

ELECTRIC DETONATION OF CHARGES

Electrical detonation can be carried out at any time from various distances. The necessary components are a source of electric power, a wire conductor and an electric blasting cap that receives the electric charge and produces an explosion.

An electric blasting cap consists of a blasting cap and incandescent fuse (electric igniter).

The incandescent fuse (igniter) is designed to detonate a blasting cap. It is a small tube with two insulated wires protruding from its end. Its other end is plugged up with a stopper – this end connects with the blasting cap. You remove the stopper and put the blasting cap into the tube. The wires on the other end are connected inside of the tube with a thin wire bridge. The bridge is located inside of an incendiary mixture. In order to produce an explosion, each blasting cap in the network requires 0.5 ampere of electric current – with a shunt connection of 1.0 ampere – wired in a series configuration.

A flashlight battery is enough to ignite an electric blasting cap. Storage batteries and blasting machines also can be used.

The blasting machines detonate electric blasting caps or detonating charges which in turn detonate the main charges.

The PM-1 Blasting Machine weighs seven kilograms. It can detonate a single charge or a group of charges. It can detonate up to 100 charges hooked into a wire network of up to two kilometers.

To produce an explosion:

Take out the key from the machine casing's pocket. To open the cover – put the key into the slot in the cover and turn it counterclockwise until it stops. Open the cover and put the key into the lower socket on the front panel and tighten the spring, carefully turning the key clockwise until it stops. After that – remove the key from the socket. Connect the trunk circuit wires to the machine's terminals. Put the key into the upper socket marked "Explosion" and turn it clockwise until it stops (About 1/4 of a turn). Hold it in that position while the spring uncoils. The explosion should follow. After that, return the key to its initial position and remove it from the socket. Disconnect the trunk wires, close the cover, and lock it with the key. Put the key back into the casing's pocket.

The PM-2 Blasting Machine weighs 2.5 kilograms. It can detonate a single charge a group of charges. It can detonate up to 25 charges hooked into a wire network of up to one kilometer.

To produce an explosion:

Take the handle from the small case located on the machine's strap. Connect the trunk wires to the machine's terminals. Put the handle into the explosion socket so that the grooves on the handle base mesh with the projections on the transmission shaft. Hold the machine by the bottom of the case using your left hand under the strap. With your right hand, quickly turn the handle clockwise until it stops and continue to hold it until the explosion occurs.

After the explosion, disconnect the trunk wires, remove the handle from the socket and return it to its case on the strap.

All electric blasting caps must be wired into a series circuit when using the PM-1 and PM-2 blasting machines. Since the failure of a single blasting cap will lead to the failure of the whole network, observe the following rules while setting up the demolition:

Check the electric blasting cap wires – their ends must be clean and the wire is not broken.

Put the electric blasting cap inside the explosive charge so that at least three/fourths of its length is inside the charge.

Make sure that the blasting cap is securely fixed to the charge and cannot fall out of it.

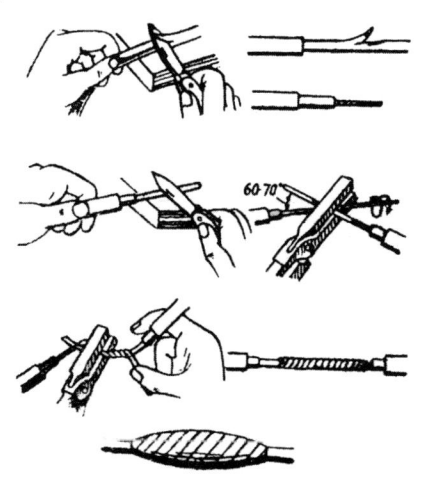

Figure 4. Splicing Wire.

Three kinds of wire are usually used: special sappers' wire; insulated electric wire; and telephone wire.

The wire leading from the electric source (blasting machine) to the charges is called the "trunk wire" and the wire between the charges is called the "end wire".

When detonating several charges simultaneously – connect them in a series using the end wires.

When conducting electric detonation of charges, you must prevent failure by meticulously joining all the charges, tightly splicing the metal wires and thoroughly insulating all splices (Figure 4). Try to lay the wire on dry areas and make sure that they do not touch each other. The trunk wire ends that are connected to the blasting machine's terminals should be cleaned to a shine and inserted securely. While doing so, insure that the bare wires do not touch the blasting machine's body and do not touch each other. And always remember to camouflage your work.

DETONATION BY EXPLOSION

This particular method can be used to set off several charges simultaneously when there is no chance to set up an electric detonation system and you do not have any detonation cord.

In this case, only one charge is detonated with a blasting cap or electric blasting cap. It is called the "active charge". The rest are the "passive" charges – (each weighing no less then 400 gram) – set down no further than one meter from the "active" charge. Put a blasting cap in each "passive" charge. The blasting caps in the "passive" charges must face the "active" charge. There should be no obstructions between the charges. When the "active" charge explodes – the rest of them detonate.

FOUGASSES AND MINES

An explosive charge can also be activated automatically – such as at the exact moment when the enemy moves over the hidden charge. For that purpose use a trip-wire fuse (UV).

The trip-wire fuse is a cylinder that contains a firing pin. The firing pin is spring-driven to strike a percussion cap. The spring is activated when the retaining pin is pulled out (Figure 5).

A fougasse – field or regular – is an explosive charge buried in the ground. While using trip-wire fuses it is possible to vary the methods of fougasse use. They could be pressure-operated or pull-action release operated.

The pressure-operated fougasse: the explosion occurs when a caterpillar track, wheel or human foot puts pressure on the fuse.

In the pull-action fougasse – one end of the trip wire or cord is tied to the retaining pin and the other end is tied to a local object so that the trip wire is some 5-20 centimeters above the ground. The wire (cord) must be camouflaged with grass, dry wood, etc. The trip wire can be tied to trees, large objects that interfere with movement, or some objects that look like they were accidentally dropped.

When a vehicle or a human foot catches on the wire or if someone picks up the dropped object – the retaining pin is pulled out and an explosion follows.

On forest roads, a tree barrier can force the enemy to remove the fallen trees. One or several of the trees can be tied to an explosive charge. As soon as the enemy moves the tree – the explosion occurs.

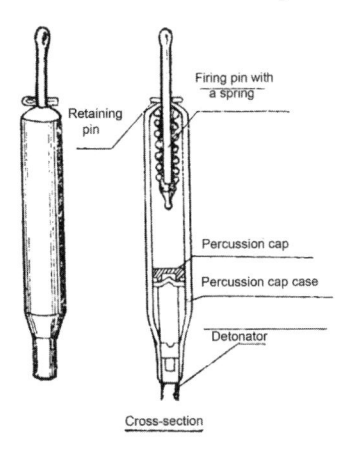

Figure 5. Trip-wire release Fuse (Cross section).

Several of the methods of emplacing fougasses are shown in Figure 6.

In the demolition business, you may need to use standard mines. They can replace fougasses. The mines can be triggered by pressure or tension-release. The possibilities for using mines are as varied as those for fougasses.

To produce an explosion after a certain period of time – use delayed-action mines. They have a clockwork circuit-closing fuse or an electro-chemical circuit-closing fuse. The alarm clock circuit-closing mines have a delay from 30 minutes to 10 hours while the electro-chemical circuit-closing mines have delay times between 10 and 35 days.

Where to Plant Mines and Fougasses

The mines and fougasses should be planted on highways and dirt roads used by the enemy. Pick the places which are difficult to detour around: embankments, dams, depressions, forest roads, forest cuts, steep slopes, etc. The weight of the charges should be from five to 100 kilograms and should be buried one to two meters deep.

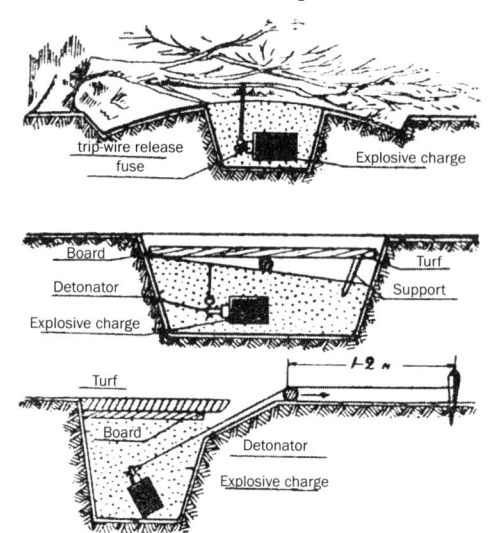

Figure 6. Various possibilities of emplacing mines and fougasses:
From top to bottom: 1 – Mining a forest road barricade;
2 – Pressure-operated fougasse; 3 – Pull-action fougasse.

Sites where fougasses are emplanted must be thoroughly camouflaged to make sure that the enemy does not notice them.

If there is a large quantity of stones around – you can build a stone fougasse – a stone-thrower on the road. The explosion of a 20-30 kilogram charge will throw a pile of stones 200-300 meters hitting enemy personnel and vehicles. Figure 7 shows how to build the stone-thrower.

Explosives and Demolition

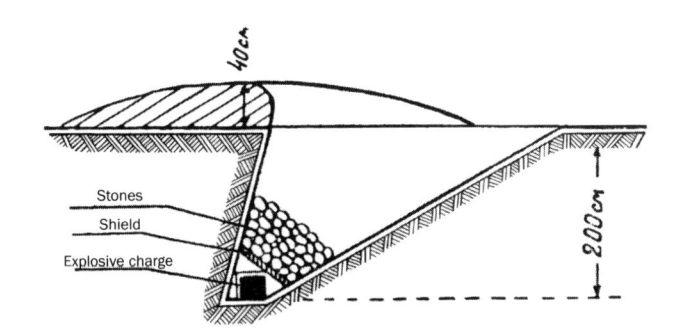

Figure 7. Stone-thrower.

It is also possible to place fougasses under water to demolish river crossings, ferries, fords, dams, bridges, etc.

During wintertime: place fougasses/booby traps on the ice of rivers and lakes where the enemy travels. Besides inflicting enemy casualties, it also destroys the crossing by breaking the ice.

HOW TO CONDUCT ARSON WITH MATCHES

First method: Take 90-100 matches (two boxes) and spread them out on a piece of cheesecloth or a regular rag. Puncture the cheesecloth or rag in many places to let air in. Saturate the cloth with any oil. Put a hemp wick inside of the matches (Figure 8). Calculate the necessary length for the wick – a hemp wick burns at the rate of two centimeters per minute. Put a piece of cloth or oakum saturated with oil around the hemp wick to reinforce the fire. Ignite the wick (it will burn smoldering without flame) and move away. The fire will start in your absence.

Figure 8. How to conduct arson with matches.

Second method: Put a box of matches inside of a can of floor wax or shoe polish. These are going to be your igniting charges. Connect a wick to the matches. Before use the charges – conduct a practical test to see how the mixture burns by burning small amounts of it.

GERMAN EXPLOSIVES

German explosives come as round cylinders or rectangular charges. You need to distinguish between them by their markings. The TNT charges have the digits 02 on them, melinite has the digits 88. All of them have one or more fuse wells for blasting caps (detonators). The openings are covered with protective paper labels. The labels have the charge codes printed on them.

The Drilling Charge (cylinder) is wrapped in paper. It's weight – 100 grams.

The Demolition Charge is wrapped in paper. It's weight – 200 grams.

The Standard Charge comes in a metal case and weighs one kilogram. The standard charge in a metal case weighing three kilograms comes in two types: one with three fuse wells for blasting caps and the other with five fuse wells.

Use the standard charges to make mines and fougasses. When you remove the label from the fuse well opening – you will see that it is threaded. You should screw blasting caps, electric blasting caps and slow-burning fuse/blasting cap combination sets into the fuse wells.

Familiarize yourself with the kinds and uses of these detonators:
1. **Blasting cap** in an aluminum tube. It is made the same way as our blasting caps. The blasting caps come in metal boxes – 100 units per box.
2. **Detonating cord** has a diameter of five millimeters. It is wound on a small wooden reel (100 meters per reel). The cord's explosive has a light rose color. The cord has a smooth waterproof covering with a bluish-green color.
3. **Bickford fuse** (slow burning). It is wound in coils of 10 meters each. It is single or dual core which can be determined by its thickness. The dual-core fuse is similar to our Bickford fuse with the gutta-percha covering. The burning speed – one centimeter per second – is the same as ours.

The friction igniter ANZ-29 is used to set off a blasting cap and ignite the Bickford fuse or gunpowder charge.

Use it as follows: Screw off the small lid on the igniter's bottom. Do it right before detonating a charge, since the lid protects the igniter's internal parts from dirt. Put the blasting cap into the slot of the cap-holder and screw the igniter into the fuse well of a blasting charge, standard charge or T-35 anti-tank mine. And what is left after that is to pull out the ring of the retaining pin. The friction igniter will ignite and produce an explosion.

Percussion-cap detonator ZZ35 is used to detonate blasting caps in fougasses and T-35 mines. It detonates by pulling a cord or wire. Here is how to use it: Put a blasting cap into the blasting cap-holding slot of the detonator. Then screw the detonator into the fuse well of the fougasse or mine. The detonator is now ready. Its upper part has a small rod. If it is pulled out – the firing pin will strike the blasting cap and an explosion follows. Remember that while installing the detonator: handle the rod very carefully.

Pull-action and tension-release detonator (double-action detonator) Z and Z-35 detonates not only when the trip wire (cord) is pulled but also if it is cut (releasing tension). Externally it looks the same as the previous one, except it has a longer rod with a small head.

The Pressure detonator with prongs is a metal tube with a sliding rod inside. The rod has pressure prongs which splay out from the rod. The prongs should be two-three centimeters above the ground.

Put a blasting cap into the blasting cap-holding slot on the detonator's bottom. The rod has an opening with a safety retaining pin. After installing the detonator – carefully pull the retainer out.

The pressure-operated detonator DZ-35 detonates from pressure on a pressure block (pedal ring) located in the upper part of the detonator. The pressure block is kept from moving down by a safety retaining pin on a ring.

To use the detonator: Put a blasting cap into the blasting cap-holder slot and screw the detonator into the fuze well of a mine or fougasse. Screw off the safety nut of the retaining pin and carefully pull it out. The detonator is now ready – an explosion will follow pressure on the pressure block.

IMPROVISED MINE

If you have captured detonators and standard charges then you can make an improvised mine. The assembled mine is shown in figure 9.

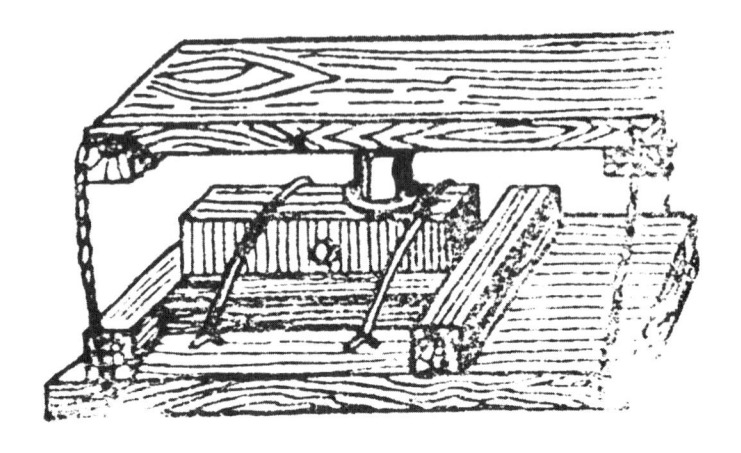

Figure 9. Assembled improvised mine.

Using pressure operated detonators you can destroy enemy tanks, cannons, etc.

Assemble the mine as follows: Prepare two wooden boards – 35 x 20 x 2 centimeters. Make four wooden cross-blocks (their length equal to the board's width) and two lengthwise blocks (their length equal to the length of the standard charge). Place the standard charge on the lower board as shown in Figure 9 and nail the blocks to the board. Secure the charge with wire. Screw in the pressure operated detonator DZ-35. Put the upper board on top of the detonator's pressure block. The cross blocks on its sides prevent the board from breaking or splitting. Fasten the upper and bottom boards with wire stays. The stays can be fixed to the boards with nails or wire staples. The mine is finished.

After digging in the mine – pull out the safety retaining pin from the detonator. When pressure is applied to the upper board the mine will go off immediately. If the mine is installed upside down – the blasting effect will be greater.

It is possible to put extra pull action detonators in the extra fuse wells of the standard charge and run trip wires from them.

Explosives and Demolition

HOW TO FELL A TREE

You need to fell trees and telegraph poles in order to build road barricades, anti-tank obstacles and for other purposes.
On the side where you want the tree to fall, make an axe cut approximately ¼ of the tree's trunk diameter. Start cutting the tree with the axe on opposite side a bit higher than the initial cut. Continue until the tree begins to sway with a hand push. Then make a strong push on the tree and it will fall in the desired direction.

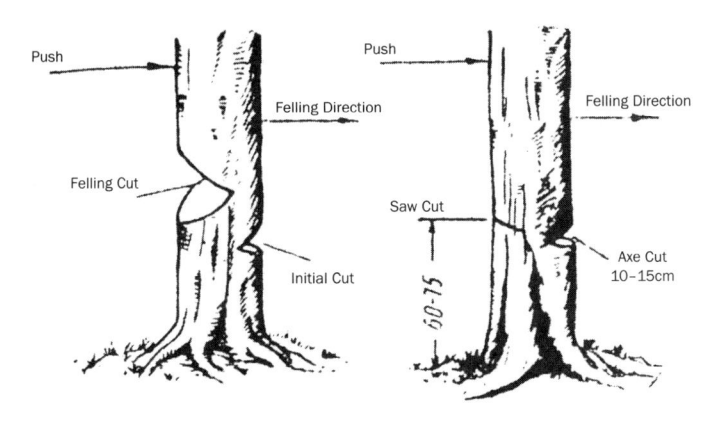

Figure 10. Felling trees.

It is better use a saw to fell a tree. Make a cut with an axe on the side that you want the tree to fell. And then, instead of cutting through the trunk with the axe – use the saw on the opposite side. When the saw's blade is completely inside the trunk – drive a wedge into the cut to prevent binding of the saw blade (Figure 10).

HOW TO TIE KNOTS

While emplacing explosives and carrying out various demolition and sapper tasks, you will need to tie dependable and strong knots. Learn how to tie them (Figure 11).
The end knot is used to connect the ends of two cords.
The straight knot is used to connect two cords.
The slip knot is used for tying auxiliary cords to stakes.

The Naytov (naval) knot is used for tying two items together.

The simple knot is used for tying two ropes together with the help of sling straps.

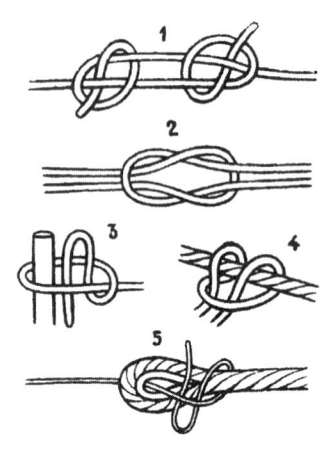

Figure 11. Knots: 1 – end knot; 2 – straight knot; 3 – slip knot; 4 – naytov (naval) knot; 5 – simple knot.

LEARN HOW TO HANDLE GERMAN MINES

Remember: the fascists use mines widely and employ them with cunning and trickery. Quite often they leave various lures in plain sight and connect them to mines. You should be careful and wary of them.

Do not enter a house which has been left by the Germans until you have inspected the ground around it. The stair steps of the porch, doors, windows, floor boards and various household objects – all of them could be connected to mines. Any attempt to move them or even a simple touch could produce an explosion. Use a long rope and a grapnel to open the door of such a house.

After entering the house – thoroughly inspect it. First, do a visual inspection, looking for the revealing signs of mines: fresh spots in the walls' plaster, evidence of disturbing the bricks in the walls or stove, fresh scratches on the floor. Also, check the electrical wires – see if there are any devices connected to them. If you find suspicious areas – check them more thoroughly.

Try to avoid all kinds of twine, rope and wire in the forest, on the roads and in the houses. They could be linked to mines. Be careful around places which show some disturbance to their uniformity. For example: small lumps of dirt on grass warn you about digging at that site. There could be a mine planted there. Be careful not to pick a rifle or other weapon left behind by the Germans, especially if it is in a highly-visible spot. The same rule applies to any other object. First, make sure it is not connected to a mine. Remember that the Germans sometimes even put mines on the corpses of their soldiers and officers.

To find mines planted in the ground, snow, sand, brushwood, or hay – use a simple probe. Find a metal rod about 1.5 meters long. Sharpen one end of the rod and bend the other for ease of use. Hold the probe at an angle in front of yourself, probing the ground around suspicious places. Push the probe carefully to a depth of about 20 centimeters. Try to direct it so that the probe will touch the mine's side. You can use a rifle with a bayonet or a sharpened wooden stake as a probe. As soon as you feel that the probe has touched some foreign object – stop the pressure – it could be a mine. Start disarming it.

You must know the main types of the German mines and how to handle them.

GERMAN ANTI-PERSONNEL SHRAPNEL MINES

a) When armed with the pressure-operated fuse, the mine detonates when pressure is applied onto the prongs protruding from the ground or onto the pressure block (pedal ring).

After finding the mine – put a hairpin, thin nail, piece of wire or regular safety retaining pin into the aperture for the fuse's safety pin – without touching the prongs or pedal ring.

Then unscrew the fuse. Make sure that the safety retainer (hairpin, wire or nail) does not slide out of the aperture. The mine is disarmed.

b) The anti-personnel mine S can also be employed with pull-action fuses (detonators).

The mine detonates if the trip wire (cord) is pulled or yanked out activating the fuse (detonator).

After finding this mine – carefully cut the wire (cord) near the pull ring of the fuse's retaining pin.

Then carefully put a hairpin, thin nail, piece of wire or regular safety retaining pin into the aperture for the Z-35 fuse safety pin and cut the wire (cord) near the fuse.

Carefully unscrew the T-joint fuse (detonator), close the central well's opening with a plug and remove the mine from its place.

The mine can also be destroyed by detonating it. To do so – carefully hook a long rope onto the trip wire (cord) of the fuse and pull the rope while sheltering behind some cover (boulder, building, bomb crater). The rope length should be 30 meters or longer.

The mine will explode four-five seconds after activating the pressure block or the trip wire (cord). Therefore, if you accidentally activate the mine S fuse and hear it crackling – immediately drop to the ground.

Remember that the mine S explodes at the height of a standing man's chest – about 1.5 meters. The mine, when it explodes, throws shrapnel pellets located inside its shell and pieces of the shell itself in a radius of up to 100 meters.

GERMAN ANTI-TANK MINE T-35

The anti-tank mine T-35 has its main pressure-activated fuse located on the top lid of the mine. It explodes if a vehicle runs over it or a person steps on it. Sometimes the mine has additional pull-action fuses – located on its side and bottom. They insure that the mine will explode if it is moved.

When you find the mine – do not apply any pressure to the top of the fuse or move the mine. Carefully clean dirt and snow off from the mine's top.

Hook a rope (at least 25 meters long) to the main fuse or mine's handle, move to a shelter (foxhole, bomb crater, behind a building) and from there pull the rope to move the mine from its place. If there are the side or bottom pull-action fuses, it will explode.

If there are no pull-action fuses, then it is possible to disarm the mine. Using your thumb, press the safety retainer of the main fuse into its place until it stops. After that, using the edge of a coin as a screwdriver, turn the screw of the vertical safety switch to the position where the red dot on the switch aligns with the white line on the fuse head (the word "swicher" is written above the white line). This will put the fuse into the safe mode.

The Germans also use delayed-action mines with clockwork circuit-closing fuses. You can detect the sound of these fuses by ear or with the help of a simple device. An ordinary drinking glass, tightly pressed with its opening against the part of the wall or floor under inspection, will help you hear the "tick-tock" of the clockwork mechanism better.

To check the ground outside of a building, you can use a so-called "water stethoscope" which can be made out of a standard bottle or flask. Fill the bottle with water so that water would is two-three centimeters from the plug. Cork the bottle with a stopper (rubber is preferable) with a piece of thin glass tube stuck through it. Put a rubber hose onto the outside end of the tube. After that – plant the bottle into the ground (the ground surface should be level with the water in the bottle) and put the free end of the hose into your ear. If there is a mine nearby, you will hear the clockwork sounds.

To disarm this type of mine: disconnect the wires that connect the clockwork mechanism with the electric battery. If you have difficulty doing that or the mine's design is unfamiliar to you – leave it in place and put security guards around it. After that, try to detonate the mine by exploding one-two demolition charges near it. Use the same method to detonate other mines as well – if there is no time to disarm and retrieve them or you are not allowed to leave them in place.

Knowing how to handle the German mines allows you to use them against the Germans themselves.

DESTROYING ENEMY'S TARGETS

Destroy the enemy's material resources and technical equipment using all available means: demolition, arson, etc.

To destroy wooden structures such as bridge piles, telegraph poles, the walls of wooden buildings – use demolition charges placed either outside the object or inside it (in a bore-hole).

To calculate the demolition charge's size – use its thickness (diameter). Measure the log's circumference with a piece of rope or your belt and divide the result by 3. That will be the log's diameter. Multiply this number (in centimeters) by itself and you will get the charge's weight (in grams). For example: log's diameter – 20 centimeters; the weight of the charge – 20 x 20 = 400 grams. When using an internal charge – bore a hole in the log. The size (depth) of the hole should be about 3/4 of the logs diameter. Put the charge into the hole. Boring the holes certainly takes time, but you can use charges ten times smaller than that required for an external explosion. To determine he charge's size for breaking squared beams – multiply the beam's thickness by its width. Example: beam's thickness is 30 centimeters and its width – 40 centimeters. The charge's size would be: 30 x 40 – 1,200 grams. As a rule – to destroy hardwood (oak) structures, the charge's size should be doubled; for underwater explosions – it should be divided in half.

If there is the need to demolish stone structures (buildings' walls, bridge piers, etc.) put the demolition charges either next to the structure (cover them with dirt) or inside the structures by hollowing out chambers in them beforehand.

When demolishing a bridge – place the charges in several locations (on pilings, spans and girders). Connect the charges with detonating cord or with an electric wire network (if using the electric detonation). Remember that if some bridge pilings are not demolished – it will ease the enemy's restoration of the bridge. For attaching demolition charges to trees, pilings and columns, see figure 12.

Burn wooden bridges if the circumstances permit. Braid straw or twigs into ropes, tie them to the bridge's pilings, pour liquid fuel on them and ignite them. Break up the bridge's flooring so that is burns faster.

Figure 12. a) demolition of a tree; b) demolition of a tree under water.

To calculate a charge's size for demolition of metal beams and piers – multiply its width by its thickness and increase the result 25 times. Example: the beam's thickness is 4 centimeters and its width – 20 centimeters. The charge's size would be: 4 x 20 x 25 = 2,000 grams, i.e. two kilograms.

It is essential to place the TNT demolition charges in rows, along the entire width of the beam. If there are not enough charges – add them without fail. If you do not have time to calculate the size of the demolition charges, then demolish the bridge with large concentrated charges (20-30 kilograms). Put them on the lower parts of the spans' lower girders on opposite sides and detonate them simultaneously. Figure 13 shows the best places to place demolition charges on bridges.

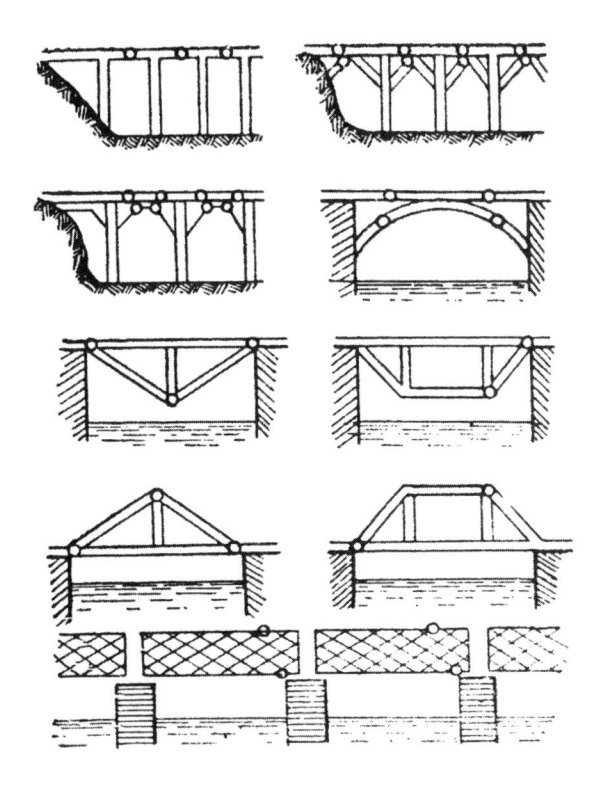

Figure 13. Diagrams of bridge demolitions.
Circles show the locations of the demolition charges.

On railroads, in addition to bridges, destroy the tracks, switches, frogs, embankments, water towers and hydrants. The railroad tracks are easily destroyed with a single 400-gram demolition charge (TNT or melinite) (Figure 14) Railroad switches should be destroyed with two charges: one between the track and the narrow end of the switch; the other – at the narrow point itself. To demolish the frog [crosspiece] – put the charge between the core joint and the track.

Figure 14. Location of the demolition charges to destroy a railroad track.

HOW TO DAMAGE WIRE
(COMMUNICATION AND ELECTRICAL)

Telegraph and telephone lines—and electrical lines as well can be damaged by destroying their poles (cut and fell them) or by felling trees onto the lines.

If you find a telephone cable on the ground – make several concealed breaks in it. It is not difficult: bend it many times in the same place until you feel that the metal core inside of its insulation is broken. Repeat this at several places.

Cut out kilometers of telegraph and telephone lines. While cutting field telephone cables – drag the end away as far as possible and tie it to any object. This will hamper the attempts to find and splice the wire. It would be even better to take a part of the wire with you.

Cut a sapling with a branch at its lower part. Cut off all branches but the lower one. Then hook the wire with that branch and make a strong pull – the wire will snap.

Break the insulators on the telegraph and telephone lines with a wooden staff – it will disrupt the normal operations of the fascists' telephone and telegraph communications.

Pull telephone or telegraph wires together at the insulators using a piece of wire – it will create a short circuit. Any communications over that line will be impossible. It will take a lot of time for the fascists to find and fix the damage.

You can disrupt wire communications using a very simple device. Tie a heavy weight or a stone or any other appropriate object to a long and strong rope. If you are using a stone – first wrap it in a piece of cloth to help tie it to the rope. After twirling the weight over your head, throw it over the wires. The rope should wrap around the wires. After that, a pull of the rope should be enough to snap the wires. You should throw the rope near the middle of the wires between the poles – the wires will snap easier at that point (Figure 15).

Figure 15. Breaking telephone and telegraph wires.

In order to damage a high-voltage electric transmission line – it is sufficient to connect it to the ground by a metal wire. Use a long piece of metal wire instead of the rope. Tie a weight to one end of the wire and bury the other end about 25 centimeters in the ground. Wet that place with water or urine. After that – throw the wire with the weight over the electrical line. The electrical current will go to the ground through the ground wire and the line will be damaged (Figure 16).

Remember: you must let go of the wire before it touches the electrical line. Otherwise you will get an electric shock.

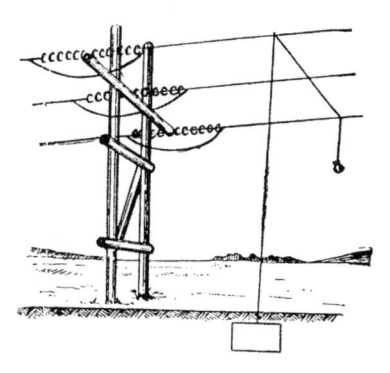

Figure 16. Damaging a high-voltage electrical transmission line.

HOW TO DESTROY FASCIST WEAPONS

If you cannot use the enemy's weapons, carry them away, hide them or destroy them.

Rifles, machine-guns, mortars. All type of rifles and machine-guns can be destroyed by removing bolts and breech mechanisms, burning the weapons or blowing them up. Destroy small quantities of rifles by:

a) laying a rifle between two supports and then striking it with a heavy object or putting your own weight on it to break or bend it;

b) Ruining the wooden parts with an axe;

c) Breaking off the sights and the magazine wells.

Large quantities of rifles are usually destroyed by burning.

Mortars and heavy machine-guns are destroyed by taking them apart. Separate the barrel from the base plate; take off the sight, elevating mechanism, etc. Hide the individual parts and assemblies or spread them around so that the enemy cannot find them.

Mortars and machine-guns can be destroyed by shooting at them. Shoot at the mortar's tube, machine-gun barrel's jacket, and other mechanisms. Fire at these weapons from a distance of 10-15 meters in order to protect yourself from possible flying fragments.

In order to destroy the mortars with certainty – use explosive charges on their barrels (tubes).

Artillery pieces. The most important parts for destruction of artillery pieces are: the breechblock, anti-recoil mechanisms (recoil brake and recuperator), axle, elevating and traversing gear, and the sights.

1. Conduct the partial destruction of artillery pieces as follows:

a) Take out the breechblock or firing mechanism;

b) Damage the breechblock and the breechblock housing by striking them with a heavy metal object, creating burrs and barbs;

c) Take out the nuts and lock nuts of the anti-recoil mechanisms and bend them by striking them;

d) Damage the traversing and elevating mechanisms.

Remember that only damaging individual assemblies and parts gives the enemy an opportunity to restore the cannon quickly. Thus, if conditions permit, try to destroy the artillery piece completely.

2. The complete destruction of an artillery piece can be achieved with demolition charges. See the table for the required size of the charges:

Guns' Caliber (mm)	**Charge Size (kg)**	**Location of Charge**
Up to 47	0.2 – 0.4	
47 – 100	0.4 – 2.0	Inside of the breech or
100 – 150	2.0 – 4.0	above the breechblock;
150 – 210	4.0 – 5.0	also along the cylinders
210 – 305	5.0 – 7.0	of the anti-recoil devices
305 – 420	7.0 – 10.0	or balancing gear

If you need to destroy several artillery pieces that are occupying combat positions or concentrated in an artillery park, then the destruction should be done by simultaneous explosions, connecting all the demolition charges to a single detonator. In such a case, the fragments could fly as far as 500 meters.

Guns can also be damaged if you pour some sand into the barrel and then fire the gun. If you pour sulfuric acid or alkali, which damage metals, into the barrel, then the gun will be ruined.

Artillery pieces can also be easily damaged if you shot their anti-recoil or balancing mechanisms with armor-piercing bullets.

Artillery depots. An artillery depot can be destroyed by detonating one of the boxes with explosives stored inside. To produce an explosion – put a slow-burning fuse/blasting cap combination (blasting cap, Bickford fuse and a piece of hemp wick) into a demolition charge. The hemp wick (two-five centimeters long) is tied to the Bickford fuse to extend the burning time. Remember that the Bickford fuse burns with the speed of one centimeter per second and the hemp wick burns at two centimeters per minute, i.e. thirty times slower. When you make the slow-burning fuse/blasting cap combination, keep in mind how much time you will need to run to a safe shelter.

Destroy stores of hand grenades, mines and fougasses in the same way.

Artillery ammunition depots can be destroyed by detonating one of the boxes containing artillery shells – the rest of them will explode by detonation. Also, the depot can be burned down.

Remember: when the artillery rounds are exploding, the fragments fly as far as 1000 meters.

Powder charges in bags can be destroyed by burning them or pouring water over them (or even better, by submerging them entirely under water). Signal and illuminating flare cartridges should also be destroyed in the same way.

Boxes of rifle and handgun cartridges should be burnt.

HOW TO DERAIL A TRAIN

First method. Screw off the nuts at both ends of the railroad track, remove the bolts and pull out the spikes from the railroad ties. The track should now be free. Move the track eight-ten centimeters to the side. An oncoming train will certainly derail.

Second method. Remove the spikes from two-three sections of track without removing the bolts at the junctures. Use a crow bar to move the tracks 10-12 centimeters to the side. This will widen the space between the tracks. Fix the tracks in their new position with the spikes or put a wooden spreader bar between them. A derailment is unavoidable.

Third method. Use this method on the embankment of a track where it makes a sharp turn. Dig holes under 15-20 ties of the outer track. The holes should be about half a tie wide and no less then half a meter deep. The ties should be suspended in the air. Disguise the evidence of your work; do not leave the dug-up dirt in piles. When the train moves over the undermined tracks, the locomotive will push the tracks down and overturn.

Explosives and Demolition

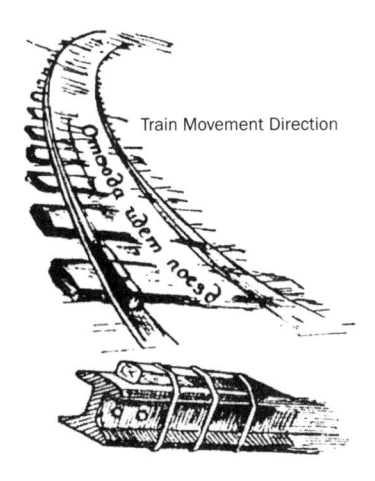

Figure 17. How to derail a train using a wedge.

Fourth method. This is the most complex method and requires preparation in advance. It used on the curves of the railroad tracks. Make a straight wedge out of a piece of dry hardwood (oak) that is 80 centimeters long, 7 centimeters thick and 5 centimeters wide. Cut one side of the wedge at angle as shown (Figure 17). Secure the wedge with wire to the top of the outer track at the curve so that the angled cut will face the oncoming train. When the train approaches the wedge, the locomotive's leading wheel will run up the wedge. The locomotive will not make the turn, but will move straight and leave the tracks.

IV.
COMBAT WEAPONS

REMEMBER THE BASIC RULES OF THE WEAPONS HANDLING

No matter what the circumstances, you must keep your weapon combat ready, i.e. clean and in working order. Always handle it with care. Your weapon must always be combat ready. Never plug the barrel's muzzle with anything – if left in, firing the weapon may cause the barrel to bulge or even rupture. Before you start cleaning the weapon – make sure that the cleaning accessories are in good order (cleaning rod, pull-through, screwdriver, drift punch, etc.).

While doing a visual inspection, look for:
Rust, scratches, dents on metal parts and dirt on the individual parts of the weapon.
Cracks and dents on the wooden parts.
Check that the main mechanisms of the weapon (bolt, sight, trigger, etc.) function properly and check the condition of the barrel's bore.
Learn the major signs of barrel carelessness and defects. You can detect them by looking through the barrel while holding it toward a light source.
1. Rust – a thin layer of dark substance on the bore's walls. If you run a clean cloth through the bore and see brown spots on it – it is a sure sign of rust.
2. Rash – small dark spots, that are specks of rust spread over the barrel's bore.
3. Bulge – this looks like a transverse dark ring (solid or intermittent) inside the bore.

INSPECTION AND HANDLING CARTRIDGES

A cartridge should be clean and without dents, cracks, burrs or green plaque. You must check if the primer is set too deeply or the bullet is not firmly fixed in the cartridge neck or if it is seated too deeply in the cartridge case.

The cartridges which are in good working order should be rubbed with clean cloth saturated with rifle oil. This should prevent them from rusting.

CLEANING AND OILING THE WEAPON

Timely cleaning and oiling of your weapon make it reliable.

If the weapon has not been used for a long while – clean it at least once every ten days. Immediately after firing your weapon, clean the bore and those parts of the weapon that have been exposed to the action of gunpowder gases. And as soon as you have a chance – do a complete cleaning of the weapon and oil it. Three-four days after cleaning, run a piece of clean white cloth through the bore – if you see traces of propellant fouling, rust and black spots – then repeat the cleaning. Otherwise just oil the bore.

Always have clean, soft cloth and oakum to clean, wipe and oil the weapon. Use the oakum only for cleaning.

Use alkali to clean those parts of the weapon that have been exposed to the action of gunpowder gases to remove their residue. Oil the weapon with rifle oil after cleaning. Remember that an excess of the oil collects dirt on the weapon and may cause its failure. To remove thickened oil from small parts – wash them in kerosene or gasoline. After washing – wipe them dry and oil.

To clean recesses, grooves, slots and other places on the weapon that are hard to reach with the standard cleaning rod or pull-through: cut a wooden stick with a knife to the required thickness, wrap a small piece of cloth (saturated with alkali, kerosene or oil) around it.

During wintertime, parts exposed to friction should be oiled with special winter rifle oil. Apply a very thin film of it with a clean cloth. A thick film of oil could harden during intensely cold weather and cause the weapon to fail.

If there is no winter rifle oil, wipe the parts exposed to friction with kerosene or the liquid from incendiary bottles (Molotov cocktail) #1 or #3: one of the ingredients in these is gasoline or kerosene.

Always carry your weapon with you and do not leave it unattended. Do not disassemble all the weapons in a partisan unit at the same time – do it in turn.

RIFLE – MODEL 1891/30

Figure 18. Rifle model 1891/30.

Purpose. This is the main weapon of the partisans. It is used to inflict casualties on the enemy by fire, bayonet or smashing him with the rifle butt.

Combat characteristics. This rifle produces the best results at ranges out to 400 meters. Its combat rate of fire is 10 rounds per minute. Its maximum range is 2000 meters.

Take care of your rifle. Under all conditions, keep your rifle clean, in proper working order, combat ready and handle it carefully.

Every day inspect your rifle and check for:

1) The proper operations of the bolt, magazine housing cover and the trigger;
2) Presence of dirt in the barrel bore;
3) Conditions of the front sight and the sight;
4) Secure fit of the bayonet.

PROBLEM	PROBLEM CAUSE	CORRECTIVE ACTION
1. Magazine housing cover opens when loading cartridges into the magazine and cartridges fell out.	Magazine cover catch is broken: its screw is loose or worn out or the catch tooth is worn.	Load the rifle without a stripper clip by putting the cartridges into the magazine well one by one. After shooting – determine the problem and repair it.
2. A cartridge jams while being loaded into the chamber.	During loading, the cartridge does not feed under the finger of the dual cut-off ejector and feeder guide. The dual cut-off ejector and feeder guide is broken.	Load the cartridge into the chamber manually. If the jamming occurs frequently – load the rifle without the stripper clip by putting cartridges into magazine well one by one. Replace the rifle at the first opportunity.
3. The cartridge feeds into the chamber too	The cartridge is damaged: its case is	Remove the damaged cartridge. If after opening

tightly – to close the bolt you need to use strong force.	dented, the primer juts out of the cartridge or the chamber is dirty.	the bolt, the cartridge still is stuck in the chamber – drive it out using a cleaning rod through the barrel. Clean and oil the chamber.
4. Misfire: after pulling the trigger the firing pin did not dent the primer.	The primer is faulty. The firing pin does not extend far enough or is broken. The hammer spring is weak, bent or broken. Oil inside of the bolt's firing pin channel has thickened.	Reload the rifle and continue to fire. If the misfire repeats itself frequently – remove the bolt, check how much of the firing pin comes out and if necessary – fix the pin's position. If the oil in the bolt has thickened or become dirty – disassemble the bolt, wipe it dry and oil it lightly with winter rifle oil. If the firing pin or hammer spring is broken or faulty – replace the rifle.
5. The cartridge case does not extract after a shot.	The extractor is damaged: its lip is worn or there is dirt or thickened rifle oil under it.	Remove the bolt and check if the extractor is broken. If it is in working order, try to remove the cartridge case by opening the bolt energetically or driving out the case with a cleaning rod through the barrel. After removing the case – clean the chamber and oil it. If the extractor is broken – replace the rifle.
6. Cartridges or cartridge cases are not ejected during reloading.	The spring of the dual cut-off ejector and feeder guide is bent. The channel of the dual cut-off ejector and feeder guide is dirty.	Remove the cartridge (case) manually and clean the dual cut-off ejector and feeder guide channel. If the dual cut-off ejector and feeder guide is broken – replace the rifle.

While moving through the forest – disconnect the bayonet to prevent it from catching on tree branches and making noise.

While cleaning the bore, insert enough oakum into the pull-through so that it will press into the lands and grooves and will enter the barrel's bore with light resistance. To do so – shape the oakum into an "eight" equal to the length of the pull-through copper part and insert half of the "eight" through the end of the pull-through. To make the oakum hold – twist it in different directions and lay it in the slots on the pull-through. If alkali is available – soak the oakum in it.

HOW TO FIX A JAM

Try to fix any jam during firing by first reloading the rifle. If the jam repeats – unload the rifle, find out what causes the jamming and fix the problem (see the table).

LIVE ROUND MARKINGS

Armor-piercing bullet – its head is painted black.

Tracer bullet – its head is painted green. The tracer bullet leaves a luminous trace after it.

SMALL CALIBER RIFLES TOZ-8 AND TOZ-9

Combat characteristics. The small caliber rifle produces less noise and has little recoil when shooting. Its design is very simple, it is easy to disassemble and it is very reliable.

Those qualities enhance many opportunities for partisan detachments to use the TOZ rifles.

The TOZ-8 rifle is a single-shot weapon and the TOZ-9 has a magazine holding five rounds. Combat rate of fire: the TOZ-8 rifle – up to seven rounds per minute; TOZ-9 – up to 10 rounds per minute. Maximum effective range – 250 meters.

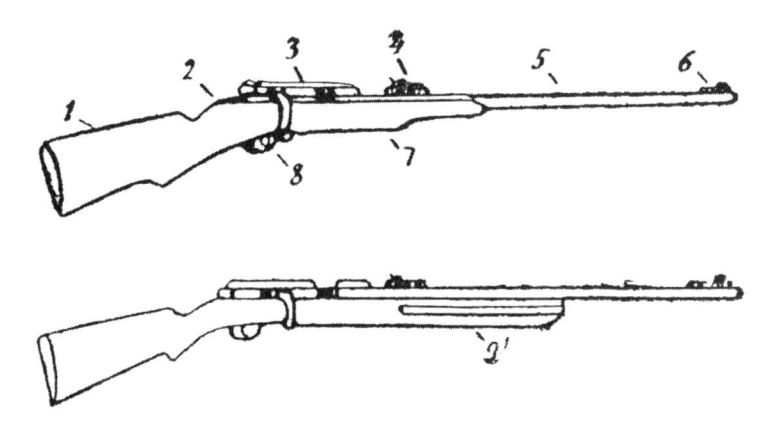

Figure 19. Small caliber rifles TOZ-8 and TOZ-9: 1 – rifle stock; 2 – grip stock; 3 – receiver; 4 – sight; 5- barrel; 6 – front sight; 7 – forestock; 8 – trigger.

HOW TO FIX A JAM

1. The cartridge does not slide into the chamber of the single shot rifle – the cartridge has not been placed correctly on the cartridge guide of the receiver, but is located on the left side of the receiver or is at an angle.

To prevent that – make sure that the rifle is not tilted to the side while loading the cartridge.

2. **Misfire** – there is no percussion compound inside the cartridge rim or the cartridge case is thicker than standard.

Open the bolt and reload the rifle.

The misfire may result from thickened rifle oil inside of the bolt, a broken or bent firing pin, or a weak or broken hammer spring. Consult the preceding table to fix the misfire.

3. The empty cartridge case does not extract from the chamber – some dirt has accumulated between the extractor and the extractor lip (in its front part) or in the grooves on the barrel for the extractor and slide.

Clean out the dirt and continue shooting.

4. The pressure required for the trigger release is not uniform – it is intermittently strong and weak – the trigger screw has not been tightened.

Tighten the screw and continue shooting.

SEMI-AUTOMATIC (SELF-LOADING) RIFLE MODEL 1940

Figure 20. Tokarev Semi-automatic (self-loading) rifle model 1940.

This rifle produces the best results at ranges out to 400 meters. Its combat rate of fire is 25 rounds per minute. Its maximum range is 1,500 meters.

HOW TO CHANGE GAS REGULATOR'S SETTINGS

You should pay special attention to the gas regulator which is located on the muzzle-attachment (Figure 21). In wintertime – set the regulator so that gases escape through the large openings, in summer – through the small openings.

To switch the regulator to another setting – remove the magazine, pull the bolt to the rear catch and engage the bolt-catch (lifting the later up with your finger through the opening in the receiver). At that point the bolt's handle will become loose. Remove the cleaning rod, disassemble the barrel band and remove the barrel jacket. Pull back the gas regulator until it stops and rotate the gas passage sleeve half a turn with a wrench. Set the gas regulator's face so that the required number shows when the weapon is held horizontally right side up. After that – secure the gas passage sleeve tightly with the wrench. Close the bolt, replace the barrel jacket and barrel band and insert the cleaning rod and magazine.

HOW TO FIX JAMS

1. **Misfire** – the firing pin is broken or does not fully extend when firing; the bolt is dirty; the hammer spring is broken or weakened or there is a bad cartridge primer.

Wait five-seven seconds after pulling the trigger, open the bolt and remove the cartridge. If misfiring continues – check the condition and extension of the firing pin, clean the firing pin chamber, the firing pin and the hammer spring.

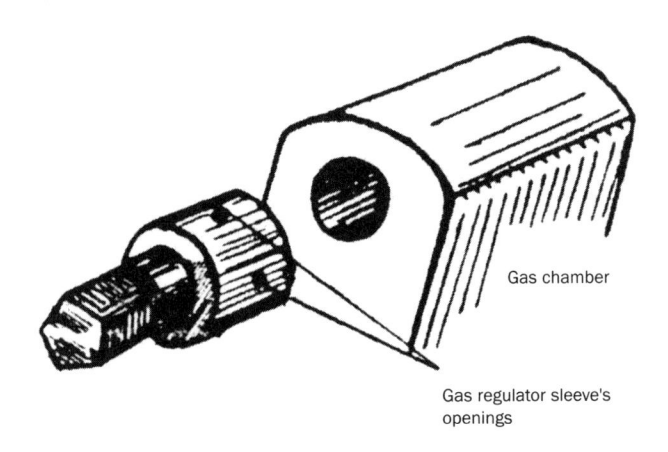

Figure 21. Gas regulator.

Gas chamber

Gas regulator sleeve's openings

2. **Cartridge case does not extract from the chamber** – the extractor housing is dirty, the extractor is broken or the extractor lip is worn; the extractor spring is broken; the chamber is dirty.

Clean the extractor housing; replace the extractor or its spring; clean the chamber and oil it lightly.

3. **Cartridge case stays in the extractor lip** - the cartridge deflector is broken.

Pull the bolt back until it stops. Remove the cartridge cases by hand if jamming continues.

4. **Cartridge case jams between the bolt and the barrel shoulder** – the extractor spring has weakened; there is an excessive gap between the bolt housing and the extractor lip.

Pull the bolt back until it stops; remove the cartridge case by hand; continue shooting. If the jamming does not stop – replace the rifle.

5. **The bolt does not fully open** – the receiver and the gas chamber are dirty.

Reload the rifle and continue shooting. If the jamming does not stop – disassemble and clean the rifle. As the least resort – use the larger opening on the gas regulator.

6. **The bolt does not fully seat** – the bolt grooves in the receiver are dirty; the forward return spring is broken or weakened.

Without pulling the trigger, push the bolt forward as far as possible and continue shooting. If the jamming is repeated – remove the bolt from the receiver, clean and oil bolt grooves of the receiver and the bolt. Continue shooting. If the forward return spring is broken – replace the rifle.

7. **A new cartridge is not loaded into the chamber** – dirty magazine; the magazine's walls are dented; the magazine spring has weakened.

Reload the rifle and continue shooting. If the jamming continues – replace the magazine.

8. **New cartridge sticks between the barrel housing and the front part of the magazine** – the magazine lips are bent.

Pull the bolt back, remove the cartridge or put it into the chamber and continue shooting. If the jamming does not stop – replace the magazine.

9. **Bolt is not held open by the bolt-catch in the rear** position and it moves forward too fast – the bolt-catch is jammed.

Change the setting of the gas regulator to a smaller opening. If the bolt-catch is broken – replace the rifle.

HAND GRENADES

HAND GRENADE MODEL 1933 (Figure 22)

Function and combat characteristics. The grenade's function – to destroy enemy personnel with fragments either during the attack or defense. The throwing range – 30-40 meters. The effective fragmentation radius: with the defensive jacket – 25 meters and without it – 5 meters.

Figure 22. Hand grenade model 1933: 1 – case; 2 – case lid; 3- shakeproof washer; 4 – central cylinder; 5 – detonator locking slide; 6 – defensive jacket; 7 – bursting charge; 8 – external cylinder handle; 9 – internal cylinder handle; 10 – insert; 11 – grooves; 12 – safety catch; 13 – striker; 14 – case base; 15 – striker spring; 16 – detonator safety catch; 17 – tape; 18 – lock nut; 19 – safety catch locking strip; 20 – defensive jacket locking strip; 21 – defensive jacket retaining strip.

Combat Weapons

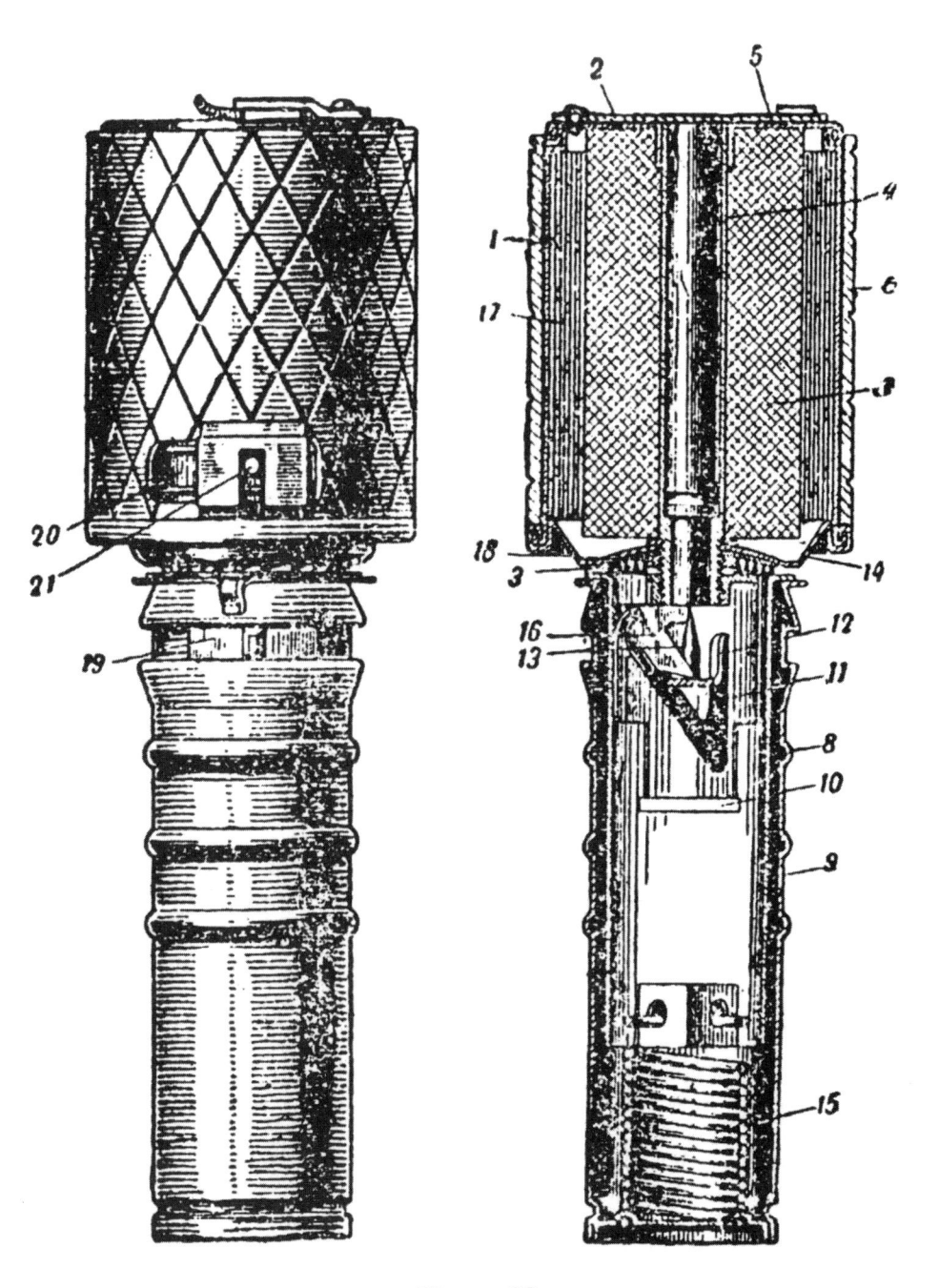

Figure 22.

HOW TO PUT THE GRENADE IN SAFETY MODE (Figure 23)

Pick up the grenade by the handle with your right hand. Use the thumb of your right hand to push the safety slide left until it stops. Then with your left hand, hold the grenade and with your right hand pull the external cylinder handle down until it stops. Turn the external cylinder right and smoothly move it forward (up). This exposes the red indicator – the grenade is in the ready mode. Use your right thumb to turn the safety slide right until it covers the red indicator. The detonating mechanism is in the safety mode.

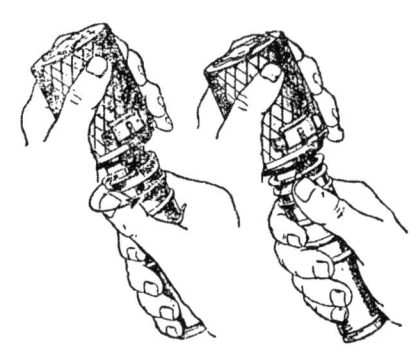

Figure 23. Putting the grenade into safe and ready modes.

HOW TO PRIME THE GRENADE

Only prime the grenade immediately before throwing it. First, put the grenade's firing mechanism in the safe mode.

After that – insert the detonator (Figure 24). Pick up the grenade by the case with your left hand with the case lid up and with your right hand slide off the detonator locking slide. Pick up the detonator with your right hand and insert it into the central cylinder so the igniting capsule is down. At first the detonator will slide in easily, but when only 7-8 millimeters of its length remains exposed, continued movement will meet some resistance. Light pressure applied with your right hand thumb will be enough to slide it completely inside of the grenade. At the same time, move the safety retainer locking slide into its place.

You cannot store the primed grenade: it could explode easily. If the grenade is primed, but not used, it should be disarmed immediately.[4]

Combat Weapons

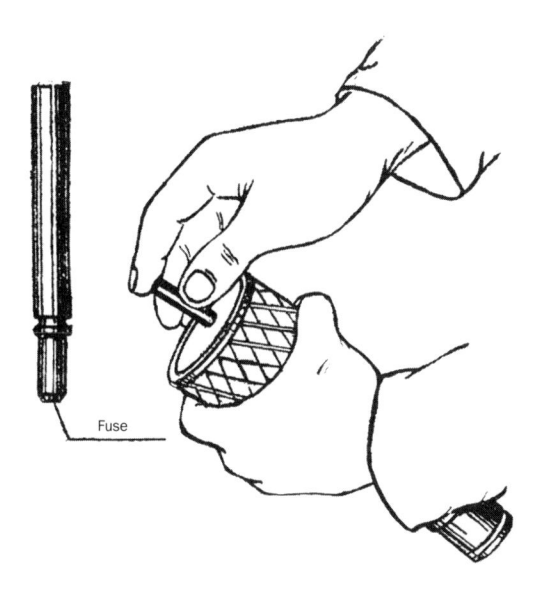

Figure 24. Inserting the detonator.

HOW TO DISARM THE GRENADE

Before disarming the grenade, check to insure that the firing mechanism is on safe (the red indicator is hidden).

Pick up the grenade by the case with your left hand and slide off the detonator locking slide. Some 7-8 millimeters of the detonator length will be exposed. With the fingers of your right hand, extract the detonator from the grenade, wrap it in paper or a rag and put it in the carrying case. Close the detonator locking slide, release the firing mechanism and put the grenade in the carrying case.

HOW TO THROW THE GRENADE (Figure 25)

Pick up the grenade with your right hand by the handle and, with your right thumb, push the safety retainer left until it stops and you see the red indicator. While still holding the safety retainer with your right thumb – swing back your arm and throw the grenade toward the target.

Only throw a grenade equipped with the defensive jacket when you are behind shelter. Otherwise – remove the jacket.

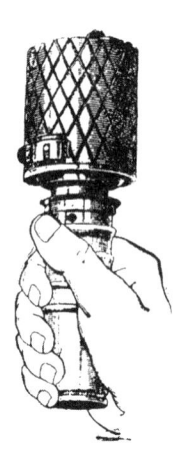

The Red Army's Do-It-Yourself Nazi-Bashing Guerrilla Warfare Manual

Figure 25. How to move the safety retainer.

DEFENSIVE HAND GRENADE MODEL F-1

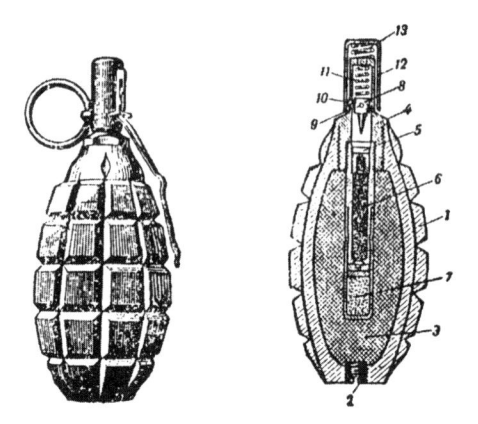

Figure 26. Hand grenade model F-1: 1 – grenade body; 2 – iron plug; 3 – explosive charge; 4 – detonator shell; 5 – detonator's igniting cap; 6 – powder; 7 – blasting cap; 8 – striker pin; 9 – opening in the striker pin for the safety pin; 10 – retaining ball; 11 – hammer spring; 12 – safety spoon; 13 – safety spoon spring.

Function – to destroy enemy personnel only from a sheltered position.

HOW TO PRIME THE GRENADE

Unscrew the inert plug from the grenade and throw it away. Check if there is a hollow space inside the explosive charge for the detonator made by the inert plug. If there is no hollow – make one with a wooden stick. After that, take the detonator and insert it into the grenade so that the detonator's tube fits inside the hollow in the explosive charge. Then screw the detonator in until it stops.

Figure 27. How to pull out the grenade pin.

HOW TO THROW THE GRENADE

Take the primed grenade in your right hand so that the lever of the safety spoon is under your four fingers. Press the lever to the grenade body with your right hand fingers. Use your left had to straighten the prongs of the safety pin and pull it out by the ring (Figure 27). Swing your hand back and forcefully throw the grenade at the target and move into a shelter. It is impossible to put the safety pin back and also it is dangerous to hold the armed grenade. Thus, after removing the safety pin – throw the grenade immediately (Figure 28).

Figure 28. How to throw F-1 grenade.

You should throw this grenade only from a foxhole or from behind cover.

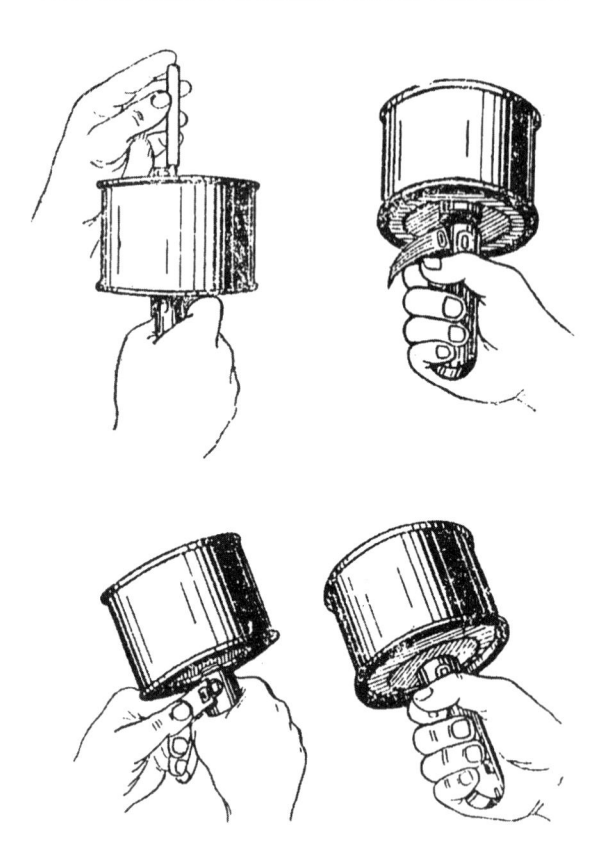

BLAST EFFECT ANTI-TANK GRENADE

Figure 29. How to throw the grenade.

Pick up the grenade by the handle in your right hand so that the safety spoon is pressed tightly against the handle.

With your left hand, open the sliding lock, slide the detonator inside the grenade and close the sliding lock. Do not apply much force while inserting the detonator – it should slide in easily.

Pull out the cotter safety pin. Throw the grenade and take cover behind in shelter.

The grenade will explode instantly when it comes in contact with a hard surface.

If the thrown grenade does not explode – do not touch it. Detonate it with another grenade or shoot it with a rifle.

Combat Weapons

HOW TO DISARM THE GRENADE

If the grenade is primed but not thrown – disarm it. To do that – without releasing the safety spoon, put the cotter safety pin back in its place and spread its prongs apart. Check that the prongs are spread apart, open the sliding lock and, holding the left hand covering the detonator, turn the grenade upside down – the detonator will fall out of the grenade. Close the sliding lock and put the grenade and detonator into the carrying pouch.

SUBMACHINE-GUNS MODEL 1940 PPD AND MODEL 1941 PPSh
(Figure 30)

Function. The submachine-gun destroys the enemy in close combat. Submachine-gun fire can be semiautomatic and automatic (short bursts of 2-4 rounds and long bursts of 20-25 rounds).

Combat characteristics. Maximum range – 500 meters. Rates of fire: semiautomatic fire up to 30 rounds per minute; short burst fire – up to 70 rounds per minute; long burst fire – up to 100 rounds per minute.

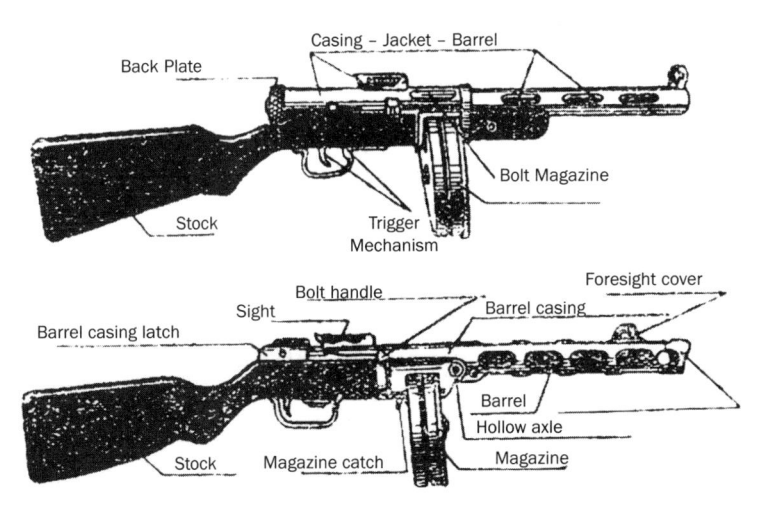

Figure 30. Submachine-guns Model 1940 PPD and Model 1941 PPSh.

The best results are achieved using single round fire for ranges up to 300 meters; short bursts of fire for ranges up to 200 meters and long bursts of fire at ranges up to 100 meters.

DAILY INSPECTION

Check proper functioning of:
1) The bolt and if the safety catch holds the bolt in both the forward and rear position;
2) The fire-selector switch;
3) The magazine catch.

HOW TO PREVENT JAMMING

1. If the situation permits, field strip the weapon after firing 500-1000 rounds. Remove fouling from expended ammunition and remove thickened rifle oil from the working parts. Oil the parts lightly and reassemble the weapon.

If the combat situation does not permit field stripping the submachine-gun, detach the magazine, set the fire-selector switch in the automatic fire mode and pull the bolt to the rearmost position. Pour liberal amounts of kerosene on the bolt through the magazine opening. Pull the trigger and the pull the bolt to the rearmost position again. Repeat this several times to thin the thickened rifle oil and gunpowder fouling.

2. During intense fire: after each 150-200 rounds, take a short break to let the barrel cool down; lightly oil the chamber or the upper cartridge in the magazine.

HOW TO FIX A JAM DURING COMBAT

1. If a jamming occurs – reload the submachine-gun and continue firing.

2. If a cartridge or cartridge case is left in the receiver – remove it by hand, reload the submachine-gun and continue firing.

3. If the jamming is the result of a faulty magazine – replace it and continue firing.

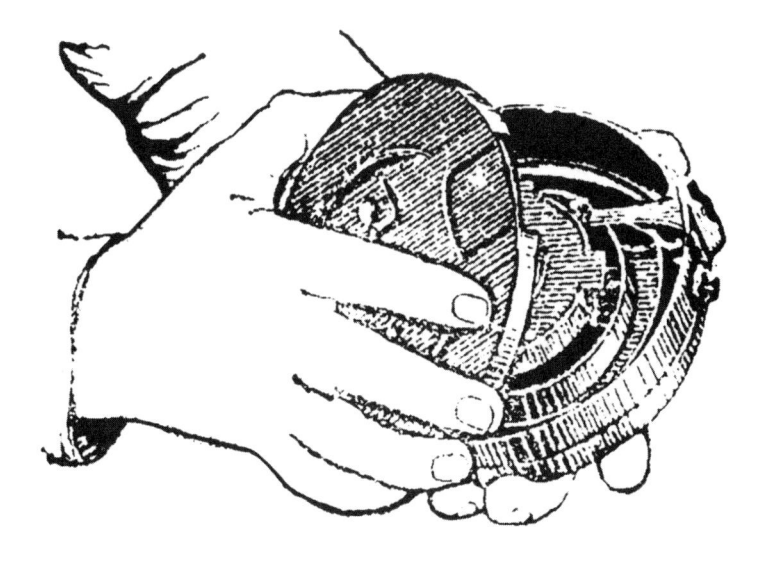

Figure 31. How to remove the magazine lid.

If the submachine-gun bolt does not fully seat in the forward position and a cartridge is in the chamber – do not drive the bolt forward by hand as this may cause an accidental discharge.

HOW TO LOAD THE MAGAZINE

1. **Removing the lid**. While holding the magazine with your left hand, use your middle finger to push the magazine catch up until it stops, then use the thumb of your right hand to turn the slide about 90 degrees. Then remove the lid while holding the magazine with the left hand (figure 31).

2. **Winding the magazine spring**. Hold the magazine in your left hand. Grasp the winding drum's lugs with the fingers of your right hand and rotate it counterclockwise (figure 32). You should hear eight clicks – the spring is wound.

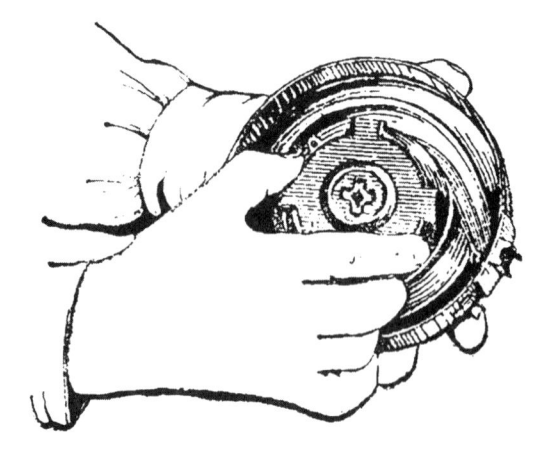

Figure 32. How to wind the spring.

Do not let go of the winding drum until you hear the click. Make sure that during the first turn of the winding drum, the magazine cartridge platform slides in the inner channel of the spiral but the spiral itself does not move.

3. **Put the cartridges into the magazine.** Take the magazine in your left hand, tilt it slightly and put 71 cartridges along all length of the spiral – in both the inner and outer channels.

4. **Release the winding device.** Take the magazine in your left hand and with your right hand turn the winding drum slightly counterclockwise. Press the magazine catch with your middle finger and release the winding device – this will put the cartridges under spring tension.
   Push down any protruding cartridges so that the cartridge heads are level.

5. **Replace the magazine lid.** Move the magazine catch to uppermost position and lock it with the slide.

FIELD STRIPPING THE PPD SUBMACHINE-GUN

1. **Remove the magazine** (figure 33). While holding the submachine-gun with your right hand ahead of the trigger, press the stock to your side with your elbow. Push the magazine catch forward with your right thumb and remove the magazine from the magazine opening.

2. **Screw off the back plate** (figure 34). Screw off the back plate with your right hand while holding the submachine-gun by the comb of the stock with your left hand. While doing this, hold the back plate in place with your left thumb to prevent damaging the thread end from the action of the recoil spring.

3. **Remove the back plate** (figure 35) along with the recoil spring from the receiver; remove the spring from the back plate cylinder.

4. **Remove the bolt** (figure 36). While holding the submachine-gun with your left hand, hold the bolt's handle with your right hand. Push the safety switch right and remove the bolt from the receiver.

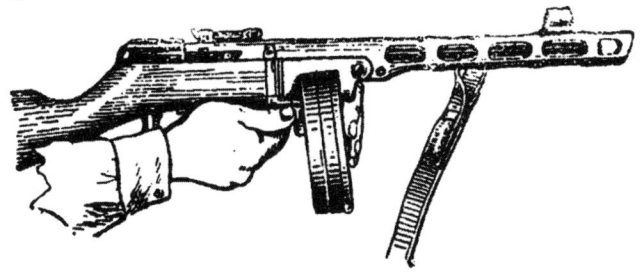

Figure 33. How to remove the magazine.

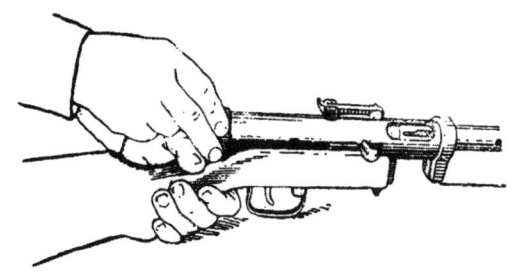

Figure 34. How to screw off the back plate.

Figure 35. How to remove the back plate.

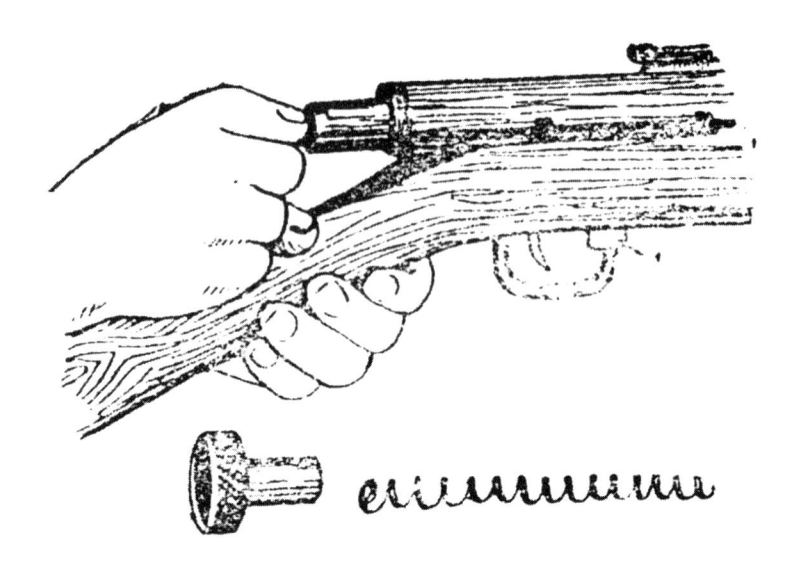

Figure 36. How to remove the bolt.

ASSEMBLING THE PPD SUBMACHINE-GUN AFTER FIELD STRIPPING

1. **Insert the bolt.** While holding the submachine-gun by the comb of the stock with your left hand, pull the trigger with your index finger and push the bolt inside the receiver. Make sure that the safety switch is positioned to the right, the upper rim of the firing pin is level with the bolt's surface and push the bolt forward until it stops; put the gun in the safe mode.

2. **Screw the back plate into the main casing.** Put the recoil spring onto the back plate cylinder, push it into the bolt's recess and screw the back plate into the receiver.

3. **Check that the gun is assembled properly.** Pull the bolt back and pull the trigger.

4. **Insert the magazine** (Figure 38). While holding the submachine-gun by the comb of the stock with your left hand tilt it to the left, while with the right hand, insert the magazine into the magazine well, slightly tapping on its bottom.

Combat Weapons

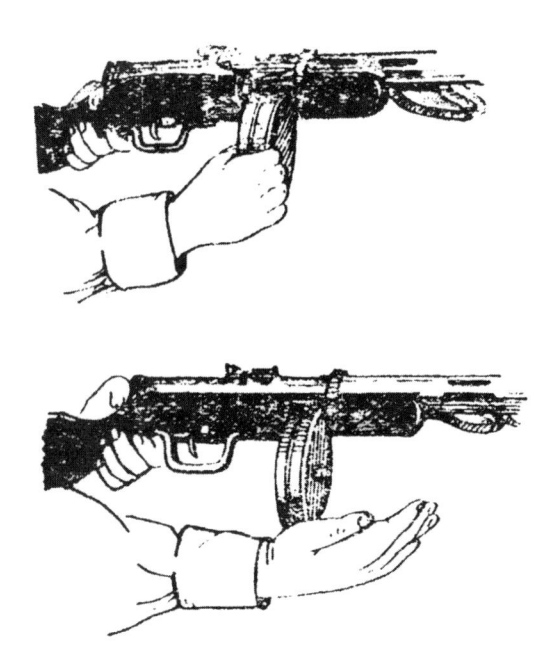

Figure 38. How to connect the magazine.

FIELD STRIPPING THE PPSh SUBMACHINE-GUN

1. **Disconnect the magazine**. While holding the submachine-gun with your right hand ahead of the trigger guard, press the gun to your side with your elbow. With your right thumb, push the magazine catch forward and with the left hand remove the magazine from the magazine well.

2. **Open the bolt cover** (Figure 39). With your right thumb, push the bolt cover latch forward and with your left hand press down on the fore-part of the barrel's jacket breaking open the cover and pushing it down (Figure 40).

3. **Remove the bolt along with the recoil spring, mainspring guide and the buffer**. While holding the submachine-gun with your left hand ahead of the trigger guard, pull the bolt handle back with your right hand. Lift the front of the bolt up, move it to the right and then remove the bolt along with the recoil spring, mainspring guide and buffer from the receiver. (Figure 41)

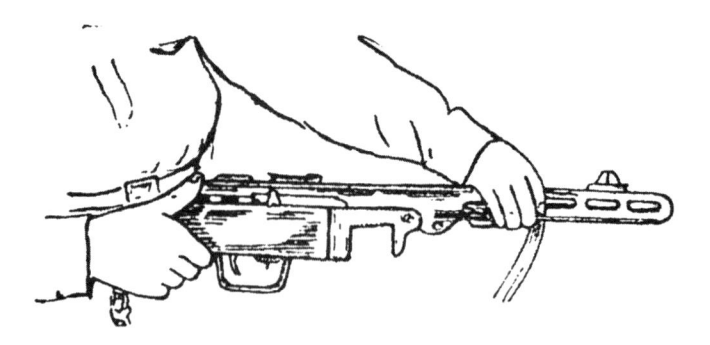

Figure 39. Opening the bolt cover – position 1.

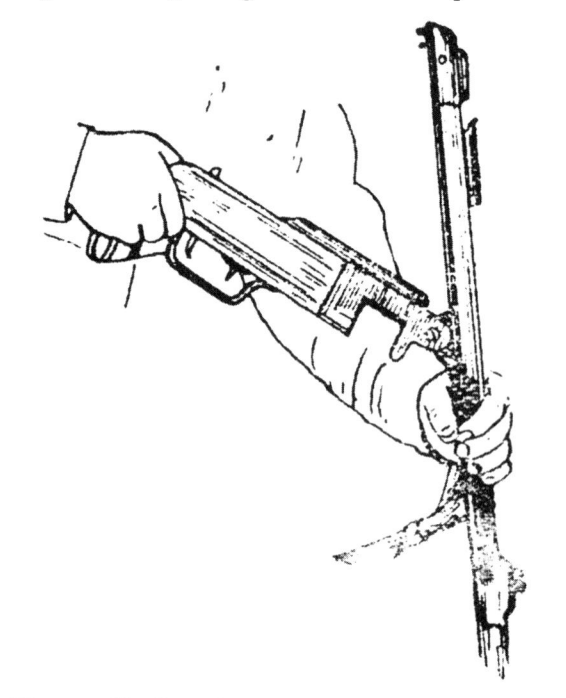

Figure 40. Opening the bolt cover – position 2.

4. **Separate the recoil spring, mainspring guide and buffer from the bolt.**

5. **Separate the buffer from the recoil spring and mainspring guide.**

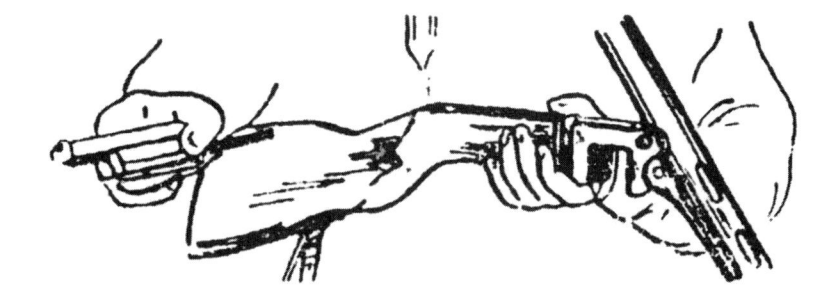

Figure 41. How to remove the bolt.

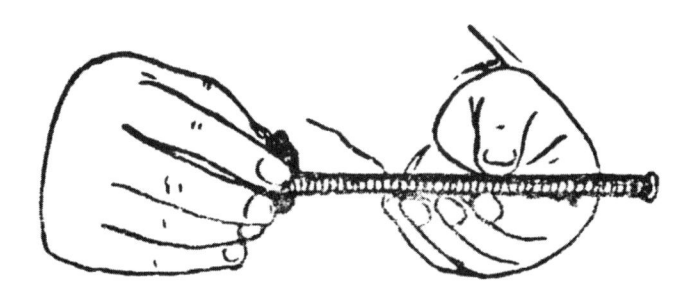

Figure 42. How to put the buffer onto the mainspring guide.

ASSEMBLING THE PPSh SUBMACHINE-GUN AFTER FIELD STRIPPING

1. **Insert the buffer into the recoil spring until the flat side is against the spring's base plate** (Figure 42).

2. **Insert the return spring into the bolt recess** (Figure 43).

3. **Insert the bolt with the recoil spring, mainspring guide and buffer into the receiver** (Figure 44). While doing so, the rear end of the mainspring guide should slide into the receiver housing. Secure the bolt back with the safety catch and pull the buffer back until it stops.

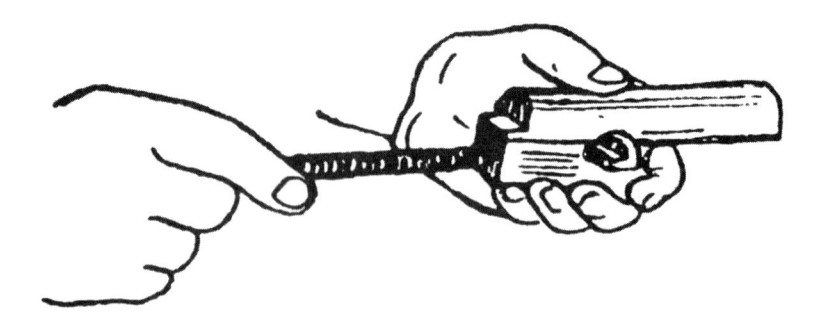

Figure 43. How to insert the bolt with the return spring, mainspring guide and buffer into the bolt recess.

4. **Close the bolt cover.** With the right thumb press the latch forward and push the bolt cover down.

5. **Release the bolt from safety catch.** While holding the bolt handle, pull the trigger with the left index finger and slowly guide the bolt forward.

6. **Insert the magazine.** With your left hand, insert the magazine opening into the magazine well. In doing so, the guide rib of the magazine should fit into the magazine catch slot. The catch itself should lock behind the rib flange.

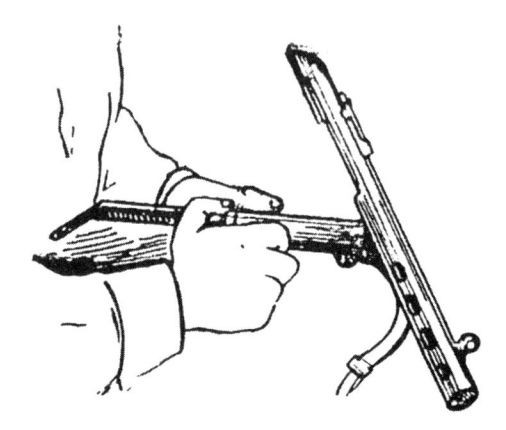

Figure 44. How to insert the bolt with the recoil spring, mainspring guide and buffer into the receiver.

LIGHT MACHINE-GUN DP (Degtyarev Pekhotny — *Infantry Degtyarev* Figure 45)[5]

Function. The light machine-gun DP is the primary automatic weapon used to destroy groups in the open and important individual targets at a range out to 800 meters and to engage ground attack aircraft at a range up to 500 meters.

Combat characteristics. Normal rate of fire – up to 80 rounds per minute. Firing is conducted in short bursts (3-6 rounds). Maximum range – 1,500 meters.

Daily inspect the machine-gun and check:

1) Is the barrel properly mounted in the receiver;

2) Are the front sight and rear sight in good working order and is the rear sight slide pulled back completely (put in the battle sight position); is the front sight cover in the proper position (the corresponding mark on the cover scale's must be aligned with the mark on the barrel jacket);

3) Is the barrel nut tightened;

4) Is the bipod properly mounted;

5) Is the upper magazine seating protected by its cover;

6) Is the stock locking pin screwed in properly;

7) Is the plug on the oil bottle screwed in properly;

8) Are the trigger and safety switch in good working order.

Stripping and assembling the machine-gun should be done on a clean ground sheet. After shooting, first clean and oil the barrel bore and bolt head.

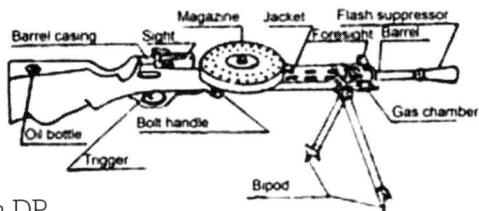

Figure 45. Light machine-gun DP.

PREVENT JAMMING DURING SHOOTING

To prevent jamming:
1) While loading the magazine carefully inspect cartridges and the magazine itself;

2) Do not let the barrel overheat and change it every 250-300 rounds;

3) In the wintertime, before shooting, oil the moving parts with winter rifle oil (if it is available); during breaks in shooting clean the gas regulator, piston cylinder and chamber; remove the thickened rifle oil from the moving parts and oil them and the chamber with winter rifle oil.

HOW TO FIX JAMMING

Try to fix any jamming by simply reloading, pulling the charging handle all the way to the rear. If the jamming repeats – unload the machine-gun, find out what the problem is and fix it.

1. A cartridge is stuck at a slant in magazine feeder slot – the magazine spring has weakened or is not wound completely; the connecting screw is not seated completely; the magazine feed-plate is loose.
Immediately replace the magazine and continue shooting.

2. A cartridge is not in the magazine feed-plate opening – the winding spring has weakened or is not wound completely.
Replace the magazine and continue shooting.

3. Moving parts do not fully seat in the forward position – the piston cylinder is dirty; the cartridge is dented; the chamber is dirty.
Depending on the problem, clean the piston cylinder; remove the dented cartridge; oil the chamber.

4. Moving parts do not move fully to the rear – the opening of the gas regulator is dirty.
Strip the machine-gun and clean it. If there is no time for that – clean the moving parts with kerosene or winter rifle oil through the receiver opening.

Combat Weapons

5. Misfire. If the misfire happens frequently – replace the firing pin.

6. The empty cartridge case does not eject – the ejector is broken. Replace the machine-gun.

7. A cartridge is stuck in the chamber or a cartridge case is left in the chamber – the extractor lip is broken; the barrel is overheated.
Clean the chamber or replace the barrel. If the ejector is broken – replace the machine-gun.

8. Involuntary automatic fire.
Disrupt the cartridge feed from the magazine by hand and wash the moving parts (especially the trigger mechanism) with kerosene. If this does not work – replace the machine-gun.

HOW TO LOAD THE MAGAZINE (Figure 46)

Turn the magazine so that its feeder opening is on top and prop it against some object. Take a cartridge into your right hand and squeeze it in your fist – leave the bullet's nose about one centimeter above the index finger. Press the magazine base cover with your right thumb; carefully shove the bullet's nose under the upper cover and insert it into the nearest slot of the cartridge rack in the cover. Use the bullet to turn the upper cover clockwise, pull the winding spring's stop catch out of the magazine feed opening (then push it down into the magazine feed opening using your left hand fingers).

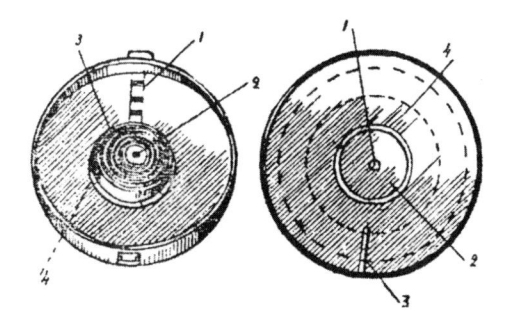

Figure 46. a) magazine base cover: 1 – loading tray; 2 – bushing; 3 – winding spring; 4 – coil.
b) magazine upper cover: 1 – bushing opening; 2 – stanchion; 3 – winding spring's hold-open catch; 4 – teeth for loading cartridges.

Take 5-10 cartridges in your left hand and insert them one by one into the magazine opening (with the cartridge bases toward the magazine stanchion). Turn the upper lid clockwise with the bullet; to do so move the bullet's nose to the next openings in the magazine disk. Hold the base plate steady in the same position – with the feed opening facing away from you.

COMPANY MORTAR MODELS 1938 AND 1940 (50 RM)
(Figures 47 & 48)

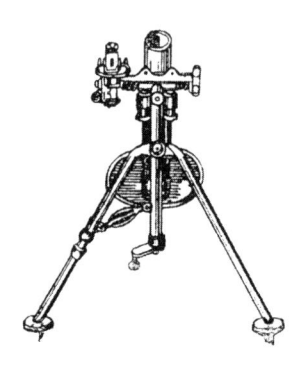

Figure 47. Mortar model 1938.

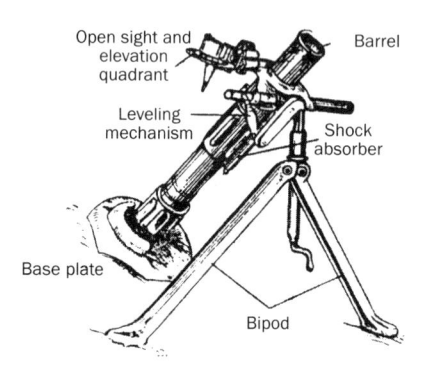

Figure 48. Mortar model 1940.

Function. A mortar is a weapon of high trajectory fire. It is used to destroy enemy personnel and firing points.

Combat characteristics. The mortar is a rapid-firing weapon. It is fairly light and possesses high accuracy. The mortar rounds fly with a steep trajectory and, when exploding, create a large number of fragments that travel horizontally for grazing fire. The fragments hit people laying on the ground in a radius of about 13 meters and standing people out to 30 meters. The mortar's range is from 100 to 800 meters.

The combat crew of the mortar is three persons: commander, gunner and assistant gunner.

Carrying the mortar (Figure 49).

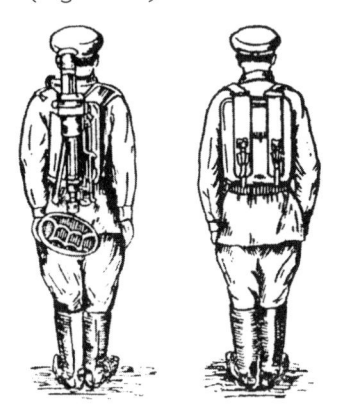

Figure 49. a) pack for the mortar model 1938; b) pack with two ammunition carrying cases.

The mortar and the rounds are carried in special packs: the gunner carries the mortar and his assistant – two carrying cases (14 rounds) (Figure 50). The mortar can also be carried in a special animal pack (Figure 51).

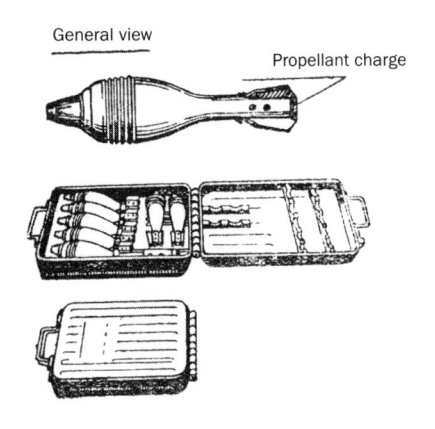

Figure 50. Mortar round and carrying case.

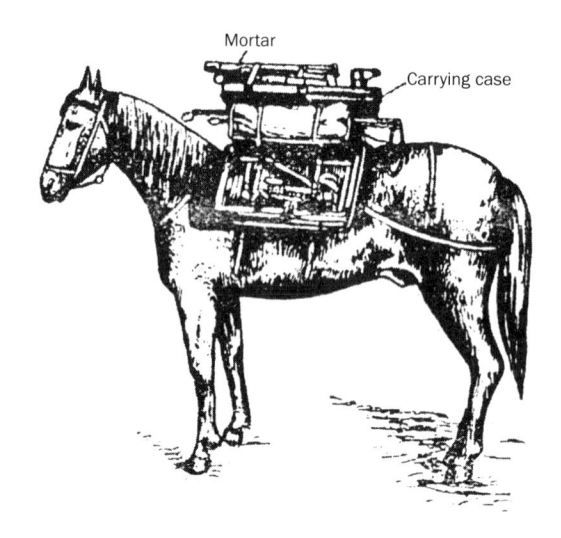

Figure 51. Animal pack.

HOW TO FIX THE MORTAR'S MALFUNCTIONS

1. Gas escapes from the barrel base breech – there is firing pin or ring erosion.

Replace the firing pin; if there is ring erosion – replace the barrel.

2. The barrel base breech is stuck – the thread on the breech piece or the barrel is dirty or worn out.

Screw off the breech piece and clean the thread. If the thread is stripped – replace the mortar.

3. Frequent misfires in the base breech end – the firing pin is very dirty or eroded.

Clean the end of the firing pin. If there is some serious erosion – replace the firing pin.

4. Frequent misfires at the open end of the mortar tube – the firing pin sways in the breech base slot.

Replace the mortar.

5. The round went down into the muzzle and is stuck inside of the barrel – the probable cause – the shock absorber clamp is fastened too tightly around the barrel.

Unscrew the shock absorber screws by several turns but make sure that the barrel does not move inside of the clamp. The round should fall and fire.

6. The elevating and traversing gears are difficult to work.
Disassemble the gears, clean them and lightly oil their threads.

7. The leveling mechanism is difficult to work.
Disassemble the mechanism, clean it and lightly oil its threads. Adjust the bipod leg stay screws by screwing them or the pivot yoke in or out.

8. The shock absorber works poorly.
Disassemble the shock absorber and clean its parts. If the shock absorber spring has weakened – replace it. Do not fire the mortar with a faulty shock absorber.

9. After firing a round, the mortar's lay is out of adjustment.
Check that the sight is firmly mounted, tighten it and continue firing. Check that the open sight is held in place by the sight latch. If not – lock it in place and continue to fire.

CAUSES OF MISFIRES OF THE MODEL 1938 MORTAR

1. The firing pin is worn out. Replace it.

2. The firing pin retains some pieces of the propellant charge (or pieces of the primer) from the previous round. Remove them.

3. The barrel is dirty. Clean it.

4. The positioning band of the mortar round is dirty. Clean it.

5. The propellant charge primer is defective. Replace the propellant charge.

6. The propellant charge is seated completely into the tail fin's tube. Push it in by hand.

ANTI-TANK RIFLE

The anti-tank rifle is a fearsome means with which to destroy the enemy's tanks and armored cars. The Red Army equipped with two models: a single-shot and a self-loading (semi-automatic) rifle. They have the ability to destroy an enemy's tank with a single shot. Both models use 14.5 millimeter armored-piercing incendiary cartridges. The best results are achieved when firing at tanks from the distance of 150 – 200 meters, though the bullet can pierce armor at a greater distance.

The Degtyarev single shot anti-tank rifle weighs 16.5 kilograms; its length – two meters (Figure 52). The crew consists of two persons – a gunner and his assistant.

It is possible to shoot five to six rounds per minute from the single-shot anti-tank rifle. The loading is done manually. The cartridge is loaded through the receiver and pushed into the chamber. Close the bolt with an energetic forward movement. If the bolt is not closed completely – it will frequently result in a misfire.

If the misfire happened while the bolt is properly closed – recock the bolt manually by pulling the striker backward. If the misfire repeats – remove the cartridge by opening the bolt to the rear and load another cartridge. If the misfire happens again with the new cartridge – check if the firing pin is broken or the striker mechanism is dirty.

When carrying the weapon on a march, put the weapon on safety. To do so – pull the striker ring backward and turn the bolt cam lug right to a 90 degree angle. When the bolt cam lug is pointed straight up – the rifle is on safe.

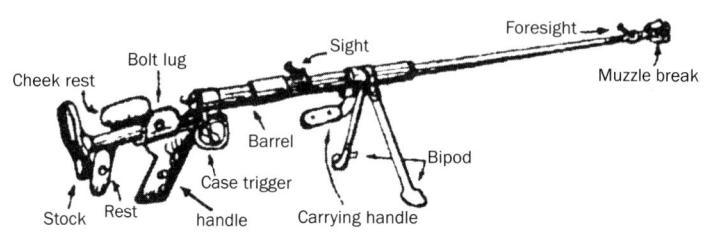

Figure 52. Degtyarev Anti-tank Rifle.

To remove the bolt when cleaning the rifle: press the stop catch which is located on the left side of the back of the receiver.

Always make sure that cartridges are lightly oiled with rifle oil. If the cartridges are dry, then misfires might occur.

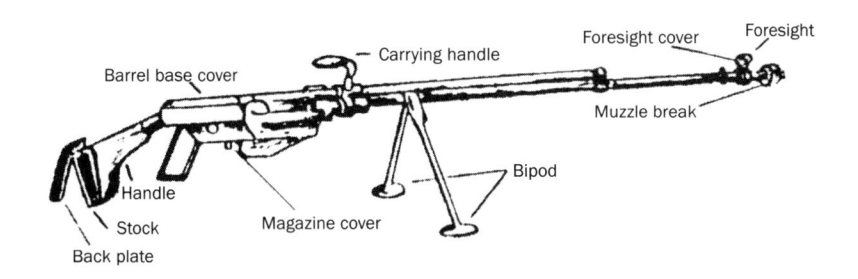

Figure 53. Simonov Anti-tank Rifle.

The Simonov self-loading (semiautomatic) anti-tank rifle weighs 20.3 kilograms, its length – 2.2 meters (figure 53). Combat (normal) rate of fire – 15 rounds per minute. Ammunition is fed into the semiautomatic rifle from a box magazine that contains a clip with five cartridges. You can reload the clip with cartridges without removing it from the rifle. The cartridges should be loaded through the upper receiver.

The anti-tank rifle's crew must prepare its firing position before engagement to reduce their vulnerability to enemy tank fire. The position should be carefully camouflaged. A simple anti-tank slit trench is a fairly safe shelter. You can take cover in it if a tank comes too close. Immediately after the tank passes over the trench, quickly fire at its rear where the engine compartment is located.

Use the anti-tank rifle to fire at the lower part of the tank turret – the ammunition is usually stored there – or at its tracks near the drive sprockets. When firing at an armored car – take aim at the engine or lower part of the turret. An incendiary armor-piercing bullet ignites or detonates tanks or armored cars when it hits the engine, fuel tank or ammunition.

The anti-tank rifle can also be used to fire at other targets– groups of enemy soldiers, artillery pieces in the open (the bullet pierces their metal shields), machine-gun fire positions and aircraft.

ANTI-TANK RIFLE GRENADE

Use the model 1941 (VPGS-41) Serdyuk anti-tank grenade when you cannot get closer than 40 meters to a tank.

The grenade has five main parts: 1) warhead with explosive; 2) striking mechanism; 3) detonator; 4) rod; 5) stabilizer. The grenade is normally disassembled when stored and carried. Assemble it before combat. Figure 54 shows how to assemble the grenade.

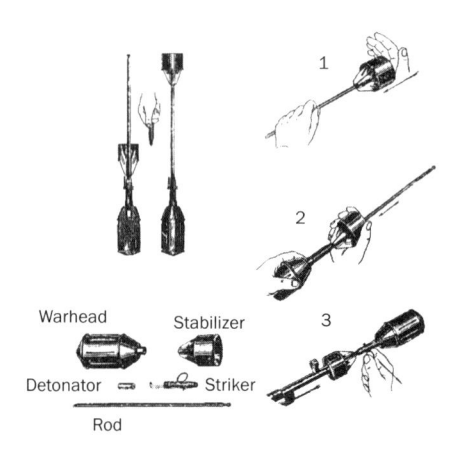

Figure 54. Anti-tank Rifle Grenade. This shows the grenade's parts, assembly and preparation for use.

Slide the stabilizer onto the rod. Screw the rod into the striking mechanism and then screw the mechanism into the warhead. You can move the grenade to the firing position in this state.

The grenade must be armed only at the firing position. To do so: 1) unscrew the striking mechanism from the warhead; 2) insert the detonator in the detonator cup; while doing so make sure that the safety pin's prongs are spread apart some 3-4 millimeter; 3) screw the striking mechanism with the detonator into the grenade's warhead; 4) slide the stabilizer onto the rod and down until the rod comes up against the detonator.

Now the grenade is ready. What remains is slide the rod into the rifle barrel. When the rod is seated inside the barrel – load the rifle with a blank cartridge (cartridge without a bullet). After that, use your right hand to pull out the safety pin ring from the grenade. Now you can fire the grenade.

The optimum use of the antitank rifle grenade is in direct fire against individual targets from 60—70 meters. You should take cover in a trench or behind a tree while firing the grenade. To engage closely grouped tanks – fire at them indirectly from a greater distance – 120-140 meters at 40-50 degrees angle of elevation.

V.

REVOLVER AND PISTOL

REVOLVER MODEL 1895

Function – for offensive and defensive close combat and hand-to-hand fighting.

Combat characteristics. Combat (normal) rate of fire: seven shots in 15-20 seconds. Weapon caliber – 7.62 millimeter.

Cleaning the revolver. Use a pull-through cord for cleaning and oiling the revolver barrel and the swing-out cylinder chambers. Slide enough oakum or clean cloth into the pull-through slotted tab so that it passes through the barrel with light resistance.

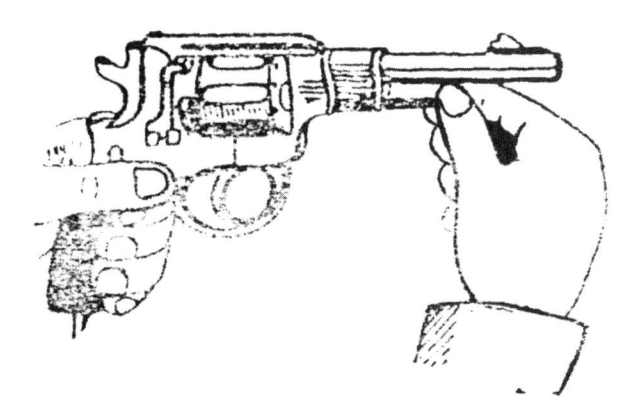

Figure 55. How to unscrew the extractor rod.

Saturate the oakum with alkali solution. Slide the pull-through cord into the barrel from the muzzle end and pull it 7-10 times through the barrel ensuring that it twists following the barrel rifling.

FIELD STRIPPING OF THE REVOLVER FOR CLEANING

Hold the revolver with your left hand and turn the extractor rod's head counterclockwise, then withdraw the extractor rod from the cartridge cylinder's axis (figure 55).

Turn the extractor rod guide until the marker on it aligns with the marker on the barrel. Remove the cartridge cylinder's axis by pulling it out by the axis head.

Swing the loading gate out and pull the cartridge cylinder out to the right.

Rotate the loading gate back into its place.

ASSEMBLING REVOLVER

Rotate the loading gate down.

Take the cylinder in the right hand, put the thumb on its back and slide the movable tube inside the cylinder.

Insert the cylinder into the frame from the right side and close the loading gate.

Turn the extractor rod guide and align its marker with the marker on the barrel. Slide the cylinder's axis into its place – the head should lie in the frame's slot.

While rotating the extractor rod guide, push it into the cylinder's axis and turn its head counterclockwise.

HOW TO LOAD THE REVOLVER

Make sure that the revolver is not cocked; if it is – un—cock it. Take the revolver into your left hand (figure 56). Swing the loading gate out and, rotating the cylinder clockwise put the cartridges into the chambers.

Figure 56. Loading the revolver.

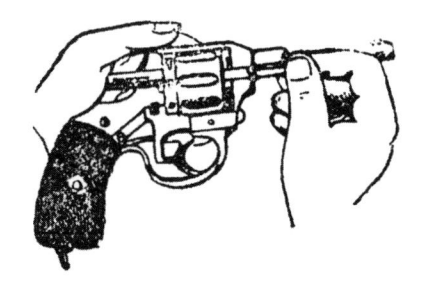

Figure 57. Unloading the revolver.

HOW TO UNLOAD THE REVOLVER

Take the revolver into your left hand (figure 57). Swing the loading gate out. Press the front end of a cartridge with your finger and push it out of the chamber. If the cartridge will not come out under your finger's pressure, unscrew the cleaning rod, turn it with the extractor rod guide counterclockwise and with a sharp strike push the cartridge out.

FIXING JAMMING

Try to fix any jamming by one of two methods: 1) cock the hammer; or 2) un-cock the hammer, holding it with your thumb.

If the jamming persists – unload the revolver and look it over. If there is a serious malfunction or damage – replace the revolver.

A misfire could be caused by one of three problems: 1) the percussion cap is faulty (set too deep into the cartridge or covered with green oxide); 2) the weapon oil has thickened; 3) the striking or firing (or both) mechanisms are dirty.

Throw away the faulty cartridge. If the revolver's mechanisms are dirty – strip it and clean it thoroughly.

PISTOL MODEL 1930

The pistol's functions are the same as the revolver. Combat (normal) rate of fire – 8 rounds per 10-15 seconds. Caliber – 7.62mm. Our submachine guns fire the same cartridges.

Cleaning and oiling the pistol is done in the same way as of the revolver. The only difference – the barrel is cleaned through the cartridge ejection aperture. A screwdriver and pull-through are the needed accessories.

FIELD STRIPPING THE PISTOL

Hold the pistol by the grip with your right hand; press the magazine catch with the thumb and remove the magazine.

Make sure that there is no cartridge in the chamber: with your left hand, pull the slide back and look into the chamber. After that let the slide forward slowly, at the same time holding the hammer with your right thumb.

Use the lip of the base of the pistol magazine to push the slide catch's spring back (figure 58) so that it is freed from the slide catch's axis. Do not remove the spring completely – leave it on the column. Press the catch axis with the index finger at its protrusion, move it and remove the slide catch (figure 59).

Remove the slide along with the barrel moving it forward on the frame's rails while holding the return spring (figure 60).

Hold the slide in your left hand with the return spring facing up and with your right hand remove the spring from the slide assembly along with the mainspring guide and ferrule.

Remove the barrel bushing from the slide assembly by turning the bushing 180 degrees.

Hold slide as it shown in figure 61. Push the barrel link forward and remove the barrel with your right hand.

Take out the firing mechanism assembly from the frame by pulling it out with your right hand.

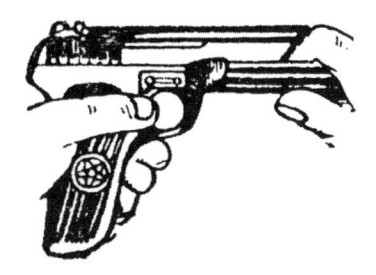

Figure 58. How to move the slide's catch back.

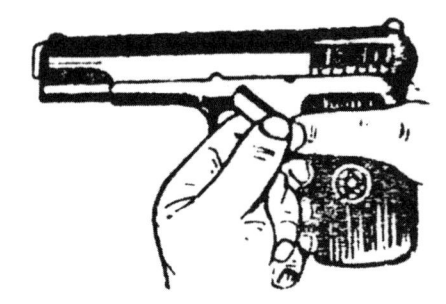

Figure 59. How to remove the slide catch.

Figure 60. How to remove the slide with the barrel.

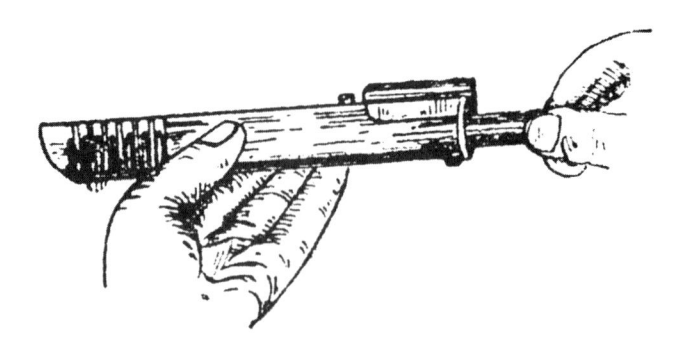

Figure 61. How to remove the barrel.

PISTOL ASSEMBLY

First, put the firing mechanism assembly into the frame. To replace the barrel – hold the slide upside down in your left hand (do not forget to push the barrel link forward). Then, insert the barrel bushing into the slide; as soon as the slide flanges are aligned with the slide assembly's edge – turn the bushing 180 degrees. To insert the return spring: push it by its ferrule into the slide's slot, flip the barrel link back, while holding the mainspring guide by the head. Then push the spring toward its ferrule and insert the mainspring guide's head between the slide's sides. Do not let the spring jump out. After that – hold the frame by the grip with your right hand, press the firing mechanism down with your right thumb and move the slide with the barrel onto the frame guiding it into the grooves. Now it is possible to insert the slide catch from the left side, while holding the slide in the rearmost position. Make sure that its axis and tooth went into proper place. Finally, push the slide catch's spring onto it axis and insert the magazine, pushing it up to the stop.

HOW TO LOAD THE PISTOL

While loading the magazine with eight cartridges – make sure that the last cartridge bullet's tip is above the front guide. Push the magazine into the grip until it stops with a click. After that – load the cartridge into the chamber – pull the slide rearmost and release.

Put the hammer in the safe mode: first put the hammer into the firing mode by pulling it back into the rearmost position. Then, holding its spur with the right thumb, press the trigger with the index finger. As soon as the hammer slides off the cocking stud, release the trigger and ease the hammer forward until you hear a light click. Now the hammer is in the safe mode.

You can load the pistol with nine cartridges. Put a magazine loaded with eight cartridges into the pistol grip. Quickly pull the slide back and release it – this will load a cartridge into the chamber. Put the hammer into the safe mode, remove the magazine, add one more cartridge and push it back into the pistol grip. Now the pistol is loaded with nine cartridges.

HOW TO FIX JAMMING

1. **The magazine will not slide freely into the pistol grip**. Wipe the magazine with a cloth and oil it. Clean and lightly oil the grip and the magazine well.

2. **The magazine falls out of the grip after being inserted**. Clean the magazine opening.

3. **The slide moves back with difficulty**. Field strip and clean the pistol, wipe it dry and oil it lightly (with winter oil – if it is wintertime).

4. **A cartridge from the magazine does not feed into the chamber**. Pull the slide back and release it.

5. **The slide does not go fully forward and the cartridge is still visible**. Push the slide forward with your hand.

6. **Misfire.** Cock the hammer and try to shoot once more; if the misfire repeats – remove and throw away the faulty cartridge by pulling the slide back sharply.

7. **An empty cartridge case stays inside the chamber**. Pull the slide back until it stops, flip the slide catch up so its tooth is fixed in the slide's slot and slide will stay in the open position. Remove the magazine by pushing the slide catch down, let the slide move forward and quickly pull it back again. If the extractor does not catch the empty case again – fix the slide in the open position just described, push the case out if the barrel with a cleaning rod. Clean and oil the barrel and chamber.

8. **After a shot, the next cartridge jams into the chamber's wall**. Pull the slide back a little and release it.

9. **After a shot, the slide stays in an open position with some cartridges left in the magazine**. Push the ridge of the slide catch with your finger and slide the catch tooth out of the slide's slot.

10. **The pistol fires automatically**, i.e. the hammer does not stay cocked after a shot. With your right hand thumb press the button of the magazine catch.[6]

Take good care of the revolver or pistol. If the revolver (pistol) has been in a wet holster – give it a good cleaning, oil it and dry the holster at the first opportunity.

BE ABLE TO FIRE AT THE ENEMY WITH GREAT ACCURACY

Pick the vulnerable spots – chest, abdomen and head – as aiming points. To take aim accurately – hold your head strait. Keep your fingers on the grip of the pistol (revolver) as it is shown at figure 62 – lightly, without effort. Do not hold the grip too tightly. Pull the trigger with the first joint of the forefinger and keep the thumb parallel to the barrel.

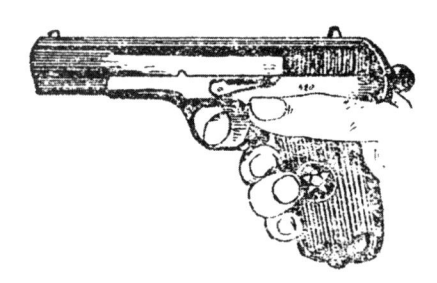

Figure 62. How to hold the pistol for shooting.

While shooting from a standing, kneeling or prone firing position – keep your hand and weapon balanced, free and without effort. If you are shooting using an aiming rest – from any position – keep your hand and weapon balanced. To increase stability, find a support for your left arm and with your left hand hold your right hand by the wrist.

BE ABLE TO WORK WITH A SHOVEL

Learn to dig in under enemy fire quickly and effectively.

Entrenching tools (small shovel, sapper shovel or pickaxe) are used for self-entrenching. If they are not available, you can use any shovel with its handle shortened to 40-45 centimeters.

HOW TO DIG YOURSELF IN

Before starting to dig in – look around carefully and determine that the position would be a good one firing position. If not – crawl sideways to find a better spot and then begin to dig in.

Put your rifle on your right side with its bolt handle down within arms reach. It will not interfere with your work and you will be able to get to it quickly.

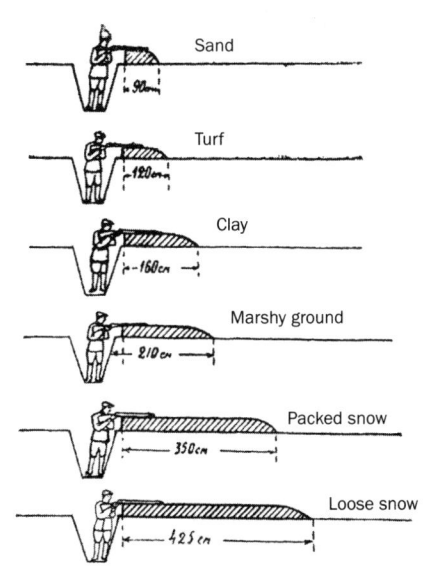

Figure 63. Required thickness of breastworks made from different materials.

Roll onto your left side without raising your head. Pick up the shovel with your left hand on the handle and with your right hand near the blade. Cut the turf using with strikes pulled toward yourself.

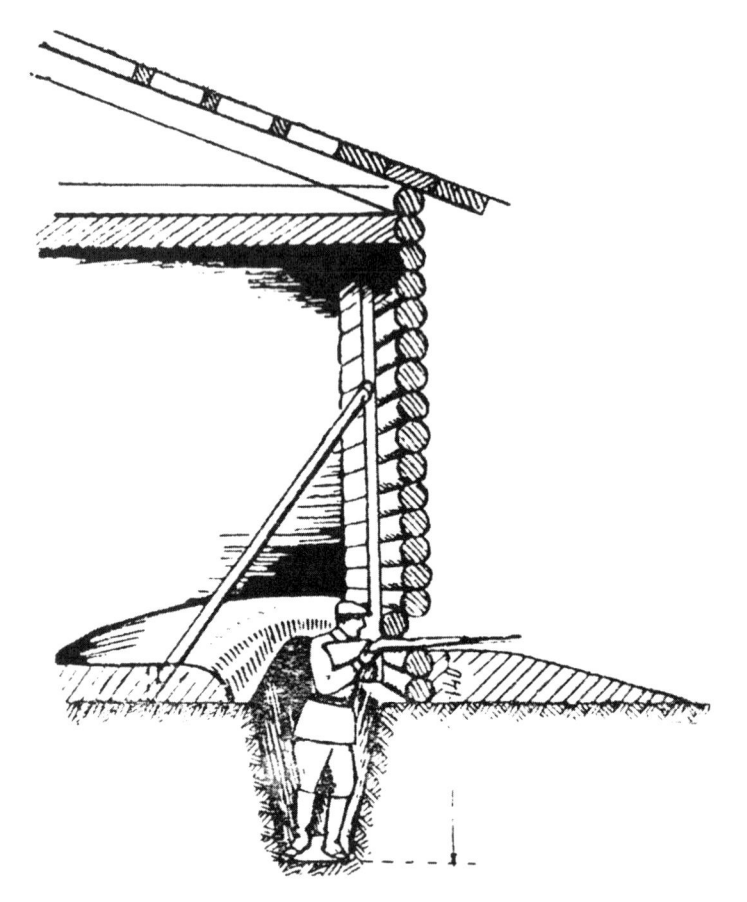

Figure 64. Foxhole inside of a building.

First throw the turf and soil forward to build a small mound (breastwork) to protect yourself from enemy fire and create an aiming rest. Then throw the soil at your sides. While digging – spread your legs slightly and keep your head close to the ground.

After digging a foxhole 20-25 centimeters deep at the front end, crawl back slightly and deepen the foxhole to protect your body and legs.

Camouflage the foxhole immediately with turf, grass, tree branches, etc. to make it undistinguishable from the surrounding terrain.

Because different materials have different resistance to a bullet's penetration, the breastwork of the foxhole will be of different thicknesses, depending on the material.

DIGGING IN SNOW

Remember: if the depth of the snow is 40-50 centimeters you can just clear the space down to the ground and pile the removed snow in front of yourself to build a breastwork. If the snow cover is deeper then that – it is not necessary to dig down to ground level. Loose snow should be compressed to make a breastwork at least 40 centimeters deep. Use the snow removed from the foxhole to reinforce the breastwork. When digging a foxhole in snow, make sure that it is clean, without soil particles. The soil's dark spots on the white background would betray your position.

USE LOCAL OBJECTS

=Remember: woods, trees, bushes, stumps, roadside ditches, etc. are your protection.

You can use wooden fences and hurdles as camouflage. Make firing openings (embrasures) in them.

To protect yourself from the enemy's bullets you can use some wooden structures – a barn, shed, etc. Dig out a foxhole under a wall inside of the building using dug out soil to build a protective mound outside of the wall (figure 64).

While preparing houses for a battle – use the lower floors and basements. Block up windows with sandbags or bags filled with soil. You will need to leave narrow embrasures for observation and fire.

VI.

BE ABLE TO USE THE ENEMY'S WEAPONS

A partisan uses not only the standard Red Army (RKKA – Worker-Peasant's Red Army) weapons, but also the weapons of the enemy. Learn to use them to beat the German Fascists with their own equipment. First, familiarize yourself with the main types of German small arms.

GERMAN MAUSER RIFLE MODEL 1898

The magazine capacity of this rifle is five 7.92mm cartridges. Loading this rifle is similar to loading our rifle by turning the bolt counterclockwise and pulling it back.

Figure 65. German rifle MAUSER model 1898.

The rifle's receiver opens to expose the magazine well. The receiver's top side has a clip stripper guide to push cartridges from a cartridge clip into the magazine with your finger.

The bolt has a lug in the rear. Turning the lug to the straight (vertical) position puts the rifle in safe mode. Turning the lug clockwise locks the bolt and prevents it from moving backward. Turning the lug counterclockwise puts the rifle in ready (fire) mode.

To remove the bolt from the receiver: turn the bolt handle up to the left and back, while pressing the bolt release the bolt stop with your thumb and remove the bolt. To reinsert the bolt, align the bolt camming lug in the bolt rails and push the bolt stop on the left side of the receiver.

Sights on the rifle include a front sight and a rear sight assembly. There are four identical range indicator sets of numbers etched in meters. One each is located on each side of the sight and two are etched on the top of the sight tangent.

Maximum effective range – 2,000 meters. Maximum range is 5,000 meters and the bullet is lethal out to that distance.

To disconnect the bayonet – press the spring catch with a finger of your right hand.

You must fire rifle without the bayonet. It is connected to the rifle immediately before a bayonet charge.

CARBINE 98-K

The carbine's combat characteristics are practically identical with those of the Mauser model 1898 rifle. It differs from the rifle in just few non-essential details (the bolt handle is bent further down, the barrel is shorter by 140 millimeters, the rear sight assembly and front sight are a bit different). The carbine is lighter and more convenient to use than the rifle. Its weight is only 3.9kg.

SUBMACHINE-GUN 28/II (SCHMEISSER)

The maximum effective range is 300 meters. It's caliber – 9 millimeter. The submachine-gun uses the same ammunition as the 38-40 submachine-gun and the Parabellum pistol.

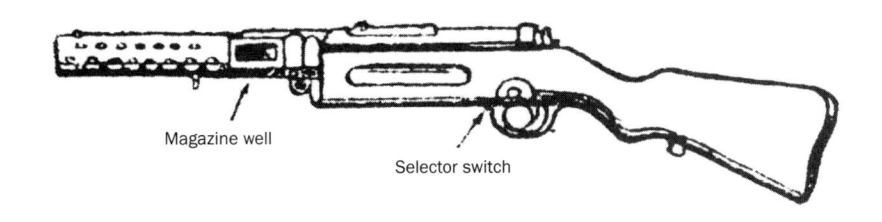

Figure 66. Submachine-gun 22/II (Schmeisser).

Loading the magazine. Hold the magazine in your left hand and with your right hand put a cartridge on the magazine platform. Then press the cartridge into the magazine with your left thumb and with your right thumb push it back flush with the magazine rear. Magazine capacity is 32 rounds.

Loading the submachine-gun. Hold the weapon with your left hand and with your right hand pull the bolt back and turn it left (up). The bolt handle will slide into the safety slot and the bolt will be in the safe mode. After that – insert the magazine into the magazine well on the left side.

To load the submachine-gun and ready it for firing – pull the bolt handle back and turn it right (down), then release it.

The tangent rear sight has ten settings – each graduated in 100 meter increments. Press the sight slide catch (on the left side) and put the slide on the desired range marker.

On the left side of the submachine-gun's trigger is a selector switch. To fire single shots – push it right. When firing single shots – release the trigger after each shot and pull it again to fire another round. To fire automatic – push the switch to the left. A short pull on the trigger produces a three-five round burst.

When changing the magazines – put the bolt handle in the safe mode (as described above). The press the magazine release catch, remove the magazine and insert another one.

Unloading the submachine-gun. First – remove the magazine. Then move the bolt handle out of the safety slot. Hold the bolt with your hand while pulling the trigger and slowly moving the bolt forward.

You should be able to quickly fix the main types of jamming. If there is a misfire, a cartridge case does not extract from the chamber, or the bolt does not seat fully in the forward position – the first action in all those situations is to reload the submachine-gun.

If the bolt still does not seat fully in the forward position- the submachine-gun is dirty and needs cleaning.

After cleaning the submachine-gun, oil it lightly with a piece of cloth saturated with rifle oil. Take extra care to oil the moving parts of the bolt.

SUBMACHINE-GUN 38-40

Caliber – 9mm.

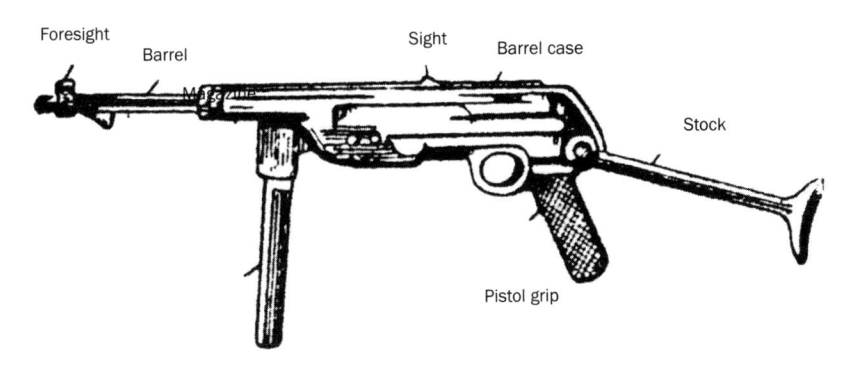

The submachine-gun has a collapsible stock located next to the pistol grip. It can be extended and then the submachine-gun becomes longer, easier to fire and more accurate. To extend the collapsible stock, find the button on the left side of the pistol grip and push it down- the stock will open.

The stock has a rounded oval butt piece to steady the weapon against one's right shoulder while firing. The stock is held in place by a mechanical button. If you need to open the stock – push it down. Pushing the stock upward will fix it in its locked closed position.

The submachine-gun uses an elongated box magazine. To load the submachine-gun, push the magazine into the magazine well located under the weapon. A spring-loaded catch holds the magazine in the weapon. The catch is located on the magazine well's left side. To remove the magazine – push the catch downward.

How to load the magazine? Its capacity is 32 rounds. Put the cartridges into the magazine one by one. When the magazine is fully loaded, a cartridge will be visible through a drilled opening with "32" stamped near it.

To shoot the submachine-gun – pull the bolt to the rearmost position. The gun is ready to fire. Pull the trigger and the gun will fire until it has no more rounds in its magazine. If you want to fire in short bursts – pull and release the trigger. The submachine-gun will fire three-five rounds bursts.

To put a loaded submachine-gun on safe: pull the bolt to the rearmost position and turn it upwards so that it stays in its special slot.

On the upper part of the submachine-gun is a rear sight which consists of two leafs. One of the leafs is fixed firmly on the receiver. It is used to fire at short ranges – 50-100 meters. The other one flips up on hinges and is used to fire at distance up to 200 meters.

The gun's muzzle is threaded. A conical collar (flash suppressor) may be screwed on to it to mask muzzle flashes during nighttime shooting.

To fire the submachine-gun:

—Flip open the collapsible stock;

—Pull the stock into your right shoulder;

—Hold the pistol grip with your right hand and the magazine with your left hand;

—Take aim at the target aligning the front sight with the rear sight;

—Pull the trigger and fire at the target.

LIGHT MACHINE-GUNS

All light machine-guns use German or Polish 7.92mm Mauser cartridges.

KNOW THE MARKINGS ON DIFFERENT TYPES OF MAUSER CARTRIDGES

A cartridge with a light-weight bullet has a **black ring** around the percussion primer seat. A cartridge with a heavy-weight bullet has a **green ring** around the percussion primer seat. A cartridge with an armor-piercing bullet has a **red ring** around the percussion primer seat. A cartridge with an incendiary bullet has a **black ring** around the percussion primer seat and the bullet's nose is chromium or black. A cartridge with armor-piercing tracer bullet has a **red ring** around the percussion primer seat and a black nose.[7]

LIGHT MACHINE-GUN MG-34

The MG-34 weighs 12 kilograms. It is 7.92mm caliber. The maximum

Be Able to Use The Enemy's Weapons

effective range is 1,000 meters. The machine-gun can fire rounds from a magazine as well as from a belt. The magazine's capacity is 75 rounds.

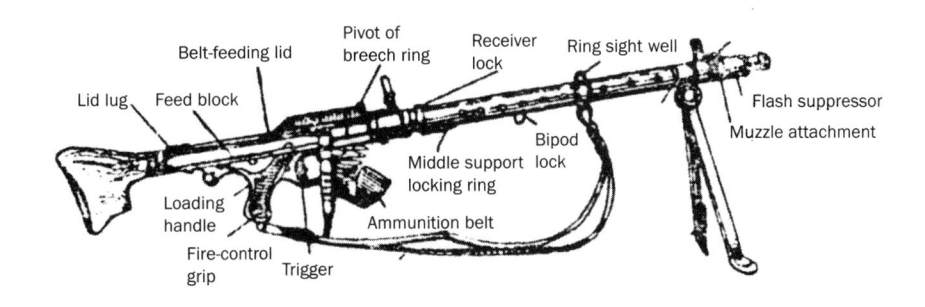

Figure 68. Light machine-gun MG-34 with belt feed.

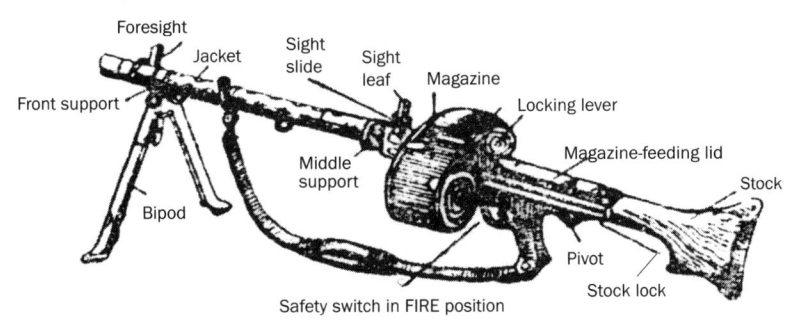

Figure 69. Light machine-gun MG-34 with magazine feed.

There are two types of machine-gun belts: a long one that holds 250 rounds and a short one that holds 50 rounds. Study the machine-gun components in figures 68 and 69.

Machine-gun with the magazine feed. Check if there is a lid for the magazine feed installed on the machine-gun (figures 70 and 71). Load the cartridges into the magazine. To do this, insert the special key into the axis pin of the winding spring of the right drum. Wind it up completely. Repeat the same procedure with the left drum. Load cartridges through the aperture that is between the drums. When the viewing hole marked 75 on the right shows a cartridge – stop loading. The magazine is now fully loaded.[8]

LOADING THE MACHINE-GUN

Pull the cocking lever to the rearmost position and then return it to the forward position. If the lever does not go back – the machine-gun is in the safety mode. You would take it off of safe. To do that – press the safety switch lever and move it forward. The red letter **F** will appear. Then hold the magazine in a position where the red numbers on the drum (0, 25, 50, and 75) are at the side closest to you. Slide your hand under the magazine sling and insert the magazine into the magazine chamber on the top lid. First insert the forward lip of the magazine and then seat the rear part with a push of the hand. The machine-gun is now loaded.

FIRING THE MACHINE-GUN

Flip up the rear sight leaf, turning it toward you. Flip up the front sight. The rear sight leaf has numbers on it. They mark the aiming distance in hundreds of meters. Adjust the sight to the desired distance by aligning the top of the sight slide with the selected mark.

Take it off safety. Fire short bursts (three-five rounds). Use sustained fire while repulsing an attack.

To fire the machine-gun automatically – pull on the lower part of the trigger and hold it until a desirable number of rounds have fired.

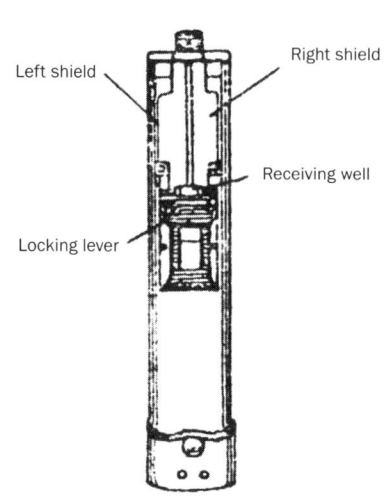

Figure 70. Magazine feed lid.

Be Able to Use The Enemy's Weapons

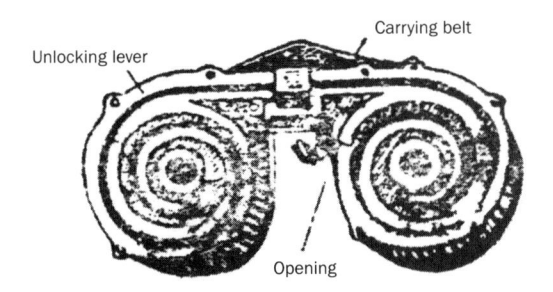

Figure 71. 75-round capacity magazine.

To fire single rounds – pull on the upper part of the trigger. After the shot – release the trigger and pull it again – the next shot will follow.
    Do not put two fingers into the trigger guard simultaneously.
    Replace the hot barrel after 250 rounds.

UNLOADING THE MACHINE-GUN

Pull the cocking lever back and let it stay in that position. Put it on safety: press the safety switch lever and move it back (toward you). The letter **S** (safety) will appear. You can put it on safety with the cocking lever in a forward or rear position.
    Hold the magazine with the right hand as shown (figure 72). Press the unlocking lever and remove the magazine by lifting it up. If the magazine does not disconnect – pull it up with the right hand, striking its bottom simultaneously with the left. If this does not work – press the magazine catch with your left thumb and lift the magazine with your right hand.

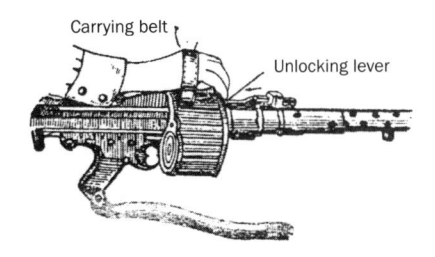

Figure 72. Removing the magazine.

Holding the cocking lever, pull the trigger and slowly let the bolt go forward from the cocked position. The machine-gun now is unloaded.

REPLACING THE BARREL

Pull the cocking lever in the rearmost position. Take it off safety (letter F). Press the barrel release lever to the right and turn the receiver to the right (Figure 73).

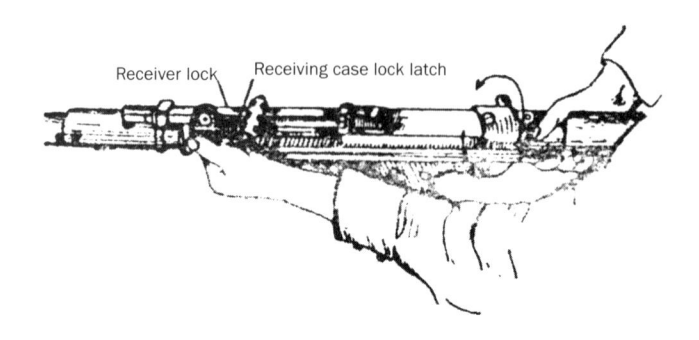

Figure 73. Disconnecting the barrel by turning the barrel release lever.

Tilt the machine-gun stock and catch the falling barrel. If the barrel does not fall out by itself – pull it out with any sharp object (hook, cartridge belt end or cartridge) and let it cool down. To prevent burning yourself, wear a glove or wrap your hand in a piece of cloth.

Put the spare barrel into the jacket and lift the stock. Push the barrel inside the barrel casing until the barrel's base is aligned with the barrel release lever. Turn the receiver sharply to the left until the barrel release lever will lock. Insert the magazine (ammunition belt). Push the cocking lever forward and take it off safety. Now you can load the machine-gun and continue to fire.

HOW TO FIX JAMMING

1. The bolt stays in the rearmost position. Release the trigger and pull the cocking lever back. If the machine-gun is set up for magazine-feeding: disconnect the magazine and align the cartridges correctly in the magazine lip. If that does not work – replace the magazine. If the gun is set up for belt feed – open the feed block cover, realign the cartridges correctly in the belt, load the machine-gun and continue to fire.

2. Misfire. Clean the machine-gun and oil the moving parts with winter rifle oil. If it still does not work – replace the bolt.

3. Empty cartridge case is not ejected. Replace the bolt and if that does not help – replace the barrel.

4. The moving parts will not go back. Fieldstrip the machinegun, clean it and oil it.

DISASSEMBLING AND ASSEMBLING THE MACHINE-GUN

Unload the machine-gun and put it on safety. Do not forget to uncock the bolt. Push the locking pin of the feed block cover all way to the left, open the cover and remove it by lifting. (If the machine-gun set for belt-feed: remove the lower part of the feed-piece by lifting it up). Holding the receiver with the left hand, press the butt latch, turn the stock 1/4 of a turn counterclockwise and disconnect the stock and pull out the spring. Pull the cocking lever back completely and remove the bolt. After that, remove the barrel as described previously (figure 73). Disconnect the sling. Separate the receiver from the jacket. To do that: while holding the barrel nut with the left hand, push up the receiver lock with your fingers. Hold the pistol grip with your right hand and turn the receiver casing clockwise completely, move it backward and remove. The machine-gun is stripped.

Assembling the machine-gun. Connect the receiver and jacket. Insert the barrel into the jacket (see HOW TO REPLACE BARREL). Put the bolt in with its head up and seat it by pushing the cocking lever forward. Insert the spring and reconnect the stock (for the belt-feed version – connect the lower part of the feed-piece). Reconnect the feed block cover by pressing its locking pin. Connect the sling. The machine-gun is assembled.

Pull the cocking lever back and pull the trigger. If the machine-gun works – the assembly has been done properly. Put the weapon on safe.

MOUNTING THE BIPOD

Forward position. Lift the front sight up. Using your left hand, push the retaining spring located on the gun jacket open. Take the bipod with your right hand and insert its support bracket into the slots in the gun jacket.

Seat the support bracket deep into the jacket slots and turn it clockwise underneath the gun. Release the retaining spring and check the bipod's proper installation.

Middle position. Lift the rear sight leaf. Push the retaining spring of the middle support open and continue as described above.

Removing the bipod. Push the retaining spring open on the jacket, turn the bipod into the upper position and disconnect it.

Use the middle support while shooting in the open. If you are shooting from foxholes or trenches – use the forward support.

Loading the belt-fed machine-gun. Make sure that the belt-feeding lid and the lower part of the belt-feeding piece are in place – the machine-gun will not fire without them (figures 74 and 76). Put the cartridges into the belt. Insert each cartridge into a link so that the cartridge slides into the link ring in the cartridge belt and holds it. You can connect another belt to the belt loaded into the machine-gun. To do this – remove the cartridge from the first link of the belt you want to connect. In that link insert the end piece of the last link from the belt in use and then replace the cartridge. If you do not have a 250 cartridges capacity belt you can make one out of shorter belts (figure 77).

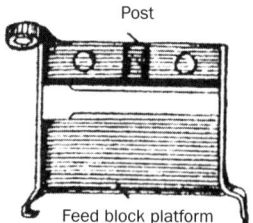

Figure 74. Lower part of feed-piece for belt-fed operation (no drum feed).

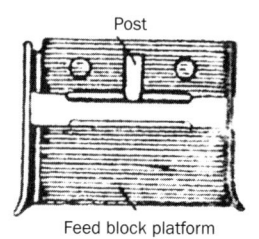

Figure 75. Lower part of feed-piece for drum-fed operation.

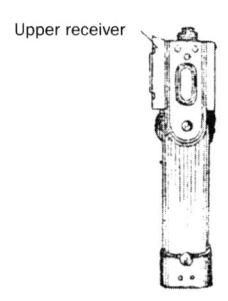

Figure 76. Feed block cover for belt-feed.

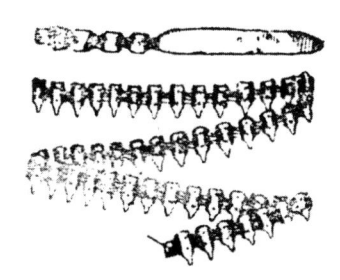

Figure 77. 50-round capacity belt.

Put the loaded belt into the feed-tray. To do this, pull the cocking lever back and then slide it forward. While holding the belt with the exposed cartridges beneath, insert the belt's tip into the receiver so the tip touches the rear end of the receiver. Push the tip further until it appears on the opposite side and then pull it through until it stops.

If the belt does not have the tip – open the receiver cover so that the cartridge belt is pressed against the rear end of the receiver. The MG-34 machine-gun works with left or right side feeding. Position the feed-slide on the top of the receiver on the left side if the feeding is going to be from the left or on the right – if feeding is going to be from the right. Hold the belt close the cover and lock it with the cover pin.

Unloading the machine-gun. Pull the cocking lever to the rearmost position. Open the receiver cover and remove the feeding belt. Close the cover and put the weapon on safe.

Sometimes the machine-gun has a lower feed-piece for belt-feeding from a drum (figure 75). You can remove the belt from the drum and use it in the same way as a belt-fed firing without the drum.

MG-08/15 AND MG08/18 LIGHT MACHINE-GUNS

Combat characteristics. Combat (normal) rate of fire – 500 rounds per minute. Maximum Effective Range – 2,000 meters. Machine-gun's weight: MG-08/15 – 17.9 kilograms; MG-08/18 – 14.5 kilograms.

The machine-guns' designs are generally the same as the Maxim medium machine-gun. The instructions from the field manual NSD (Nastavleniye po strelkovomu delu)-38 "Medium Machine-gun MAXIM Model 1910" should be applied to handle them.

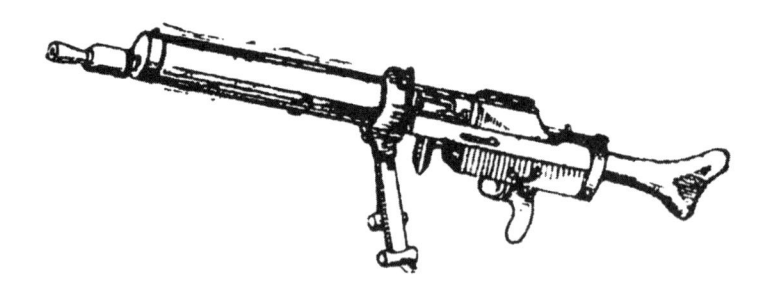

Figure 78. Light machine-gun MG-08/15.

Mount the magazine box assembly containing the machine-gun belt to the right side of the weapon using the special guide ribs.

Use 7-12 rounds bursts when firing the MG-08/15 and 3-5 round bursts when firing the MG-08/18. The latter is air cooled and that excludes having to fill the cooling jacket with water.

When disassembling the stock: first remove the upper bolt then rotate the stock so that the rear cross-piece is down.

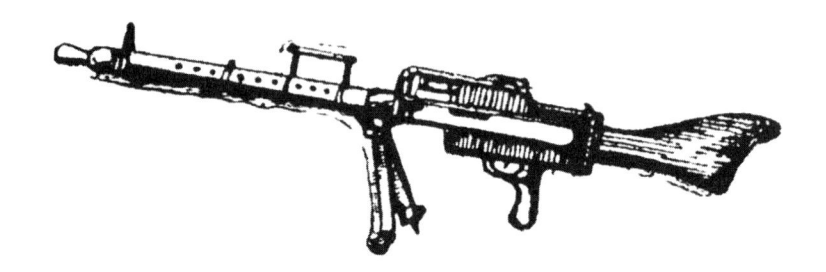

Figure 79. MG-08/18 light machine-gun.

MG-13 (DREYSE) LIGHT MACHINE-GUN

Combat characteristics. Combat (normal) rate of fire – 550 rounds per minute. Maximum effective range – 1,200 meters. Weight – 12 kilograms. Magazine capacity – 25 rounds.

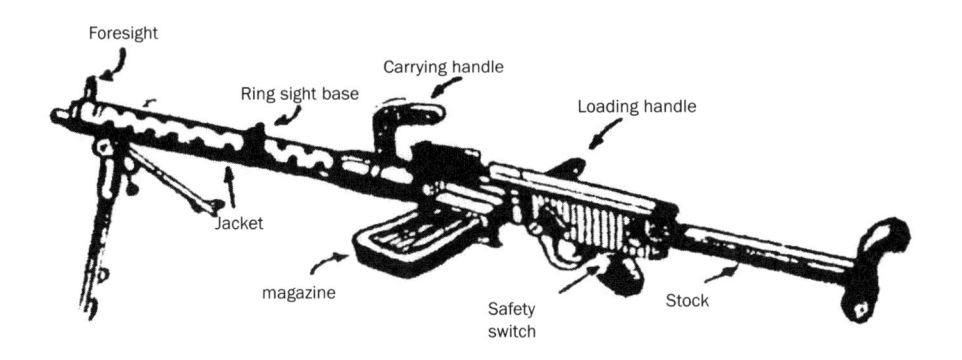

Figure 80. MG-13 (Dreyse) light machine-gun.

Loading the machine-gun. Stand the machine-gun on its bipod. Press the latch on the rear of the receiver to open its cover. Then insert the magazine into the receiver with the left hand – first the shorter front part and then the longer rear part. A light click will let you know that the magazine is inserted correctly. Pull the cocking lever to the rearmost position and release it. The hammer is now cocked and the bolt has seated a cartridge in the chamber.

Set sights. Flip up the front sight. The rear sight leaf has marks indicating aiming distances in hundreds of meters. Press the slide catch with the right thumb and index finger and select the distance by moving the slide.

To fire automatically – pull the lower part of the trigger. After a three-five round burst, release the trigger. To fire single shots – pull the upper part of the trigger.

Changing the magazine. Press the magazine catch and push the magazine forward and to the left, remove it and insert another one.

Unloading the machine-gun. After removing the magazine, pull the cocking lever back several times to make sure that there is no cartridge in the chamber. Pull the trigger.

If you move with the loaded machine-gun – do not forget to turn safety mode ON. You need to move the safety-catch thumb piece (located on the left rear part of the trigger housing) back to the S letter.

The bipod can be located in the forward or middle position. To change the bipod location – press the leaf spring on the cooling jacket's bottom, turn the bipod upward and disconnect it. After that – insert the bipod in the required place with its legs up, press the leaf spring into the jacket and turn the bipod downward.

HOW TO FIX JAMMING

1. **The trigger is not moving.** Take it off safety.

2. **Misfire.** Reload the machine-gun by pulling the cocking lever back and releasing it.

3. **The cartridge is stuck in the chamber.** Pull the cocking lever back and turn the machine-gun to the right side. If the cartridge does not fall out – disconnect the magazine and remove or properly insert the cartridge.

4. **An empty cartridge case has not ejected and is stuck in the chamber.** With a sharp movement, pull the cocking lever back and release it.

5. **An empty cartridge case remains stuck in the chamber.** Knock the case out of the chamber with a cleaning rod and check if the ejector is in good shape.

6. **The bolt moves with difficulty.** Check the firing mechanism's cleanliness. If the return spring is broken – replace it.

FIELD-STRIPPING THE MACHINE-GUN

1. Take out the magazine.

2. Cock the hammer by pulling the cocking lever back and releasing it.

3. Press the locking pin, open and lift up the receiver cover.

4. With your left hand, press the rear locking latch right and move the butt stock and the trigger assembly mechanism downward.

5. Turn the locking pin of the trigger assembly mechanism toward yourself, lift the accelerating spring and turn it outward.

6. Pull back the moving parts and separate the bolt.

7. With both hands, remove the barrel along with the barrel casing.

8. Separate the barrel casing from the barrel by pressing the connecting bolt and moving it to the right.

Assembling the machine-gun is done in the reverse order.

ZGB-30 (ZB vz.26) LIGHT MACHINE-GUN

Combat characteristics. Combat (normal) rate of fire – 550-650 rounds per minute. Maximum effective range – 1,000 meters. It is the lightest German machine-gun. It weighs only 9.6 kilograms. Magazine capacity – 20 rounds.[9]

Loading the magazine. Pick up the magazine in your left hand and with your right hand press the cartridges one by one under the magazine flange with the bullets facing toward you. Hold the magazine in the same position while unloading it. Push the cartridges out with your right thumb and push them forward from under the flange.

Loading the machine-gun. Stand the machine-gun on its bipod. Push the magazine housing cover forward. Insert the forward part of the magazine first and then strike its rear part with your palm – you should hear a light click.

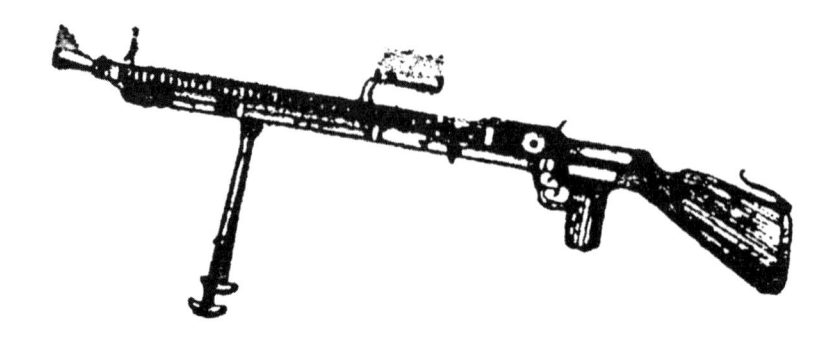

Figure 81. ZGB-30 (ZB vz.26) light machine-gun.

Make sure that the front retaining lug of the magazine fits into its corresponding slot in the magazine receiver. Pull the cocking lever rearward.
There is a rear sight drum on the left side of the receiver. Look for the numbers that appear inside the drum's window. They show the aiming distance in hundreds of meters.
To fire the machine-gun automatically – put the selector switch to the "20" number. The selector switch is located on the machine-gun's left side above the trigger guard. Fire in three-five round bursts. To fire single shots – put the selector switch to "1". Putting the selector switch to "0" will turn the safety mode ON.

Unloading the machine-gun. First, take out the magazine. Then hold the pistol grip with your left hand and pull the trigger while using your right hand to slowly move the bolt to the forward position. Close the magazine housing cover.

HOW TO FIX JAMMING

1. **The bolt does not move forward.** Turn the safety mode OFF.

2. **Misfire**. Pull the cocking lever back and remove the misfired cartridge.

3. **The next cartridge is stuck in the chamber**. Pull the cocking lever back. If the stuck cartridge does not fall out by itself – remove the magazine and remove the cartridge.

4. **The bolt goes forward slowly**. Make sure that the firing mechanism is clean. If the return spring is broken – replace it.

STRIPPING THE MACHINE-GUN

1. Remove the magazine.

2. Remove the barrel: first turn the lever of the barrel sleeve coupling (located on the left side) up, then holding the barrel by the handle, push it forward and separate it from the body.

3. Locate the lock for the breech and trigger assembly in the upper rear part of the receiver. Push it right.

4. Push on the stock with the trigger assembly down.

5. Pull the cocking lever back.

6. Pull back the bolt with the piston rod and its extension and remove them.

7. Separate the bolt from the piston rod.

Assemble the machine-gun in reverse order.

S-18 ANTI-TANK RIFLE (SOLOTURN)

Combat characteristics. Combat (normal) rate of fire – up to 10 rounds per minute. Caliber – 20mm.

This is a self-loading (semi-automatic) rifle for fighting tanks, armored vehicles, etc. An armor-piercing bullet of the rifle pierces armor 31mm thick at a distance of up to 200 meters. The magazine capacity is 10 rounds.

How to load the magazine. Hold it with your left hand and with your right hand load the cartridges into the magazine follower so that the bullets' tips are pointed to the magazine end without the flange. Push the cartridges down until the magazine is full.

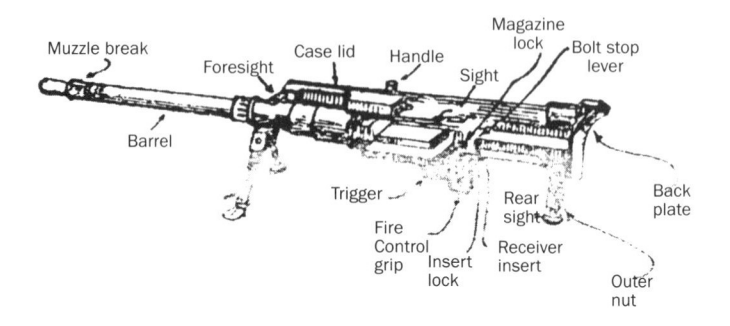

Figure 82. S-18 anti-tank rifle (Soloturn).

To unload the magazine: hold it with your left hand with the bullets' tips pointed away from you and with your right thumb push the cartridges out one by one.

How to load the rifle. Turn the cocking lever up with your right hand and pull it back to the rearmost position until it clicks. Then move your hand onto the pistol grip. Insert the magazine into the magazine slot (on the left side) with your left hand and ram it into the place with a palm strike. The magazine insertion releases the bolt. The bolt moves forward from the return spring's pressure, strips a cartridge out of the magazine, loads it into the chamber and locks the breech. The rifle is now loaded and ready to fire. Make sure there is a muzzle brake at the end of the barrel – firing without one is prohibited.

You should shoot the rifle from the prone position. First, press the stock against your shoulder firmly. There is a rear sight located in the stock. To adjust the rifle elevation precisely – turn the outer nut of the sight. Then hold the pistol grip firmly with your right hand and pull the trigger with two fingers. The shot and automatic reloading will follow. To shoot another round – release the trigger, aim the rifle and pull the trigger again.

The bolt will stop in the middle position and automatically eject the magazine when it is empty. Insert another magazine and continue shooting.

How to unload the rifle.
Move the magazine catch forward and remove the magazine. Turn up the cocking lever, pull it back until your hear a click and then remove your hand. At that moment the cartridge that was in the chamber should be ejected to the right. Push the cocking lever forward – the rifle is unloaded.

HOW TO FIX JAMMING

1. **The cartridge is stuck in the chamber.** Move the magazine catch forward and remove the magazine. Pull the cocking lever back, remove the faulty cartridge from the chamber, align the cartridges' positions in the magazine and load the rifle again.

2. **Misfire.** Remove the faulty cartridge and reload the rifle.

FIELD STRIPPING THE RIFLE

1. Press the barrel lock with your left hand and remove the barrel by turning it from you with your right hand and pushing it forward.

2. Move the receiver cover lock forward and open it.

3. Press the lower breech release toward the breech lock and move the breech lock left until it stops.

4. Push down the outer nut of the rear sight, pull the bar back and flip down the rear leaf sight.

5. Remove the bolt from the receiver and remove the barrel assembly.

Using a screwdriver or drift, turn the barrel nut left and separate the bolt from the barrel receiver.

Reassemble the weapon in the reverse order.

LUGER PARABELLUM PISTOL

The Parabellum pistol is the personal weapon of all German army officers. The same model comes in two different calibers – 7.65mm and 9mm.

Loading the pistol: holding the slide with a thumb and index finger pull it back (Figure 83). Figure 84 shows how to move the slide forward.

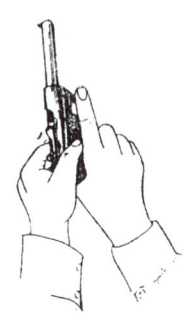

Figure 83. How to pull the slide back.

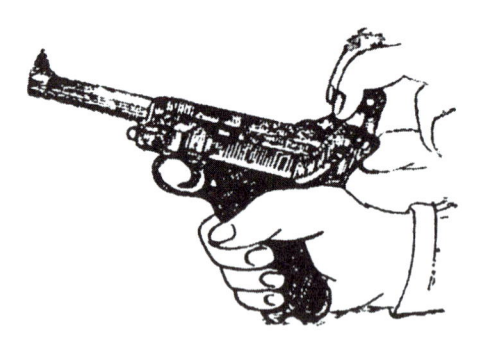

Figure 84. How to move the slide forward.

The safety switch is located on the left side of the grip. It moves between two dots – the upper and lower. When the switch is on the lower dot – the pistol is on safety and cannot be fired. Move the lever to the upper dot which has a word FIRE in German – the safety is off and you can shoot.

Loading cartridges into the chamber is possible in both positions of the safety switch. Insert the magazine into the lower part of the pistol grip. It holds 8 rounds. The magazine automatically locks into the grip.

You can conduct aimed fire at a distance up to 50 meters. The bullet is lethal out to 300 meters.

M-34 HAND GRENADE

Combat characteristics.

Weight – 310 grams

Blast effect radius – 3-6 meters

Effective fragmentation radius – 10-15 meters

Distance the grenade can be thrown – 35-40 meters.

The M-34 German hand grenade (figure 85) is an offensive percussion-fused grenade.

The grenades are issued to soldiers in the combat zone primed and ready to employ.[10]

Throwing the Grenade (Figure 86)

1. Take the grenade in your right hand (Figure 86).

2. Put your left index finger into the ring.

3. Turn your right hand with the grenade 90 degrees from yourself (causing the ring to turn), so the safety pin is freed from the safety catch.

4. Pull out the ring with the safety pin.

5. Throw the grenade.

The grenade is safe as long as the safety pin is not pulled out.
    The grenade has two safety devices: one is removed when the ring is pulled and the other one pops off during the flight.
    The grenade explodes at the moment it strikes any object. Disarming the grenade is forbidden.

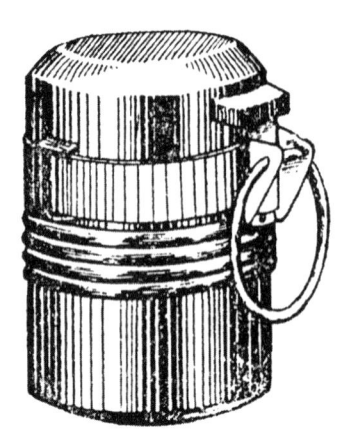

Figure 85. M-34 hand grenade.

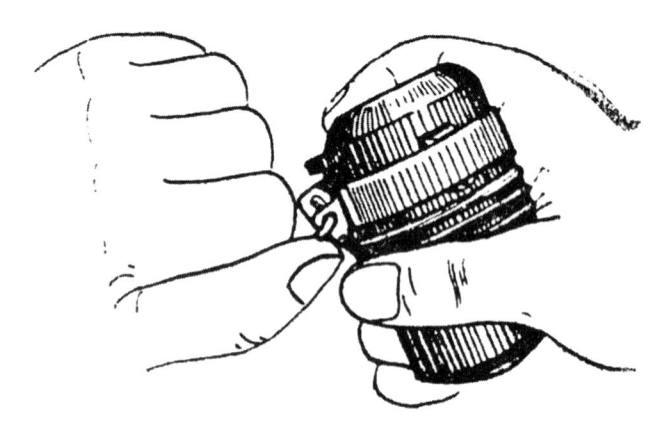

Figure 86. How to throw the grenade.

M-24 HAND GRENADE

M-24 hand grenade is an offensive grenade that has a time fuse. It consists of a cylindrical body which holds an explosive charge and a handle with the ignition mechanism.

The grenade is carried by a special clip on its body. It weighs 500 grams and it does not have a fragmentation sleeve.

Arming the grenade. First unscrew the handle from the body. In the lower part of the ignition mechanism is a cylindrical socket. Insert a percussion cap into it.

Then screw the handle back into the body using extreme safety precautions. Avoid jolts and sharp impacts. The grenade is armed (figure 87).

To throw the grenade – take it into your right hand. Use your left hand to screw off the safety cap from the bottom of the stick. There is a porcelain ball underneath. While cocking your right arm to throw the grenade, grasp the ball with your left hand and pull out the arming cord (figure 87). Then throw the grenade immediately, because it will explode in 4.5-5 seconds.

The grenade can be thrown 30-35 meters and the effective fragmentation radius is 10-15 meters.

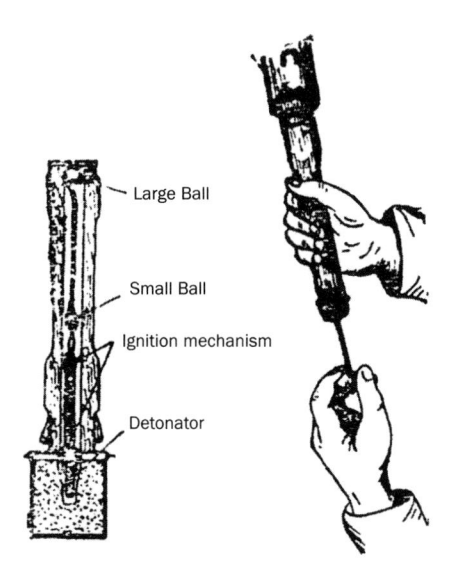

Figure 87. M-24 hand grenade.

How do you disarm the grenade?

Carefully unscrew the handle from the body. Remove the percussion cap from the ignition chamber. Wrap it in paper, cotton or a piece of cloth and put into a bag to protect it against impact or falling out. Connect the handle to the body again.

Always carry unarmed grenades and keep and carry the percussion caps separately from them.

EGG-SHAPED GRENADE MODEL 1939

This is an offensive grenade with a time fuse. It weighs 220 grams.

When preparing the grenade for throwing, first screw out the detonator base with the safety cap (figure 88 shows the safety cap in the left hand) and check the ignition channel. There should not be any foreign objects or dust. Then unscrew the safety cap from the time fuse (figure 88). Slide the percussion cap into its place. It is possible that saw dust or bristles may be in the open well of the percussion cap. If so, turn the cap upside down so that these objects fall out by themselves. If they do not, put the cap aside. It is unusable. Do not use any object to remove the foreign objects from the cap.

Carefully slide a good percussion cap onto the time fuse (figure 89). Then screw the igniter (time fuse and percussion cap) into the grenade and secure it with the nut (figure 90). The grenade is ready to throw.

Screw off the safety cap from the igniter (it will stay suspended on a cord). Hold the grenade in your right hand. Seize the cap between the index and middle fingers of your left hand, then cock your arm [pulling on the cord] and throw the grenade toward the target. Remember that it will explode four seconds after throwing.

Sometimes the grenades will have igniters already inserted in them. You need to be able to disarm them. Screw the igniter out of the grenade body. Carefully slide the percussion cap off the time fuse and wrap in cotton waste. Slide the safety primer tube over the time fuse and screw the assembly back into the grenade body.

Unarmed grenade should be carried separately from percussion caps.

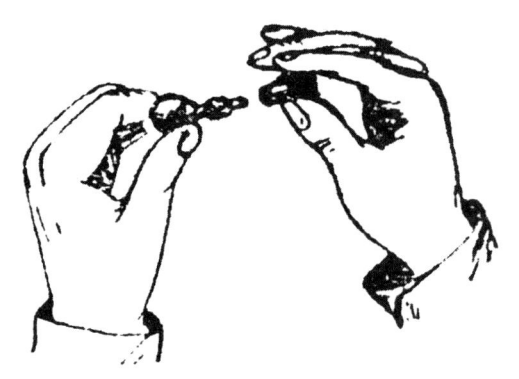

Figure 88. How to unscrew the safety cap.

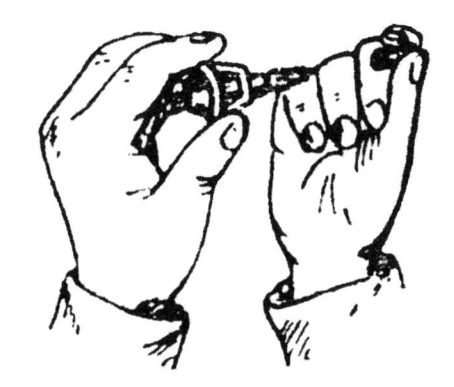

Figure 89. How to screw in the detonator.

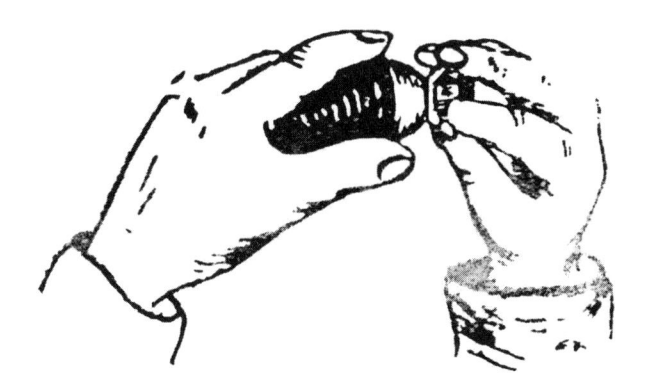

Figure 90. How to fix the detonator with the nut.

VII.

RECONNAISSANCE

REMEMBER THE BASIC RULES OF PARTISAN RECONNAISSANCE

You see everything but nobody sees you. If you let the enemy discover you – you betray the entire detachment. Operate covertly.

Remember: you are in the enemy's rear area and your detachment is not far away. The enemy may not give you a chance to break contact and then you will destroy your detachment.

The value of reconnaissance lies in carrying out the mission exactly. If you've started surveillance of the enemy – always see it through to the end. As far as possible, try to verify all information yourself. Only an accurate reconnaissance report is useful to the detachment.

It would be better if you do not take a rifle or other large and cumbersome weapon on the reconnaissance mission. Put a pistol in your pocket and hide grenades under your clothes. If you must take a rifle – always carry it in your hands, ready to use.

If you meet a stranger on the way – be extremely careful with him. He can betray you to the enemy. Talk to him carefully. Ask your most important questions in passing, gradually. After leaving him, move off the main route and return to it after making sure that there is no surveillance behind you.

While on reconnaissance, use the locals' help if you have true friends among them who help the partisans. A local will able to get information faster, especially about the enemy located in an inhabited point.

If a fight with the enemy is unavoidable – always try to destroy them completely. Search the fascists' corpses; pick up all their documents and individual correspondence. If there is no chance to carry their weapons away with you, then hide them in a secluded place. Search the ground in the area of the encounter – there may be some documents or packets that the enemy threw away. Hide the enemy's corpses and cover up traces of the battle – that will hamper the fascist attempts to locate his soldiers and pursue you. If you cannot destroy the enemy – try to get away from him.

Do not go directly to your detachment but disguise the true direction of your withdrawal using maneuvers to confuse the enemy. Avoid any encounter with large bodies of the enemy force. When you discover their approach – hide and do not disclose your location for anything. After the enemy passes you – inform the detachment and continue to carry out your original mission.

While on reconnaissance, you might encounter a group of strangers. Do not loose your head and act rashly. First make sure you are safe. Order them to put their hands up or to drop their weapons. Keep your weapons, especially a hand grenade, at the ready. Do not approach them until you are sure that there is no threat. The enemy is cunning and perfidious. He could be dressed in any kind of clothing, even in a Red Army uniform.

Try to walk inconspicuously. Do not leave tracks behind you. Avoid stepping on the wet ground – your tracks will be very visible in it. Go around that place. Remember that in early morning your tracks will be visible on the dewy grass. Avoid moving through thick undisturbed grass. Do not cross forest clearings but move along the forest's edge.

Remember: the fascists use hunting dogs to track the partisans. Take all measures to leave as few traces as possible behind you.

WHILE ON A RECONNAISSANCE MISSION YOU MUST FIND OUT

About the enemy. Where is he, in what strength, how are his forces deployed and what is he preparing to do? Where is his headquarters, fuel supplies and officers' quarters?

About the terrain. Are there covert avenues of approach to the enemy? What are conditions of the roads, bridges, etc? Which combat systems would prove the most advantageous?

About the regional population. What are political opinions of the locals? What is their attitude toward the fascists? Where are the trustworthy people who will help the partisans?

WHEN TO GO ON A RECONNAISSANCE MISSION

The best time is just before dawn. The sentries and patrols in the enemy camp are tired and their attention wanes, they have trouble seeing.

Night, fog and bad weather
re the faithful assistants of the scout.

MOVE BY STEALTH

While walking on grass, put your weight on the entire sole of your foot, not on your heel. Then your step will be inaudible.

When walking on hard soil put your weight on your toes first and then slowly lower your heel.

On soft soil, do the opposite: first put your weight on your heel and then lower your toes quietly and slowly.

While walking on grass, pick up your feet over the grass, otherwise it will rustle. (Figure 91).

DO NOT SNEEZE OR COUGH LOUDLY

If you feel like sneezing while on reconnaissance – pinch the bridge of your nose strongly. If this does not work – quickly remove your head gear, cover your face with it and only then sneeze. Also cough into your hat.

Figure 91. Move by stealth. Step like this: 1) on soft soil; 2) on hard ground; 3) on grass.

RECONNAISSANCE OF A RAVINE

First go to the ravine's rim and make sure that there is no enemy at the edge. Examine the ravine's slopes from the top. After that go down into the ravine, search the bottom and after that – the opposite rim.

RECONNAISSANCE OF AN INHABITED POINT

During reconnaissance of a settlement, it is a good idea to use the help of someone living there- someone who is true friend. If there is no such friend – the partisan must do it himself.

Approach the settlement with care. Make sure that there is no enemy.

Approach buildings from the side where the outbuildings, backyards and gardens are located, not from the front.

When entering a house, have a hand grenade at the ready. Do not shut the door tightly behind you. Leave a lookout in the yard.

If there are people in the house – first call the owner out and question him. Always stand where they cannot shoot at you from the windows and doors.

Leave the settlement by going in the direction that is the opposite of your real destination.

ROAD RECONNAISSANCE

You need to determine the following about a road: if it is not paved with asphalt or stone – what kind of dirt road is it – sandy or hard ground; what is its width in paces; where are the bridge locations and what material are they made of – wood, steel, stone; are the bridges in good condition; what is the size of the bridges; what kind of terrain is in proximity to the road – open or close, dry or marshy; what kind of enemy units move on the road – infantry, cavalry, tanks or truck columns?

RIVER RECONNAISSANCE

When approaching a river look over its banks – are they steep or gradual; visible or covered with vegetation? Find out about its bottom – is it sand, stone or covered with silt? Take notice of the bridges – what kind are they and what size? Determine where there are fording sites and their width.

Figure 92 shows how to measure a river's width. Stand near the river facing the opposite bank (A) and select some object there, such as a tree (B). Turn right and count 50 paces along the bank. Mark your last step by driving a stake into the ground (C). Then move 50 more paces in the same direction (D). Then again turn right and count your paces while periodically looking at the tree and stake. When you see the tree and stake in a straight line – stop (E). The distance from D-E is equal to the river width.

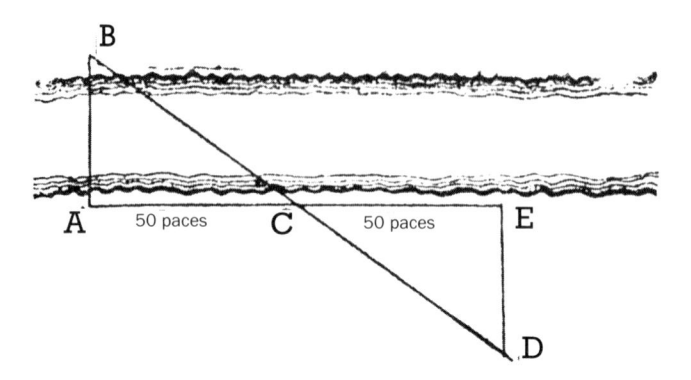

Figure 92. How to measure a river's width.

To determine the river's depth – drop a stone tied to a rope from a bridge or boat.

To figure out the river current's speed – do the following. Drive into the ground three stakes along the bank six paces from each other. Drop a small piece of wood near the first stake. Look where it is after 10 seconds. If it did not reach even the second stake – the current is slow. If it passed the second stake – the current is moderate and if it passed the third stake – the current is fast.

While crossing a river try not to leave tracks, especially near the path leading to the ford.

RECONNAISSANCE OF SWAMPS

You need to find out if the swamp is passable.
   The swamp can be crossed if:
– thick grass mixed with sedge covers the swamp (you can even move a vehicle across it during the dry season);
– pines grow in the swamp;
– the swamp has a solid growth of moss and a thick cover (up to 30 centimeters) of *ochyosy* – old decomposed moss. It will hold the weight of tracked vehicles.
   The swamp can be crossed with difficulty if:

– there are frequent small puddles of stagnant water within the moss (movement is possible by stepping from one moss clump to another and along the dirt ledges on which bushes grow);
– the swamp has growths of *pushitsa* – the grass that after flowering produces fluffy heads like dandelions;
– the swamp is covered with thickets of brush, birch, willows, alder or spruce.

The swamp is almost impassable if:
– the swamps are covered with reeds;
– grasses are floating on the top of the water.

It is easy to cross a frozen swamp. Measure the snow cover's thickness with a stick. Break through the ice with an iron bar and measure its thickness.

The grassy swamps freeze through quickly and solidly and the ice there builds a strong solid crust. The mossy swamps with layers of *ochyosy* freeze slower compared to the grassy ones and the ice tends to crack and give way. Mossy swamps with growths of brush are better for crossing. The swamps with tussocks freeze unevenly. Swamps covered with growths of alder or willow freeze poorly. The edge of a swamp freezes worst of all.

BE ABLE TO RECOGNIZE THE ENEMY

A scout must know the basic signs which let him determine the enemy's presence, location of his auxiliary services, etc.

An inhabited point is occupied by the enemy if there are foxholes, wire obstacles; or telephone and telegraph wires strung up near the settlement. A lot of traffic, dogs' barking, horses neighing – all this suggests that the inhabited point is occupied by a military unit. But if there is dead silence in a village and not a single person is seen on the streets – this is also suspicious: there could be an enemy ambush.

Enemy headquarters are usually located in individual buildings: schools, clubs, mansions, machine-tractor stations, former village soviet buildings, collective farm offices, etc. The fascist staff message centers are usually set apart from the headquarters to prevent a concentration of foot and mounted couriers, motorcyclists and communications vehicles.

Indicators of a headquarters: 1) a thick net of telephone and telegraph wires – many of which are colored and covered with rubber insulation; the wires are suspended on poles and trees or laid on the ground and they meet together at the headquarters; 2) a sizable number of enemy officers in the area; 3) the presence of radio stations, staff message centers, cars and special command and control vehicles which the fascists camouflage among bushes, trees, in barns and in sheds.

The higher is the headquarters – the more prevalent are these indicators.

The constant movement of motorcyclists, couriers and vehicles indicates the presence of a staff message center nearby. Look for the enemy headquarters in the area.

Field radio station – the antennas or radio towers are visible; motors and electrical generators produce a constant sound; there are couriers delivering radio telegrams.

Enemy airfield: 1) active – you can find it by the sound of motors, by seeing aircraft taking off and landing; seeing signal lights and flares, anti-aircraft artillery and machine-gun positions nearby; 2) reserve – you can determine this from prepared landing strips; from all kinds of construction – dug-outs, fuel storage facilities, repair sheds, etc.; the alternative airfield is usually guarded by sentries.

Chemical weapons – see the "Protection from chemical attack" chapter.

BE ABLE TO READ TRACKS

A walking person or group leaves various signs. You can find out who had been passing by using those signs. If you find a scrap of newspaper in a foreign language, a cigarette butt with an unfamiliar label, a tin can with foreign wrapper or a lost button from a foreign uniform – the enemy has been there.

But what branch of service? You can find that out reading the tracks on the ground.

Infantry – leaves trampled-on earth. The more troops passed through – the more trampled-on is the ground. If the infantry moves off the road – it makes a narrow trail – people move in single file, rarely two or three abreast (a person moving in a thick forest breaks branches off at his height).

Cavalry – leaves clear impressions of shod hooves. You can see horse manure. (In the forest cavalry breaks branches off at the height of a mounted man. At the places where a horse had been tied to a tree you can see the gnawed bark on that tree).

Animal-drawn transport leaves wheel tracks; the carriages move in a single file one behind another.

Artillery – leaves wheel tracks that are wider than that of carriages and their impression is deeper.

Automobiles leave tire impressions which are especially visible on wet ground.

Tanks leave tank tracks.

It is very easy to read tracks in the winter. They leave good imprints on the snow.

WHAT IS THE ENEMY STRENGTH?

It is possible to determine enemy strength by the length of moving columns of various branches.

Infantry. A company stretches out to 200 meters; a battalion – up to one kilometer and a regiment – up to three kilometers.

Cavalry. A squadron has a length of 150-200 meters; a regiment – up to three kilometers.

Artillery. A battery has a length of 300-400 meters; a horse-drawn artillery battalion takes up to one kilometer and mechanized artillery battalion takes up to 2.5 kilometers; a horse-drawn artillery regiment takes up 4.5 kilometers and a mechanized artillery regiment takes up to 12 kilometers.

A mechanized armored infantry platoon stretches out to 700 meters and a battalion takes up 2.5 kilometers.

Tanks. A company takes up a kilometer and a tank battalion takes up to three kilometers.

HOW TO DETERMINE THE ENEMY'S INTENTIONS

Indicators of an offensive. New enemy troops, artillery and tanks arrive. Trains arrive and unload at railroad stations; the empty trains move back toward the enemy's rear area. The enemy hastily repairs roads and bridges and builds new routes. Preparation for river crossings is accompanied by work to fix approaches to the river, to collect boats, ferries and logs. Logging and raft construction is an indicator of preparations for a river crossing.

Indicators of withdrawal. The locals always know about preparation for a withdrawal. It is the same experience ins all wars. Food and fuel supplies are moved to the rear area. The enemy damages roads, demolishes bridges and destroys river crossings. The enemy signalmen remove telephone and telegraph lines. Empty railroad cars, automobile and horse-drawn transport arrive from the rear area. Loaded transports and trains move toward the rear area.

KEEP COMMUNICATION WITH YOUR OWN FORCES

On a reconnaissance mission, there is always a chance that you will need to pass an important dispatch to your detachment. If there is no a courier available – use audio and light signals.

When leaving on a reconnaissance mission, agree with the detachment commander what each audio signal will mean: a shrill whistle, thumping a tree with a stick, imitation of a bird song or dog barking, shots with even intervals between them, etc. Always remember that those signals will also be heard by the enemy. Be careful with them. The audio signals can be used better at night, in fog or a blizzard.

You can use your arms to pass signals. Remember the main ones (Figure 93).

1. Attention. Lift a hand to the head's height.

2. SEE, HEAR (confirmation). Lift both hands to the head's height and lower them down.

3. REPEAT, did not understand (request). Lift both hands to the heads height and move crosswise before face.

4. EVERYONE HEAR! (assembly). Lift an arm completely, move in circles above the head and sharply pull it down.

5. DEPLOY! (to deploy and develop unit into formation). Several times move the arms from the front to the sides.

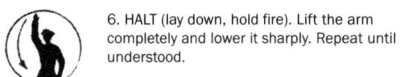

6. HALT (lay down, hold fire). Lift the arm completely and lower it sharply. Repeat until understood.

7. CONTINUE TO MOVE. (forward in the new direction). Lift one hand to the heads height while making several energetic moves up and down with another arm extended and stop if pointing in the new direction.

8. OPEN FIRE. Stretch both arms to the sides at the shoulder level and hold until understood.

9. DELIVER AMMUNITION. Lift the arm above the head and move it from side to side.

10. MOVE RIGHT (LEFT, FORWARD, BACK). Lift extended arm up above the head and lower it several times to the shoulder level pointing in the desirable direction.

11. SEE ENEMY. Extend the arm horizontally to the enemy's direction and hold it until receiving confirmation.

12. PATH IS SAFE. Several times lift the arm to the shoulder level and lower it.

Figure 93. Hand signals.

RAID

A reconnaissance mission with the goal of capturing prisoners is called a raid.

If there is time available – learn in advance what the enemy organization is: where the guards and secret posts are located; when the guards are changed; what the enemy courier routes are; where the officers' quarters are; etc.

Find the most likely places to capture a prisoner: 1) forest trails and roads used by the enemy signalmen and couriers; 2) outskirts of the inhabited points where the enemy soldiers go to collect firewood; rivers where the enemy goes to swim, water horses; 3) near the enemy bivouacs – trails to field kitchens, horse hitching posts and latrine trenches, etc.

The best time for a raid is during a dark night.

When going in the raid carefully inspect your weapon. Take some grenades and a dagger. Do not take a rucksack or knapsack with you. It there is plenty of moonlight – it would be a good idea to darken the shiny parts of your weapons – cover them with soot or clay.

The raid's success depends on surprise. The scouts or a raiding party should covertly approach the enemy and carry out their mission with a bold assault.

Jump the enemy without yelling "HOORAH".[11] Try to operate silently, using only "cold steel" – daggers, bayonets. Use the hand grenades and firearms only as the last resort: if the enemy takes refuge in a house, if there are a lot of them or if they are trying to escape.

When operating as a raiding party, one group takes prisoners and the other one stands guard, protecting their comrades and covering their withdrawal with the prisoners.

It is the best if you can capture an officer or a courier with a dispatch to the enemy headquarters. Disappear with the prisoners as quickly and silently as you came.

VIII.
CAMOUFLAGE

You must be able to mask (camouflage) yourself during any season, day and night, on any terrain in order to make yourself invisible to the enemy. Remember some simple methods of camouflage.

CAMOUFLAGE FROM ENEMY AIRCRAFT

As soon as you notice the enemy aircraft approaching, look around for buildings or trees which produce shadows. Try to hide in the shadows immediately and you will be invisible to the enemy aircraft. To camouflage yourself even better – hug the wall or tree.

It is called "camouflage by shadows". It also can be used to hide from ground observers during the day or on moonlit nights when the human body produces a shadow which increases the risk of detection by the enemy.

If an aircraft has caught you unprepared or there are no shadows – squat or lay down on the ground. Remember the main thing: do not move when the aircraft is above you. A moving person is easily detected from the air because movement is noticeable against non-moving objects. If you have a chance – throw something over yourself to make your silhouette indistinctive to enemy aircraft.

ADAPT TO TERRAIN

Adaptation to the terrain is one of the most important camouflage methods. Learn to use any natural feature and fold in the ground as a natural shield, protecting you from the enemy (Figure 94).

Every small knoll, hummock, ground pit, ravine, depression or shell (bomb) crater may serve as a good shelter from enemy detection. Natural features will also conceal you: a tree, bush, stump, large boulder, fence or wattle fencing near an inhabited point.

Remember the basic rules of how to adapt to the terrain:

What routes to move on? Try to avoid moving on roads where the enemy can detect you easily. Even during the daytime, a well-traveled and hard-packed road looks like a white ribbon, and your dark silhouette will catch the enemy's eye. Move through the forests, using ravines, trenches and hollows.

How do you conceal yourself on the move and during halts? While in the forest, use the trees' trunks and shadows for cover. Avoid forest clearings and crawl across cuttings in the woods. Move "leap frog" from one tree to another staying in their shadows while going along a forest road. Do not go beyond the forest's edge but conduct surveillance of the enemy from the forest's depth using tree trunks or bushes as your cover. When climbing a tree, make sure that there is a wall of thick branches behind you. Never settle down in a separate tree with sparse branches. Do not stand or sit in the tree trunk's fork – your silhouette will be visible even during nighttime against the background of a lighter sky. But, if the tree has fallen down, a good spot to lie down is behind the tree fork, a twisted branch or a split end.

Figure 94. Adaptation to the terrain: left – correct; right – incorrect.

Avoid taking cover behind a separate growing tree: it is a good reference point for an enemy observer. But if you are forced to stay near a separate tree or at the forest edge and in the enemy's view – then try to stand looking like the tree: if its trunk is gnarled and twisted you should take a similar posture.

During halts in the forest, stay between large tree trunks. They will cover you from the enemy observation even during daytime.

In new-growth forest within enemy view, bend over or crawl when moving through it, because upright movement is very noticeable.

In a ravine, move along the shaded side close to its edge.

You can move upright in a ditch only if it is deep enough to hide you completely. In those places where the ditch is shallower, always move bent over and sometimes even on all fours or crawling along until you reach a deeper section again. Make sure there is a bush, tall grass or a knoll – not a clear space – before looking out of the ditch. Your head would be clearly visible against the sky's background. The enemy will detect you immediately.

While scouting in fields or on plains – lie down behind the hummocks, knolls or bushes. Look out from behind these so that the enemy will not detect you. Do not look over the top of a knoll, bush or boulder – always do it from the shadow side. Move your head out slowly because a quick motion could be noticed by the enemy.

When scouting at a forest edge, move near a stump or move near a haycock in the field – tightly press against them on their shadow sides and do not break their silhouettes.

If you find yourself in an open forest glade – move through it by fast short bounds until you reach some natural cover.

If you scouting near a fence – position yourself at the side of a post; if you are near trees – stay close to the roots; if you are near a building, position yourself at the base of the garbage pile; if you are near an embankment, position yourself at its base. When taking cover behind local objects of irregular shape – try to adjust your posture to merge with their silhouettes. Do not betray yourself by abrupt movement.

In mountainous terrain, keep yourself in the shadows of the boulders and vegetation; take cover among the bushes and stone piles. Do not move near the mountain crest where your figure would be visible against the background of the sky.

If you are moving through a grain field, a thick growth of reeds or through tall grass – bend down. Spread the grain ears apart slowly and carefully and try not to rustle them. It would be a good idea to coordinate your movements with the wind's gusts which create waves over the field – by moving along with those waves you could protect yourself from an enemy observer. Use any extraneous noise to cover your silent advance.

In an inhabited point, take cover behind fences or on the windowless side of a building's wall.

When taking cover behind a fence do not show yourself but observe the enemy through a narrow slit or make a peep hole. At construction sites, ruins or burned-down spots, take cover behind logs, piles of building materials, foundations or the ruins of destroyed buildings, under burnt boards and rafters. In doing so, try to stay in the shadows – you will be less noticeable.

When entering a house and moving to an attic or roof – comply with all the rules of camouflage rules there as well.

Do not lean out of room or attic windows but conduct your observation from some depth inside, protected by the internal darkness.

When located on the roof, take cover behind a chimney and only stick your head out on the shadow side.

At night, position yourself in a low-lying area for better observation. Position yourself where you will not be noticeable but can see everything and everyone very well.

Use all means to adapt to the terrain. But if it is not enough – use artificial camouflage.

ARTIFICIAL CAMOUFLAGE

At any season of the year, there is abundant material for artificial camouflage. You should learn the correct use of the most dependable of those. Those are:

During summertime, use tree or bush branches, reeds, tall swamp grass, haycocks of mowed grain in the field, etc.

To camouflage yourself well using bushes or grass – use branches of the same bush or same grass. Pick some branches and make an artificial bush out of them. You can crawl unnoticed while holding it in front of you. Use a tuft of wheat in the wheat field as cover. Cover yourself with sedge in the swamp and carefully move foreword.

Your figure should blend into the background of any terrain. Use green while operating in green forests or bushes. Use straw or burlap for cover when you are in a field that has turned yellow.

THE SIMPLEST CAMOUFLAGE CAPE

Bast fringe is simple and dependable camouflage material.

Make a wide and fluffy fringe out of bast and cover your head and shoulders with it. This is sufficient to camouflage yourself on yellowish terrain. You can make a camouflage robe by fixing bast into a rope net.

One can use pieces of cloth instead of bast. Sew mottled rags onto a net or throw during summertime. Your silhouette will blend into the background from a distance. One can make capes out of straw, corn stalks, reeds or hay. They can be tied together with cords or bast.

UNDER ENEMY FIRE

If you plan to make a dash under enemy fire – pick out some cover on the terrain beforehand: a knoll, bush, boulder, hollow, ditch or shell crater. Rise slowly from your original shelter without attracting the enemy's attention by abrupt movements. Once you are on your feet – run as fast as possible. Drop like a stone when you are finished running. Always try to drop three to four meters distant from your chosen shelter. Then crawl covertly toward it. If you would run directly to the shelter, the enemy may mark the place and shoot you when you rise again.

During the bound, do not swing your arms – it will make you easily noticeable. Immediately after stopping, cover your head with leaves, grass or branches. Do not forget that sticking your head up will betray you. Side-to-side head movements are especially noticeable.

Try to change your firing position frequently. This is one of the best methods to camouflage your location.

The closer you get to the enemy, the shorter and faster your bounds should be. Even if you find yourself in the totally open space, you can avoid an aimed shot with rapid bounds (no longer then three-five seconds each). The enemy needs no less then six seconds to aim and shoot.

When you reach 30 meters distance from the enemy, you will be able to kill him with a hand grenade or attack him with a bayonet.

WINTER CAMOUFLAGE

In the winter, use white color in the snow as the best method of camouflage. In wintertime, a white robe will serve as a good camouflage. One can make such a robe from a bed sheet, tablecloth, drapery, etc. Wearing the white robe allows you to become totally unnoticeable to the enemy if you do not make quick moves. Try to move slowly. Make halts more often and stay motionless.

Wearing a white robe in the snow makes you unnoticeable even if you are walking at your full height. But if you have a green forest background or another dark background behind you – that is a different matter. In such cases, it would be better to crawl pushing your way through the snow with your head. Also you can dig shallow trenches in the snow and move through them by bending down to the snow's level.

If white robes are unavailable, then you can throw snow over each other while staying in the observation post.

DESTROY ENEMY'S TANKS

The brave do not fear tanks. The more fearlessly you meet the enemy's machine, the easier it is to destroy it. Find the fascist's tanks and destroy them.

The tank's motor provides the tank's movement. Put the motor out of action – and the tank does not go any farther.

The motor uses gasoline. Do not let them bring gasoline to the tanks on time – they will stand immobile.

If gasoline in the tank is not completely spent, try to ignite it – the tank will catch on fire.

A tank's turret rotates and the turret's gun moves by elevation and depression. Try to jam the turret and the weapon. Then the enemy will not be able to use aimed fire.

The air to cool the engine goes into the tank through special slots. All moving parts and hatches have slots and are not closed tightly. If you pour flammable liquid inside the slots of the tank – the tank will ignite.

The tank has vision slits and viewing instruments equipped with visors. Cover them with dirt, fire at them with any weapon to jam the visors.

To increase its cross-country performance the tank is propelled by tracks. Try to destroy the tracks or driving sprocket.

As soon as the enemy crew comes out – attack them with any available weapon using bullets, grenades or bayonet.

WHAT ARE A TANK'S WEAKNESSES?

The crew cannot hear well due to the tank's noise.
　　The crew has poor visibility because they have difficulty seeing through vision slits and viewing instruments – especially when they are on the move.
　　It is difficult to conduct aimed fire from a moving tank because of the tank's rolling and shaking. The maximum effective range while moving is only 400 meters. The tank is forced to make short halts to increase firing accuracy.

FASCIST TANKS' VULNERABLE SPOTS

Those are:
– tracks and suspension, driving sprockets;
– vision slits;
– hull roof plate and hull floor;
– engine compartment.

Concentrate your main strikes at them. Carefully look at figure 95 and memorize the places to fire at, or to throw grenades and bottles with inflammable liquid at, to put the tank out of action.[12]

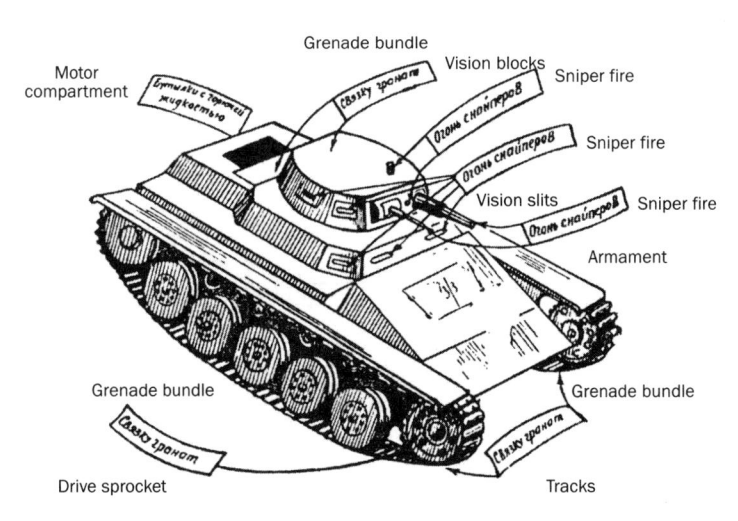

Figure 95. Tank's vulnerable spots.

PREPARE TO MEET THE TANK

The sooner you detect the tank, the easier it is to destroy it.

During the day, rely on your eyes rather than your ears. At night you can hear tank engine's noise up to 900 meters away – if it is quiet; if the wind is blowing in the tank's direction – up to 450 meters; if the wind is blowing from the tank toward you – up to 1.5 kilometers.

The sound of a moving tank can be heard at even greater distances.

And now the tank appears. Do not bustle around or run from one place to another; carefully hide yourself and blend in with the terrain to become unnoticeable. Hide in a depression, ditch, trench, shell crater or – as the last resort – behind a bush or knoll.

Prepare to meet the tank and destroy it using all available means.

Learn where the fascist tanks are, sneak up on them and destroy them.

BULLETS AGAINST TANK

It is possible to put enemy tankettes, light tanks or armored trucks out of action by firing at them with a rifle or 7.62mm machine-gun.

Open fire from 100-300 meters distance. Aim at the tank's vision slits – well aimed fire at them will hurt the crew members with fragments and spalling.

Especially accurate riflemen (snipers) fire at the vision blocks and fire control equipment.

Use heavy caliber machine-guns to fire at fuel tanks and the tank's side armor where it is thinner then the front armor plates.

When firing on heavy tanks with very thick armor, take aim at the vision slits, viewing devices and fire control equipment.

FIGHTING TANKS WITH GRENADES

Destroy enemy tanks with hand grenades by throwing them from 25-30 meters distance. The best choice is an anti-tank grenade. Throw it from behind a shelter. Aim at the tracks, drive sprockets, engine hatch cover or top of the turret. If you do not have an anti-tank grenade – throw several grenades (anti-personnel) bundled together beforehand.

Make a bundle in this manner. Tie five armed grenades that are on a safe mode together with a strong twine (wire, cable): four grenades should have the handles pointed in the same direction and the fifth – with the handle in opposite direction) (figure 96).

Hold the bundle by the fifth grenade's handle and throw the bundle at the tank. The fifth grenade explodes first and detonates the bundle.

One can make a bundle out of three Model 1933 hand grenades. Remove the defensive [fragmentation] sleeves and screw off the handles of two grenades; throw the bundle using the third grenade's handle.

After throwing the grenades, get down into your shelter.

Anti-tank rifles and rifle-propelled anti-tank grenades are also good weapons to fight tanks with.

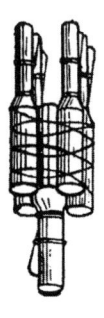

Figure 96. Five grenade bundle.

If there is a chance – sneak up close to the tank and destroy it by putting explosives and anti-tank mines on the vulnerable spots.

INCENDIARY BLEND #1 AND #3

A bottle filled with incendiary blend #1 or #3 is a simple and reliable way to destroy a tank (figure 97). It is flammable. Handle it in the following manner:

1. Prepare the bottle for throwing: tear off the paper from the matches' ends on the bottle's side.

2. Lit the matches on the bottle.

3. Throw the bottle at the tank.

INCENDIARY LIQUID KS

A bottle filled with KS liquid is a formidable weapon against tanks liquid (figure 97).

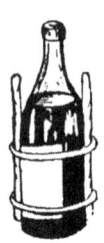

Figure 97: Left – bottle with KS liquid; middle – bottle with incendiary blend liquid; right – homemade bottle with gasoline.

There is no need to ignite the liquid; when the bottle is broken the KS liquid ignites spontaneously.
Be careful handling the bottle.[13]

BOTTLE WITH GASOLINE

You can prepare a bottle with gasoline yourself. Do that this way:

1. Pour any kind of gasoline or mix – half gasoline, half kerosene – into the bottle.

2. Do not fill the bottle completely – leave 8-9 centimeters empty from the top, because gasoline expends when heated.

3. Plug up the bottle tightly.

4. Soak oakum, cotton or a rag with gasoline and tie it to the bottle's bottom along with matches. Insulation tape is best suited for that purpose, but if it is not available – use a cord as shown at figure 97.
When a tank approaches within 15-20 meters distance from you – light the matches and throw the bottle.
When throwing the bottle aim at the tank's vulnerable spots – the engine compartment or vision slits (tanks usually have their engines in the rear).[14]

BARRIERS

Make tree barriers on forest roads.

Cut several trees with a saw on one side of the road and several – on the other one. Do not cut them completely through. Leave one-quarter of the trunks uncut, so the trunks will be connected to their stumps. The stumps should be 50-80 centimeters tall. Fell the trees so they fall across the road. It is better if the trees crisscross with their tops pointed toward the enemy. Make the barrier depth 15 meters. Then wait to ambush the enemy. Destroy the halted tanks using all available means.

If anti-tank and anti-personnel mines are available – put them into the barrier. This will keep the enemy from pulling the barrier apart. If the crew gets out of the tank to pull the barrier apart – kill them with bullets and grenades.

The enemy tanks will try to move around the barriers. Make booby traps and mine obstacles on the possible bypass.

TANK TRAP

Dig a three meter pit in the ground. The pit should be 5.5 meters wide at its top and 1.5 meters wide at the bottom. The pit needs a covering. Lay four not-too-thick logs (girders) as the covering's support – two of them should be at the edges and the other two between them. Put thin poles on top of the girders, cover them with branches and throw a dirt layer on top of that. The covering should hold the weight of a person or carriage but collapse under the tank's weight.

Carefully camouflage everything on the trap's top. Remove the dug-out dirt, level the surface, cover it with turf or with snow in wintertime.

You should stay close to the trap. Destroy a tank which falls into the pit with grenades or bottles filled with inflammable liquid. Shoot the escaping crew.

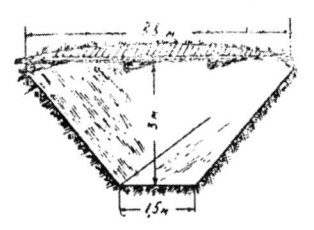

Figure 98. Tank trap.

FIGHTING ARMORED TRUCKS

Fight enemy armored trucks in the same manner as you fight his tanks. Throw grenades under the vehicles', aiming at the rear (driving) wheels and at the turret rack. Throw a bottle filled with inflammable liquid at the armored truck's front – where the motor is. Remember: the average armor on the armored truck is no more then 10 millimeters thick – it can be pierced with rifle and machine-gun armored-piercing bullets. Open fire at a distance of no more then 300 meters. Fire on heavy – four-axle – armored trucks from a shorter distance aiming at the vision slits.

If you encounter an enemy truck – shoot the driver, throw a bottle [filled with an inflammable liquid] at the radiator or driver's cabin; throw a grenade under the wheels. If there are many enemy soldiers in the truck, it is better to use an anti-tank grenade to make sure there are no survivors.

USING WIRE AGAINST A MOTORCYCLE

The best method to knock down a motorcyclist is to stretch a wire across his path. Choose a strong tree along the forest road. Tie one end of the wire to that tree at one meter's height. Pull the wire across the road and stand near another tree across from the first one.

When you hear the approaching enemy motorcyclist – pull up and tighten the wire, wrap its end several times around the tree and prepare for an ambush.

The motorcyclist will be knocked off the motorcycle when he strikes the wire. Then you can kill or capture him.

WINTER OBSTACLES

Snow rampart (bank). Use snow ramparts (banks) to fight enemy tanks during the wintertime. You can make them if there is a snow blanket at least 25 centimeters thick. The rampart should be 1.5 meters high and four meters long. When a tank hits the obstacle it is going to ground itself on its hull bottom and its tracks will start slipping. The best time to build the ramparts is during thaws. To hold the snow on these ramparts, use straw and brushwood-sticking them into the snow blanket. Those ramparts should be built on forward slopes, lowlands, forest edges and in bushes. It is a good idea to build two-three ramparts, especially near roads.

Combine the snow ramparts with forest barriers and mines. Try to plant the mines at a slant on hard surface. Then they will explode under the entire tank's body.

Ice covering. Pour water on those slopes that are more than 15 degrees steep. You will get an ice mound – the tank will spin around on it. One can start making the ice covering at minus 5 degrees (Centigrade), but it is better if it is colder.

Make the ice covering in front of snow ramparts and on river and creek banks.

Holes in the ice. On rivers and lakes make holes in the ice. Their width should be four meters and their length five to six meters. Cover the hole in the ice with poles and branches and cover these with snow. Such a hole will not freeze for a long time and it is unnoticeable from a moving tank. It is a very reliable tank trap. The distance between traps should be two-two and a half meters.

FIGHTER GROUPS

Fight tanks in groups of four to six people. Two or three members of the group throw bottles or grenades from behind shelters. The rest shoot crew members who bail out.

When conducting an ambush in the forest, place part of the group up in the trees. If the ambush is located at a narrow pass where vehicles cannot pull off the road, first kill the leading and the trail vehicle in the column. You will trap the column. It will make destroying the rest easier.

IX.

HOW TO FIGHT ENEMY AVIATION

Constantly look for enemy aviation – it will help you detect an enemy aircraft long before it approaches.

You can hear the aircraft's motor from 9-12 kilometers distance. With good visibility, the aircraft can be seen from seven-nine kilometers away.

Try to determine the direction that the aircraft is coming from by its sound. Simultaneously warn your comrades about an enemy air raid, prepare to fire at the enemy and take some measures to camouflage yourself (see CAMOUFLAGE chapter).

Fascist aircraft divided into five main groups:

1. **Fighters** – their mission is to conduct air-to-air combat, but they also fire machine-guns at ground troops and drop small bombs on them while decreasing their altitude to 300-200 meters –and sometimes even lower.

2. **Bombers** – drop bombs and fire machine-guns at ground troops; they can fly as low as 500 meters and even lower.

3. **Dive-bombers** – drop bombs while diving like a "falling rock" at the target; then they make a sharp climb to regain altitude (come out of the dive). Remember that the best times to down a dive bomber are during the start of the dive and at its end.

4. **Reconnaissance aircraft** – conduct observation and terrain photography. Bombers and fighters can also carry out reconnaissance missions.

5. **Transport aircraft** – are used to move cargo and troops and drop and land airborne troops.

Be able to recognize enemy aircraft by their identification markings (figure 99).

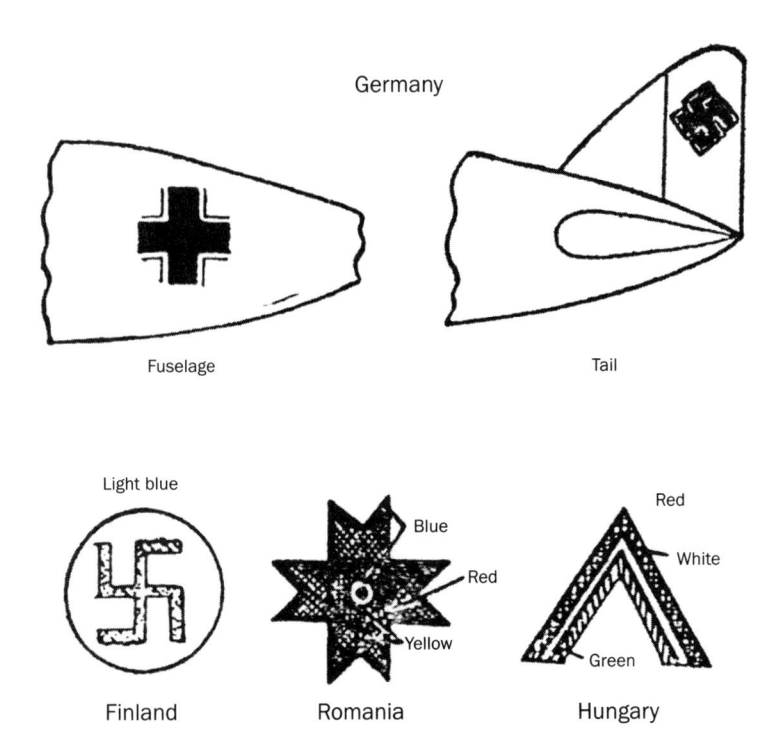

Figure 99. Identification markings of enemy aircraft.

1. **German airplanes** have a black cross on their wings and fuselage and the fascist swastika on their tails.

2. **Finnish airplanes** have a blue swastika inside of a white circle.

3. **Rumanian airplanes** have a straight yellow cross with forked ends; in the cross' center are three circles: outer – red, middle – yellow and inner – blue.

4. **Hungarian airplanes** have a triangle (chevron) made of three bands: outer – red, middle – white and inner – green.

Keep in mind that the enemy is treacherous and will not hesitate to paint the Soviet identification sign – the red star on its aircraft.

Learn to recognize the main types of German airplanes by their silhouettes and sizes.

FIRING AT AIRCRAFT

Remember: fascist airplanes sent to fight the partisan detachments fly at low altitudes. When the enemy aircraft appears – quickly occupy a nearby position to fire at the airplane. If there is no shelter (dug-out, shell crater, trench, etc.) hide inside the shadows. Do not raise dust – it will compromise your camouflage. Do not occupy a position near roads or poles with wires – enemy aviation frequently attacks such places. Avoid being near explosives and flammable objects – ammunition storage, explosive materials, kerosene and gasoline.

Know that rifle and machine-gun fire is most when the aircraft altitude is less than 800 meters.

When acting alone, be composed and take a good aim. When firing an automatic weapon, use short bursts of six-eight rounds; when firing a rifle – shoot as fast as you can.

When acting as a part of a group – open fire on the commander's order.

You can fire at aircraft from any position: lying on your back, kneeling or standing or with the weapon supported. Use the lying on your back position when the aircraft passes over your head. If it is diving at you or comes out of a dive, a kneeling or standing position is better.

Figure 100. Firing at an airplane while lying on your back.

To support your weapon, use tree branches, a pole with a fork, a bipod made out of two sticks tied at their upper ends (fork), a wattle fence, a house porch, a bridge railing, etc. When firing at aircraft with a bipod-equipped machine-gun, use dug-outs, pits, ravines, ditches, slopes or embankments.

When firing from a rifle or a light machine gun, set the sight on 5. When firing a submachine gun, set the sight on 2.5. When firing a heavy machine gun, set the sight on 6. When firing an antitank rifle, set the sight on 4.[15]

Learn to pick the most appropriate moment to fire at an aircraft. The simplest way is to fire at a diving aircraft or at the aircraft as it is coming out of its dive. When it is diving, aim at its nose; when it recovering, aim at its tail. When the aircraft is hedge-hopping – fire at it while lying on your back when the aircraft is directly overhead.

HOW TO TAKE A LEAD

If the aircraft is flying horizontally, take a lead while aiming your weapon i.e. aim ahead of the aircraft. Why is this necessary? It takes time for a bullet to reach the target. During that time, the aircraft will fly dozens of meters forward and the bullet will pass behind the target. Because of this, you need to know at what distance you should lead the aircraft in order to hit it.

Here is a simplified method of how to determine the lead aiming point. Estimate by eye the approximate distance to the aircraft (give or take a hundred meters). Use the table to determine the lead aiming point. For the sake of convenience, the lead is given in aircraft fuselage lengths instead of meters. Numbers in the table show the number of aircraft fuselage length that should be placed between the aircraft and the lead aiming point in order to hit the aircraft (figure 101). There is a different lead for different types of aircraft even when they are flying at the same altitude. The explanation is: the average speed and fuselage length differ between bombers, fighters and transport airplanes.

Memorize the table. Practice aiming at flying aircraft. After some practice, you will find it easier to find the lead aiming point by eye.

Types of aircraft/ Range (m)	Lead aiming point in "fuselages"		
	Fighters: Av. speed ~120m/sec; Fuselage length: 8–12m.	Dive-bombers and mediumbombers: Av. speed ~95m/sec; Fuselage length: 11–17m.	Heavy bombers/cargo planes: Av. speed ~80m/sec; Fuselage length: 23–25m
100	1½	1	½
200	3	2	1
300	5	3	1½
400	7	4	2
500	9	5	2½

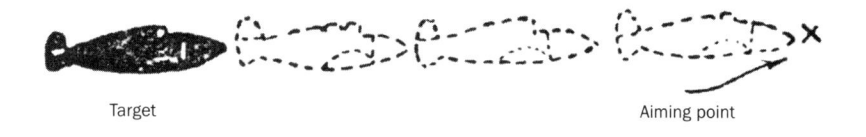

Target Aiming point

Figure 101. How to aim at flying aircraft.

SHOOTING AT PARATROOPERS

Learn to kill fascist paratroopers while they are in the air. Destroy them as soon as they approach the maximum effective range of rifle and machine-gun fire (500 meters distance from you).

A paratrooper's descent speed is six meters per second. He is also being moved laterally by the wind. Take a lead aiming point below the target and to the side of the wind's direction (figure 102).

If the wind is light, use the following rule. When the paratrooper comes within 300 meters distance from you, lead him four-five figure lengths down and three figure widths in the drift direction (figure 102). When the distance to the paratrooper is 500 meters, lead him three figure lengths down and five figure widths in the drift direction. Remember that firing at the parachute canopy is useless.

How to Fight Enemy Aviation

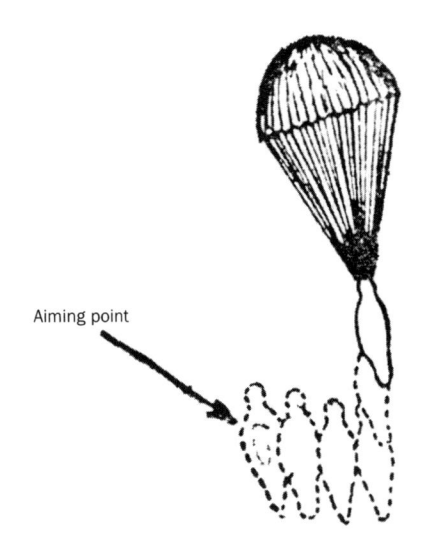

Figure 102. How to aim at a descending paratrooper.

Destroy the landing paratroopers. Kill them before they have a chance to free themselves from their harness suspension straps and can use their weapons or escape.

X.
ANTI-CHEMICAL PROTECTION

Always remember that the German-fascist troops can use poisonous gas. Look for the following signs to detect a gas attack:

1. When the gas is sprayed from an aircraft, one can see dark stripes behind airplanes which quickly disappear.

2. When the enemy drops chemical bombs from aircraft or fires chemical artillery (mortar) shells filled with persistent chemical agents, you can see some drops spread around the craters. If the shells are filled with non-persistent agents, then their explosions produce characteristic clouds. Remember that the chemical round's explosion is not as loud as that of a high-explosive round.

3. If the enemy releases chemical agents from its location, you can see flashes, fire and smoke moving toward you.

4. When chemical gas is released from a cylinder, there are whistling and hissing sounds.

Remember that, besides these methods of distribution, poisonous gas can be delivered by grenade-launchers, hand grenades and rifle grenades. In the event of a chemical attack, have all of your chemical protection equipment ready.

If you detect the signs of a chemical attack, put on your gas mask and prepare to use all available protection.

HOW TO RECOGNIZE CHEMICAL AGENTS

Detect chemical agents by smell and some external signs.

1. **Yperite** (mustard gas) – has a garlic, onion or mustard smell. It leaves dark-brown oily drops after use. Poisoned vegetation wilts and turns

yellow approximately a day after contact. The gas persists for several days in thick grass and bushes; during wintertime it can persist for several months (depending on the conditions).

2. **Lewisite** – smells like geraniums. It persists on the terrain from two to ten hours during the summertime and for several days in the winter. Exposed vegetation changes its color to a grayish brown.

3. **Phosgene** – smells like moldy hay or rotten fruit. It persists on open terrain for no longer then 10-20 minutes. In the forest and in places protected from wind, phosgene may persist for two-three hours or longer.

4. **Diphosgene** – has a smell that is very similar to phosgene. It differs from phosgene by being more persistent: it stays on open terrain for 30-90 minutes during the summertime. In the forest and in places protected from the wind, diphosgene may stay up to 12 hours. It affects yours eyes quite noticeably.

When ammunition filled with phosgene and diphosgene explodes, it produces dense white clouds that slowly expand and stay in low areas.

5. **Chloracetophenone** (CAP) is non-persistent when it is dispersed as a gas. When it is spread in small particles on the terrain, it can produce irritation for two-three days. It smells like violets or bird cherry. It can be identified by its effect on the eyes (it produces sharp pain and heavy tearing). When it is dispersed as a gas, it is a bluish-white cloud with blurred edges.

6. **Adamsite** – is a poisonous gas with no smell. It can be recognized by its yellowish-green cloud with distinctive edges. Adamsite immediately produces irritation of the nose, throat and bronchi.

7. **Aquinite (chloropicrin)** – is dispersed in steam. Its vapors can be detected only by their effect on the eyes: it produces heavy tearing and in large quantities it can cause coughing and symptoms of general poisoning.

8. **Prussic acid (Hydrogen cyanide)** – is a steam-like toxic agent that smells like cherry pits or bitter almond. It is almost impossible to detect low concentrations of prussic acid. Its vapors can be detected by a

scratchy throat, a bitter taste in the mouth (bitter almond), dizziness and nausea. In small quantities it is almost harmless. A high concentration of it causes death almost immediately.

Remember that your gas mask is the first and best chemical protection equipment. It will protect you from all known toxic agents. When putting your gas mask on, hold your breath. Then exhale sharply and then breathe normally.

When you are detecting toxic agents by smell, try to do so with only one-two inhalations. Further inhalations dull your sense of smell and it increases your danger of exposure to poison. Determine what the toxic agent is in this way: Put on your gas mask. Then, after a deep exhalation, slightly pull your mask away from your face near your ear using your index finger. Simultaneously squeeze the corrugated respirator tube shut with your other hand. Inhale slightly with your nose and determine what the toxic agent is. Continue to squeeze the tube and exhale sharply to push the toxins out of the mask. If you cannot determine what the agent is – try it again after a short break.

GAS MASK CARE

Protect your gas mask from humidity, blows and impacts. Do not store it near a fire or hot stove. Do not put foreign objects into the respirator haversack. Remove the gas mask from the haversack and let it dry after a strong rain. Also dry the haversack. Do not put heavy objects on the mask and do not use it as a seat, pillow or support.

Prevent the mask's eyepieces from becoming fogged-over. Use fogging-resistant celluloid film inserts and special "pencils". If those are not available – use dry soap.

How to use celluloid film inserts: 1) Carefully wipe the eyepieces inside; 2) Check if there are scratches on the inserts – if there is a scratch do not use the insert; 3) exhale at the insert and find out which side of it fogs; 4) put the insert under special the clamps of the eyepieces bracket clip with the misting side to the glass.

How to use the special "pencil": 1) Wipe the lenses with dry cloth or handkerchief inside until they are completely transparent; 2) run five streaks on lenses in the shape of Roman numeral III (three vertical and two horizontal); if the "pencil" leaves very thin streaks then make 10- 12 of them; 3) exhale on the lenses to fog them and rub the streaks with your fingers until the "pencil's" substance is spread evenly onto the lenses; check out if it works properly by exhaling on the lenses – if the lens stays transparent then it is prepared right.

Use dry soap in the same fashion as the "pencil".

HOW TO USE A DEFECTIVE GAS MASK

If the gas mask started letting toxic agents in, try to find the problem and fix it until you get a replacement.

Begin your check with the respirator filter canister. Exhale and clamp the corrugated tube near the canister. Try to inhale slowly. If the poisonous air does not come in, then the canister is faulty and everything else is in good order. Then hold your breath, pull the canister out of the haversack and look it over. When you find a puncture or a hole – cover it with a handkerchief, overcoat flap or plug it with a piece of soft bread or dirt – then begin breathing. Replace the damaged canister as soon as possible.

If after clamping the corrugated tube, the poisonous air still comes into the mask then the mask or the tube is faulty. Check them with your hands quickly. If you cannot find the damage or it is impossible to cover the damage with your hand (the lens is broken or the corrugated tube is damaged) then do the following: remove the canister from the haversack, screw it off of the corrugated tube, shut your eyes tightly, pull off the mask, put the canister's neck into your mouth. While holding the canister with your right hand, hold your nose with your left hand and resume breathing calmly.

Figure 103. How to breath with a faulty outlet valve.

If the mask itself is damaged, you can use another technique: hold your breath, shut your eyes tightly, take off the mask, turn it inside out; then put the upper extension of the T-shaped joint into your mouth while holding it with your left hand. Use your right hand to hold your nose and breathe through your mouth.

If the mask's damage is small – clamp the damaged place with the fingers or palm and hold until you can replace the gas mask.

When the outlet valve is damaged (in the gas mask with a helmet face-piece): press the valve against the joint's opening (figure 103). Make strong short exhalations – the air will come out behind your ears. If there is a mask with the face-piece only – close the lower part of valve holder, make energetic exhalations and air would come out behind your ears.

IF YOU DO NOT HAVE A GAS MASK

Make a homemade "gas mask".

Take a piece of cloth or cheesecloth; fold it several times to the size that will allow you to cover your face from the chin to the eyes. Put several layers of cotton inside it and sew it in quilt-like with thread. Sew strings onto the corners so that you can tie the "mask" around your head. When a chemical weapons alarm sounds, soak the "mask" in 2% soda solution or in water, cover your face and breath. Try to leave the contaminated zone because this mask will protect you for a short period of time (no more than 15-20 minutes).

A towel folded several times, a couple of handkerchiefs or even a simple piece of cloth could serve as an improvised gas mask. Soak them in a 2% soda solution, press it to your mouth tightly and quickly move out of contaminated area.

If the soda solution is not available – use regular water.

PROTECTIVE CAPE

Use a protective cape to protect yourself from s blister gas spread by aircraft (mustard gas, Lewisite).

It is made like a sleeveless raincoat with a hood. There are pockets for your hands sewn inside the cape's edges, so that you can to wrap it tightly around yourself. Some capes have a throat flap with a button. The accordion-style folded cape is carried in the haversack compartment.

In a case of chemical weapon alarm, put on your gas mask. Then remove the cape from the haversack, unfold it behind your back and cover your head with the hood. Straighten the cape at edges, put your hands in the internal pockets and wrap it around yourself.

While removing the cape, do not touch its external surface to protect you from contamination. It is better to do it by standing with your face into the wind, lift the cape up, spread your arms wide and throw it off. Bury or burn the contaminated cape.

Remember to take care of the cape: do not crush it, keep it from moisture and strong heat.

CROSSING A CONTAMINATED ZONE (CZ)

Closely woven and tightly closed clothing can protect you from droplets of gas during your exit from the CZ. Buckle up all buttons and hooks on your overcoat, quilted coat or short coat. Wrap a cord, cheesecloth or bandage around coats' flaps. Lift your collar and wrap it around with a scarf or towel. Tie up the sleeves tightly at the wrists. If you have gloves (better – made out of leather or fur) – wearing them is a must.

To protect your feet, do the following. If rubber boots or shoes are not available, wrap a thick cloth around the shoes (oilcloth works even better). Tie wooden planks to the shoe soles. One can use several layers of folded paper to wrap around the shoes. All of those wraps should be fixed tightly so that you will not need to adjust them while exiting the CZ. Remember that all those improvised protective means can hold the toxic gas off for 10-15 minutes; after that they could become a source of contamination themselves. Take off the "protective clothes" as soon as possible (after crossing the CZ) and try to wash your body with warm water and soap. Take your clothing off carefully, without touching it with your hands.

Use dirt, sand, dung, ash, coal or saw dust from uncontaminated areas to cover the contaminated soil; make planking to cross it with boards or bricks.

If there is no chance to avoid the contaminated surface – cut the upper layer of soil (10-15cm thick) ahead of you with a sapper shovel and move on that narrow clean strip. Throw the contaminated dirt to the side as far as you can.

If you need to cross the CZ during a fight, moving by bounds and lying down on the contaminated soil, you must use a simple ground mat. Weave it out of straw, brush, reeds or grass. And remember: when carrying the ground mat, hold it by its clean uncontaminated upper side; make the bounds as long as possible and move fast. When digging yourself in, throw the soil further away than usual.

FIRST AID TO A POISONED GAS VICTIM

First, put a gas mask on the poisoned person and move him carefully out of the contaminated zone.

Learn the initial symptoms of poisoning for each of the toxic gases and render first aid according to the type of gas used to poison him.

SYMPTOMS OF CONTAMINATION BY BLISTER GAS

Yperite (mustard gas). There are no symptoms during the initial stage of poisoning (from two-three hours up to 24 hours). That is the so-called latent period. Later, if the person has been contaminated with gas vapors, redness comes to the eyes along with tearing, swelling of the eyelids and light sensitivity (Ò‚ÂÚÓ·ÓflÁÌ‚). This is followed by a stuffy nose, hoarse voice, throat irritation, a light cough and redness to the skin – especially at the skin folds. Itching and a burning sensation follow. If the gas' droplets get on the skin, these areas will first redden and hurt.

A person hurt by mustard gas should be given first aid as soon as possible. The droplets of the gas must be removed immediately without spreading them or rubbing them into the skin. Apply cotton or dry sand to the contaminated spots and let these absorb the liquids. Then wipe the spots with kerosene, gasoline, manganese oxide potassium or warm water with soap.

Use the personal CW decontamination set to treat the skin. There are two types of sets.

The first is a small box with six gauze spheres. Inside of each sphere is a smaller box with a special liquid skin decontaminant for gas. Besides these spheres there are three small ampoules with inhalants to treat a damaged respiratory tract; a metal wedge to puncture the gauze spheres; and a piece of gauze to wipe the eyes. Here is how to use the set:

Anti-Chemical Protection

1. Squeeze and crush the gauze sphere with your hand or puncture it with the metal wedge while holding the sphere over the contaminated spot on the skin.

2. Wipe the spot with the sphere two-three times without unrolling the ball.

3. Unroll the ball, remove the crushed small box's parts and continue to wipe the skin with the gauze for about two-three minutes.

4. If the gauze dries up prematurely – take another sphere and use it like the first one.

5. While wiping the skin, do not apply pressure on it. After the decontamination is finished, wash the spot with water.

If the upper respiratory tract is damaged (coughing, sneezing and a stuffed nose are symptoms) – use a glass ampoule from the small compartment of the box. Crush it with your fingertips – do not remove the gauze cap. Then inhale the contents until the irritation stops. If, after 10-15 minutes, the irritation does not stop – use a second ampoule. If still wearing a gas mask, push the crushed ampoule under the mask during exhalation. To do that, slightly pull on the mask's edge near the right ear.

A new type of decontamination set is contained in a metal box. It contains two large ampoules with liquid that are used to decontaminate mustard gas (Lewisite) on the skin. Use the ampoules as follows. Pull the ampoule from the box by the bag's loop and strike it with force flat on a hard object, then shake it 10-15 times. Squeeze the ampoule with your hand (without removing from the bag) and soak a tampon in the liquid as your pour it out. Wipe contaminated skin spots with the tampon. There are several tampons in each box.

Also use the liquid from the ampoules to decontaminate contaminated parts of your clothing. When the cloth is soaked through, wipe it with the bag without removing the ampoule. Use a second ampoule as needed.

The box also contains four small ampoules to treat the irritated respiratory tract by inhalation. Use them in the same way as the ampoules in the older set.

Wash the poisoned person's eyes with a 2% soda solution or with a solution of regular salt (one gram of salt per liter of water); or use just clean water. Always use large quantities of the solutions or water and strong jets of them. The poison victim should gargle with the same liquids to clear his throat and mouth and to wash out his nose.

Lewisite. Lewisite vapors immediately irritate the eyes, nose and throat; this is followed by tears, stuffed nose, heavy drooling, nausea and vomiting. When Lewisite droplets get on the skin, there is a burning sensation almost immediately. There is no latent period. The blisters from Lewisite are whitish or reddish in color – a difference from mustard gas which produces yellow (amber) colored blisters.

The first aid for a poisoned person is same as for mustard gas.

SYMPTOMS OF POISONING BY CHOCKING GAS

Phosgene and diphosgene. Initially, after exposure, there is a light cough and shortness of breath, pallor, weakness, chest pain, and a foul taste when smoking. Then the symptoms disappear and the victim feels well. But after several hours, pulmonary edema develops and the victim feels a shortness of breath.

Aquinite (chloropicrin). The initial symptom of chloropicrin poisoning is a strong irritation to the eyes. This is followed by pulmonary edema.

How to render first aid to the victim of chocking gas. Put a gas mask on the victim immediately and move him out of the contaminated area. Do not let the victim move by himself – it intensifies the poisoning. Make breathing easier by removing the victim's equipment and belt plus unbuckle all his fasteners. If his clothing still smells of gas – remove it and let it dry out. Wrap the victim in something (but not too tightly) to warm him up and let him rest completely. If there is a chance – give him a hot drink. Do not perform artificial respiration under any circumstances.

SYMPTOMS OF POISONING BY SUFFOCATING GAS

Adamsite. Produces sharp burning and tickling sensations in the nose and throat, non-stop sneezing, pain in the chest and jaws, heavy drooling and stuffed nose. The symptoms increase for a minute, followed by dizziness, loss of balance and heavy vomiting.

First aid: leave the contaminated atmosphere. Wash the eyes with a 3% solution of boric acid or 2% soda solution or salt solution (one gram per liter of water). Gargle the same solution to clean out the mouth and throat. If the solutions are not available – use boiled water. It is helpful to sniff the substance from the small ampoule of the decontamination set to ease respiratory tract pain.

Chloracetophenone (tear gas). Causes tearing, sharp pain to the eyes, light sensitivity and compulsive blinking.

First aid – same as for Adamsite poisoning.

SYMPTOMS OF POISONING BY A BLOOD AGENT

Prussic acid (Hydrogen Cyanide). The victim begins feeling a sore throat, has a bitter taste on his tongue and has numbness in his mouth, pain in the back of the head and chest pain. This is followed by dizziness, nausea and vomiting. This turns into convulsions and breathing stoppage. All those symptoms develop very fast over the period of several minutes.

First aid. Move the victim from the contaminated area immediately. Lay him down on his back and open his clothing over his chest. Rub the chest and other body parts energetically. Moisten the forehead and temples with cold water. If the victim stops breathing – apply artificial respiration after cleaning out the mucus and vomit from his mouth.

DECONTAMINATION
(LIQUIDATION OF THE CHEMICAL ATTACK AFTER-EFFECTS)

Try to protect your weapon from contamination by droplets of gas. Cover it with a cape, overcoat or tent so that it does not hamper your ability to use it. When crossing a contaminated area, do not let your weapon touch the contaminated soil, vegetation and other objects. If the toxin gets on your weapon – decontaminate it immediately.

PARTIAL WEAPON DECONTAMINATION

Wear a gas mask when decontaminating weapons. Protect your hands with gloves (rubber gloves would be the best). Wrap your fingers inside (or outside) of the gloves with bandages, rags, etc. Use dry oakum or rags to wipe off the droplets from those spots on the weapon you will need to touch. Do not spread the droplets. The persistent toxins are easily dissolved in gasoline and kerosene. It does no good simply to wipe up droplets with those liquids. Saturate oakum or rags in the solvent, moisten the contaminated parts of the weapons and then wipe them completely with dry rags. Repeat the procedure three-four times. Remember that the solvent does not neutralize the toxins – it only dissolves them and, consequently it acquires their poisonous properties. Because of this, do not sit or kneel at the decontamination site. Act carefully to prevent drops of the solvent getting on you. Do not touch unprotected body parts with your gloves. After decontamination, remove drops of the solvent from your clothing and boots with dry oakum. After that, carefully wipe your clothing and shoes (including soles) with fresh solvent and wipe them dry.

Use the decontaminating liquid from the gauze ball (large ampoule) from the decontamination set. Follow the same rules for decontamination with the solvents.

After decontamination is finished, take off your gloves and wipe your hands with liquid from the decontamination set. Bury the gloves and used materials or burn them.[16]

Wash your hands, face and neck with water and soap. Remember, that the toxic substances penetrate deeply into wood. After decontamination wrap the wooden parts of the weapons (stock, etc.) with cloth or rags for a day.

COMPLETE WEAPONS DECONTAMINATION

Take the same precaution measures as for partial decontamination. Mix gasoline and kerosene in equal proportions (make one liter of the solvent for one rifle). Pour the solvent into 2 jars. You need to fully field strip the weapon. Put all small metal parts of the weapon into first jar, clean them thoroughly, wipe them dry and apply rifle oil. Clean the barrel, cleaning rod and bayonet two-three times, using the solvent from the first jar, then repeat using the second jar (with the clean solvent). Wipe them dry and oil. Wipe the wooden parts and accessories of the weapon several times with the solvent.

After finishing that, decontaminate your body, clothing and shoes, as described in the PARTIAL WEAPON'S DECONTAMINATION part.

Destroy the used materials. Three to five hours after the decontamination, repeat the field strip of the weapon. Clean it with alkali and oil it to prevent rust.

DECONTAMINATION OF PERSONAL ITEMS AND FOOD

1. If an area contaminated with non-persistent toxins, use ventilation. Open all windows and doors in a building to create drafts. To speed up decontamination, light a conventional or kerosene (large or small) stove; start a bonfire if it is possible.

Move clothing and shoes outside for ventilation. Do the same with food stuffs.

Meat and fat (grease) which have been contaminated with diphosgene droplets cannot be used – they are spoiled.

Cease ventilation efforts when there is no longer any smell of the non-persistent toxins and the symptoms produced by their presence are gone.

2. While decontaminating objects contaminated by persistent toxins, apply all the precaution measures as with the weapons decontamination.

Boil cotton, linen and wool mixture in a 2% soda solution. After decontamination wash and iron them.

Boil rubber items in clean water; rinse with warm water and dry. Boil for an hour in an iron caldron (large can) in the open air or in a well-ventilated room. Otherwise the toxins in the vapors may hurt you.

Clothing made out of military cloth or other woolen fabrics should be decontaminated with hot air or steam for three-four hours at a temperature of 85-95 degrees (Celsius).

Footwear, leather, fur items, cotton quilted coats, pillows, mattresses, etc., should be decontaminated at a temperature of 60-70 degrees (Celsius) for eight hours.

Do not decontaminate heavily contaminated items – burn them. Foods contaminated with mustard gas vapors should be aired until the gas' smell is gone. Eat it only after boiling or frying.

If food is contaminated with Lewisite vapors or any persistent gas' droplets, it must not be used – it should be buried or burned.

Canned food and preserved food tightly sealed in jars and bottles can be eaten. Just wash the can, jar or bottle with hot soapy water and wipe it with decontaminating liquids. You can open it after that.

Avoid drinking water from wells and bodies of water on contaminated terrain. Tie a stone wrapped in a clean cloth to a pole and lower the pole into the water until it reaches the bottom. Move it several times across the bottom, pull it out and look at the cloth. If there are droplets of toxins or their smell – the water is contaminated. Put a warning sign at the place and warn your comrades.

DESTROY FASCIST CHEMICAL MEANS

When operating in the enemy's rear area, thwart his preparations for a chemical attack. Find and destroy German chemical storage, transport for poisonous gases, chemical shells, bombs and cylinders for the toxins' release.

Identifying signs of the fascists' chemical means:

1. A large number of metal barrels, large cans or cylinders which may have the following identification markings:

   - tear gas – white stripes or circles;

   - irritating gas – blue stripes or circles;

   - choking gas – green stripes or circles;

   - blister gas – yellow stripes or circles.

The same markings are used on chemical artillery and mortar shells and bombs.

2. Large glass ampoules shaped like aviation bombs.

3. Railroad tank cars without visible markings of poisonous gas. All tank cars must be destroyed with no exception.

4. Automobiles and truck tanks which carry a painted elephant silhouette (usually yellow in color).

5. Various cylinders and rubber hoses. When installed in trenches, dug-outs, niches and other fortifications they are a reliable indicator that the

enemy is preparing for a chemical attack.

Destroy the enemy's chemical means as follows:

1. Fire at metal barrels, cans and cylinders using rifles, machine-guns and submachine-guns. Try to puncture them several times at the top and bottom. Then the gas will leak out. Destroy a chemical storage (depot) completely using explosions and fire.

2. Destroy railroad tank cars and tank trucks, chemical shells, bombs and glass ampoules using grenade bundles, mines or explosive charges.

Take great care in doing so. While destroying a chemical depot always stay on the windward side to avoid a chemical cloud coming at you. If there is a chance – use a gas mask and protective cape. Try to pick a small cylinder or ampoule as a sample and send it to a Red Army unit for investigation.

XI.

HAND-TO-HAND COMBAT

THRUST WITH A BAYONET

"On Guard!" position. It is the main position for quickly stabbing and striking the enemy. Put your left foot one step forward. Slightly bend your legs at the knees to make them springy. Hold the rifle at the lower stock ring with your left hand and at the small of the stock – with your right.

The hands are held the same in the "On Guard!" position while moving at a walk or a run.

Short thrust. While in the "On Guard" position, draw your arms back as far as you can – they are "cocked". Then quickly move your arms forward while pushing the bayonet toward the target and stabbing the enemy. Your feet should not move. Use the short thrust when the surrounding environment confines your movements: in trenches, thick brush and narrow passageways.

Medium thrust. Move your arms and rifle forward while simultaneously making a lunge with your forward leg and straightening your rear leg. The impact should coincide with the time when your front foot strikes the ground.

Use the medium thrust when your movements are not confined.

Long thrust. The body and legs move in the same way as the medium thrust. Make an additional extension with your arms: direct the bayonet toward the target with your left hand while pushing the rifle forward with your right hand and make impact. Both hands will be extended to the utmost forward position at the moment of impact.

Use the long thrust to kill the enemy from a longer distance, about three paces.

PARRY A THRUST

Parry to the right. When the enemy is thrusting at your chest's right side, deflect his weapon to the right with your rifle stock's fore-end. To parry – move your left hand sharply forward and to the right and immediately make a thrust yourself.

Parry to the left. When the enemy is thrusting at your chest's left side, deflect his weapon to the left with your rifle stock's fore-end. To parry – move your left hand sharply forward and to the left and immediately make a thrust yourself or strike him with the rifle butt swinging it forward from behind.

Parry downward. When the enemy is thrusting at your stomach or lower – deflect his weapon downward with your rifle stock's fore-end. To parry – make a sharp push with both arms down and forward and to the left or right side. After the parry, make a fast thrust with both arms or thrust with a lunge, if the enemy has stepped back.

Parry upward. Use it when the enemy aims at your face. With a sharp move of your left arm, lift your rifle up and forward and deflect the enemy's weapon upward. Then thrust at his stomach.

STRIKE WITH YOUR RIFLE BUTT

Strike with your rifle butt from above. Seize the rifle near its muzzle with your left hand and near the lower stock ring with your right. Swing your rifle over your head. Slightly bend your legs at the knees. Then straighten them up, shift your body weight to your forward foot and then bring down the rifle butt on the enemy with all the power of the movement.

Use this strike when you have no bayonet or when fighting several opponents.

Know the protection against this strike: quickly swing your rifle overhead with its magazine facing forward.

Smash forward with your rifle butt. Invert your rifle with the butt forward and the magazine positioned upward. Your left hand should be bent and pressed tightly against your chest's left side; the right hand extended forward. Simultaneously, move your right foot forward and smash the enemy in the face with your rifle butt.

Strike with your rifle butt from the side (swing). Move your rifle so that its muzzle is on the left side and lowered and the stock – on your right and higher; the magazine turned toward the enemy. Step forward with your left foot. Strike your enemy's head with the rifle butt while pivoting your body on the toes of your left foot and stepping forward with your right foot. This strike is easier to perform after parrying the enemy's rifle to the left.

SLASH WITH A SHOVEL

A shovel is a wonderful weapon for hand-to-hand combat.[17] With the shovel you can shield yourself from the enemy's strike and parry his bayonet thrust. The shovel's sharp edges make it a fearsome slashing weapon. It is especially valuable in a fight in a crowded environment.

When fighting an enemy armed with a bayoneted rifle, take a waiting position. Your first goal is to parry the enemy's thrust; the second – seize the enemy's weapon, constrain him and follow this with a quick slashing attack.

KNIFE THRUST

Knives, daggers or bayonets are all formidable weapons in hand-to-hand combat. They are especially useful during fights in close contact with the enemy: in covered trenches, group fight, thick brush or water. The knife gives you an opportunity to confidently defend yourself or to attack the enemy armed with any kind of "cold steel" weapon.

The first thing is to deflect the enemy's strike; then grab the enemy's weapon and make a retaliatory thrust at the enemy.

Figures 104 and 105 show the techniques of such fights.

Hand-to-Hand Combat

Figure 104. Knife thrust: upper picture – deflecting an enemy rifle down and to the right; lower picture – seizing the enemy's rifle and striking him with a knife from above.

DISARM THE ENEMY

Even an unarmed partisan does not retreat from a fight. Repulse the enemy's attack, disarm him and strike him.

How to take away a knife. First method: If the enemy's knife thrust comes from above, catch his armed hand in a "fork" (figure 106).

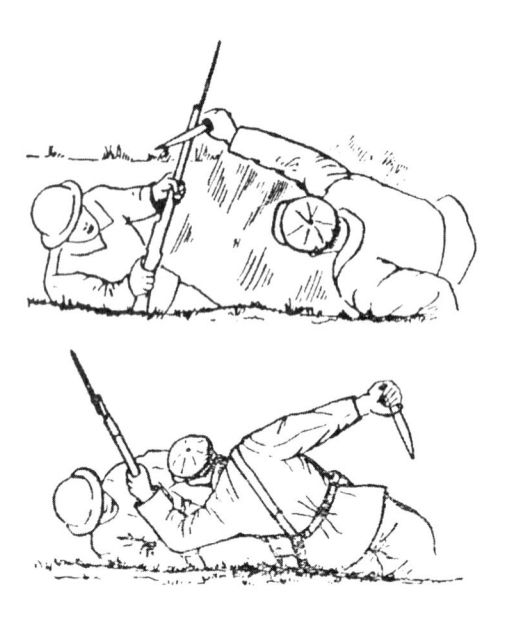

Figure 105. Knife thrust: upper picture – deflecting an enemy rifle upward; lower picture – seizing the rifle and stabbing the enemy in the abdomen or chest.

Always hold your right hand over your left hand. Disarm the enemy by pressing your right thumb into the bent joint of his little finger and pressing your left thumb into the fourth finger joint. Twist the enemy's hand counterclockwise and away from you while continuing to pull his hand toward you and still pressing his joints with your thumbs (figure 107).

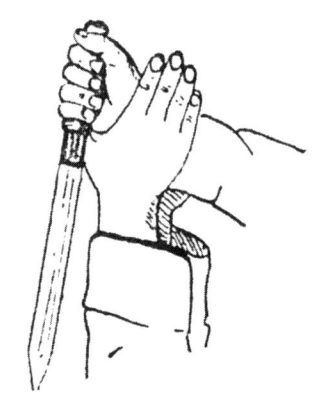

Figure 106. "Fork" hold.

Using this technique you can trip the enemy over your leg or sweep his legs with yours (figure 108). Strong pain will make the enemy to drop the knife and leave him disarmed.

SECOND METHOD. Hold the enemy's hand with your left hand while seizing his left elbow with your right hand and pull him toward yourself while simultaneously striking his chin or abdomen with your head.

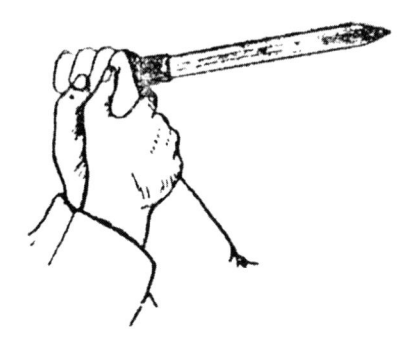

Figure 107. How to twist the enemy's hand.

Figure 108. Twisting the enemy's hand followed by tripping him over your leg or sweeping his legs.

Defense against a shovel. As the enemy strikes at you with a shovel, seize his armed hand with the "fork" or put your left arm (bent at the elbow) against his forearm. Then seize his arm inside of the elbow and strike his chin with your fist or head.

How to take away a pistol. While the enemy is threatening you with a pistol from a short distance, step forward and to the left with your left foot while moving your body left simultaneously. Deflect the armed hand of the enemy away from you with your left arm then seize his hand (figure 109a). Immediately grab the pistol barrel with your right hand and sharply twist it to break the enemy's index finger. While doing that, kick the enemy with your leg (figure 109b).

How to take away a rifle. Deflect the enemy's weapon with your forearm. Grab his rifle with both hands (figure 110a), yank it toward you; simultaneously kick the enemy in his legs or groin or strike his chin with your head (figure 110b).

If you've deflected the rifle to your left – seize it with your right hand under the enemy's left arm and continue as shown at the picture. Try to pull the enemy's left hand off the rifle and snatch away the rifle while kicking the enemy in the groin.

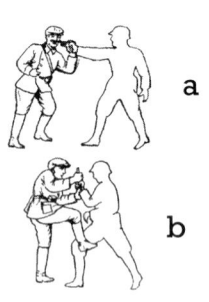

Figure 109. How to take away a pistol.

Figure 110. How to disarm the enemy after deflecting a rifle to your right: a – Seizing the rifle with both hands; b – Yanking the enemy toward you while striking his chin with your head.

XII.

RENDERING FIRST AID

HOW TO BANDAGE A WOUND

To dress the wounds, use the individual first aid packet which consists of two gauze pads and a bandage. One of the pads is sewn to the bandage and another one can be slid along the bandage it hangs on.

To dress the wound, open the packet; pick up the bandage with your right hand while holding the bandage end with the fixed gauze pad in your left hand. Do not touch and do not soil the pad's surface which is going to be in contact with the wound. If it is a perforated wound – put one gauze pad on the bullet's entrance wound and the other one on the exit wound. If there is one opening – put both gauze pads on it.

Tighten the pads onto the wound by winding the bandage around them. Unroll the bandage with your left hand going from the right to the left.

If you do not have a first aid packet, then you can use a clean towel, kerchief, etc. to dress the wound. Cover the wound with a kerchief or piece of cloth and bind it with something.

WINTERTIME BANDAGING

Do not remove clothing from the wounded in the winter. Cut the clothing at the wound with a knife or scissors. Pull apart the clothing at the wound, cover the wound with the bandage and tie it up under the clothing. Then pull the edges of the cut cloth together, fix them with a safety pin or close it with something.

Do not bandage the wound too tightly in the wintertime because the wounded area could get frostbitten.

BLEEDING

It is easy to stop light bleeding by elevating the wounded body part or bandaging the wound.

If blood spurts out of the wound fountain-like, then an artery is damaged. Press the artery tightly with your fingers.

If the wound is in the hand – press the shoulder artery; if the wound is in a leg, press the artery in the groin. You can find the artery by checking the spurts of the flowing blood (pulse). You should keep pressure on the artery for a short time only (several minutes), because your fingers will get tired. During the break time, find a towel, wide belt, etc. and use it to bind the arm or leg tightly in a tourniquet.

It is possible to use a "twist". The tourniquet or "twist" should not be kept in place more than for two hours because the limb, left without blood flow, will face the danger of necrosis.

BONE FRACTURES

Put splints on the broken limb. You can use tree branches, sticks, cardboard, plywood, etc. as the splints. If there is a wound at the place of the bone fracture – first dress the wound and then apply the splints.

BRUISES

Put a cold compress on the bruise (ice, snow). Next day put a hot compress on the bruise.

If there is a bruise to the abdomen – send the patient to a doctor.

DISLOCATIONS

Do not try to fix joint dislocations if you do not have the proper experience. It should be done only by a doctor. To provide first aid to a dislocation: put the damaged limb in the most comfortable resting position and then put a cold compress on the joint. Send the patient to a doctor as soon as possible.

FIRST AID FOR DROWNING

The lungs and stomach of the victim are filled with water and it must be removed. Pull the victim onto your knees and press his chest – clean the sand and scum from his nose and mouth beforehand. After that, apply artificial respiration until the victim begins breathing. Simultaneously rub the body of the victim with a wool cloth, shirt, mitten, etc.

ARTIFICIAL RESPIRATION

Lay the patient on his back and put a rolled-up service blouse or other piece of clothing under his shoulder blades. Pull the tongue out of the victim's mouth and tie it to his chin with a kerchief. Hold the patient's arms near his elbows and move them back – this produces an artificial inhalation. Then press the patient's arms to the patient's chest – this produces an artificial exhalation. Repeat those movements 16-18 times per minute until the patient begins to breathe on his own.

Stop administering artificial respiration only if there are definitive signs of the patient's death (rigor mortis, necrotic spots).

BURNS

For a light burn – rub some lard (unsalted) on the burned area.

With a heavy burn, the skin is covered with blisters. Do not puncture those blisters. Apply a bandage on the burn – if it is possible – soak the bandage in pure alcohol or vodka.

With even heavier burns the skin and flesh underneath are charred. Bandage the hurt area and send the patient to a doctor.

Take a great deal of care when undressing the burn victim to spare him pain. Do not rip off the parts of clothing which are stuck to his burn – cut the cloth off around them.

HEATSTROKE AND SUNSTROKE

The first symptoms of impending heatstroke are: weakness, unsteady walk, dizziness and redness of the skin.

Remove the field equipment from the patient, place him in a sitting position in the shade, loosen his belt, unfasten his collar; sprinkle his face and chest with water and give him some water to drink.

A person affected by heatstroke or sunstroke looses consciousness and falls down. Lay him down in the shade elevating his head slightly and apply all the measures described above. Do not give him anything to drink until he regains consciousness.

To prevent heatstroke: before a march on a hot day, eat a heavily salted piece of bread and repeat this at lunch.

Sunstroke is similar to heatstroke. Apply the same measures to help the stricken as with heatstroke. To prevent sunstroke, always cover your head.

EVACUATION OF THE WOUNDED FROM BATTLEFIELD

Carry the wounded from battle by crawling, while carrying him chest down on your back or pull him behind you on a greatcoat, rain cape, etc. (figure 111).

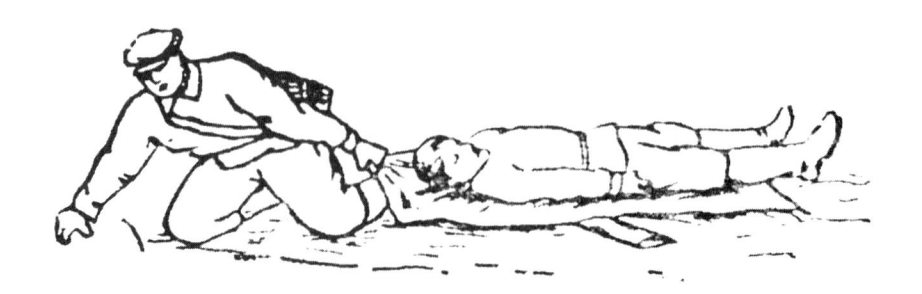

Figure 111. Evacuation of the wounded from a battlefield.

In an area protected from enemy fire, carry the wounded as shown in figure 112. The second method should be used when carrying an unconsciousness person. If you have a helper – carry the wounded as shown in figures 113, 114, and 115.

At the first opportunity carry the wounded on a stretcher. The wounded are usually carried feet first on stretchers. The bearers should not move in step.

Rendering First Aid

Figure 112. Carrying the wounded on the back.

Figure 113. Carrying the wounded with two people.

Figure 114. Carrying the wounded on an arm chair.

Figure 115. Carrying the wounded using straps.

FIRST AID FOR SICKNESS

Cough. In a case of a heavy cough, take Dover's powder – one pill three times a day. If it is a dry cough – take codeine – one pill three times a day. It would be a good idea to drink some hot milk with soda (1.5 teaspoons soda per a glass of milk). If you have a cough – dress warmly and do not smoke outside.

Flu. Take aspirin, calcex or sulfanilamide (white) – one pill three times a day. Gargle with a solution of rivanol [ethoxydiaminoacridine lactate-(one teaspoon per glass of water)]. We also recommend drinking a shot glass of vodka or wine.

The flu is contagious, therefore try to keep the patient in a separate room or separate him from healthy people with a drape made of a bed sheet, greatcoat, etc.

Vomiting. If the vomiting is the result of some stomach illness – take mint drops (20-25 drops per dose). If the vomiting is the result of headache or head bruise – lay the patient down and put a cold compress on his head.

After vomiting, the patient should receive only liquids or thin foods (warm or even hot): milk, tea, broth.

If the vomit contains blood – provide the patient with complete rest, put a cold compress on the upper stomach and heating pads on the hands and feet; the patient's head should be lowered. Do not let him eat or drink. After the bleeding stops – give the patient only thin (and cold) foods: milk, cream and raw eggs.

Diarrhea. First, give the patient a purgative (two tablespoons of castor oil or a solution of one tablespoon of Epsom salt in half a glass of warm water). Put something warm on his stomach – a hot water bottle or heating pad. Give the patient warm or – even better – hot drink, thin food. Do not let him drink milk. Three times a day, give the patient one pill of salol [phenyl salicylate] or salol with tannalbin.

Bloody diarrhea. Give the patient a purgative (two tablespoons of castor oil). Feed him thin food for the first two days. Do not give him milk. Then feed him broth and oatmeal. Give him salol or salol with tannalbin (one pill three times a day). If he still has a bellyache – put something warm on his abdomen.

Bellyache. If there is no bleeding – apply a heating pad. Give the patient salol with belladonna (1 pill three times a day).

Food poisoning. Induce vomiting – tell the patient to insert two fingers deep into his mouth and tickle his throat. Then have him drink three-five glasses of water with soda. Vomiting will follow. After that, give the patient a laxative (one tablespoon of Epsom salt per half of glass of water). Put a heating pad on his abdomen. Give the patient lots of hot drink. He should take one pill of salol three times a day. If the patient experiences general weakness – give him some caffeine (one pill three times a day).

Muscle inflammation. Apply mustard plasters or rub the muscles with ammoniated soap liniment. Give the patient aspirin or salicylic sodium – one pill three times a day. The patient should wear warm clothes.

Angina. Wrap the patient's neck with something warm. Give him lots of warm drink (heated milk, etc.). He should take aspirin or sulfanilaminde- one pill three times a day. The patient should gargle frequently with rivanol solution (one pill per glass of water).

Fainting spell. Lay the patient on his back without a pillow; unfasten his collar and belt; apply heating pads to his hands and feet. Vigorously rub his body, arms and legs. Wipe his temples with a piece of cotton saturated with liquid ammonia. Have the patient smell the liquid ammonia (put several drops on the cotton and place it under the patient's nose). When the spell is over – give the patient a hot drink and valerian drops with camphor (20 drops per dose) or caffeine (one pill three times a day). If the patient stops breathing during the fainting spell – give him artificial respiration.

XIII.

MARCH AND BIVOUAC

FOOTWEAR AND FOOT CARE

Protect your feet on the march. It is important to take care of all your clothing – but it is especially important to take care of your boots. Boots or shoes should not be too tight or too loose. Grease your footwear with fat as frequently as possible. They will be softer and will last longer.

Wash your feet any time you can – it will prevent blisters and bruises. Cut your toenails short.

FOOT WRAPPINGS

Foot wrappings works better on the march then socks. But one needs to know how to wrap his feet with them. If it is done improperly, then any rough fold or hem could quickly give you a blister.

Crumble the foot wrappings in your hands before putting them on your feet to make them softer. Spread the wrapping on a flat surface and put your foot on it close to one of the edges. Take the front corner of the wrapping's shorter part with your right hand; then wrap it around the upper part of your foot while sliding the corner under it. After that, pull the longer part of the wrapping with one hand and transfer it to another hand. Continue that procedure, gradually wrapping the foot around while smoothing the folds on the instep and sole. Wrap the foot's front, sole and heel then pull the free end up, along the shin. Then wrap the shin with the wrapping's end. (See figure 116)

Figure 116. How to put on a foot wrapping.

If you wear half-boots instead of boots, then the wrappings' ends should be outside of the half-boots and tied to your leg with puttees.

The foot wrappings should be made out of sheeting or linens. During the wintertime, they should be made from flannel or light wool cloth. The wrapping's width should be 35 centimeters and its length – 60-65 centimeters. For the half-boots: the width should be 30 centimeters and the length 45-50 centimeters.

PUTTEES

If factory-made puttees are not available, then you can make them yourself. It is not that complicated. Take an appropriate fabric and cut it into stripes with a width of about 10-12 centimeters and a length of about 1.5 meters. Hem the puttees' edges. Sew on a string 30 centimeters long.

Roll up the puttee into a roll and begin to wrap the puttee around your leg from the lower part upward. The first two turns should cover the half-boot's top and the third should go up on the leg. Take care to wrap the puttee tightly around the leg. Make the initial five-six loops tight and the following looser to prevent the puttee interfering with blood circulation. After wrapping your entire calf, secure the puttee's end with the string.

DRINKING REGIME ON THE MARCH

Before going on the march fill your canteen with water. If you do not have a canteen – make one yourself: sew a cover around a bottle and sew on loops to carry it on your waist belt.

Do not drink too much water. It would be best, during the first two-three hours of the march, to skip drinking at all. Remember: the more you drink the more you sweat. Then you will feel thirsty and soon will be weakened. Slake your thirst completely only during the long halt. But, on the move, only drink two-three mouthfuls of water at a time.

Do not miss a chance to refill your water supply during the march. Remember that not just any water is drinkable. The best kind is spring water. One can use river water as well. Not every well can be used for drinking water. If there are well beaten paths to a well one can hope that the water in it is drinkable. If a well looks abandoned – avoid it.

Do not drink water from ponds, small lakes and swamps – it is unhealthy.

In the wintertime, you can produce water from snow by melting it in a mess tin. Do not swallow snow – you can get a sore throat.

CROSSING A RIVER

It is easy to find a ford that is in frequent use. A roadway that ends at one bank and continues on the opposite indicates the beginning and the end of the ford. The presence of small ripples on the surface of slow river indicates a shallow spot. If the river has rapids, a ford is usually located below the drops. Fords are rarely present on rivers flowing through marshy areas. Reeds, sedge and scum are fair indications of a swampy bottom and are unsuitable for crossing.

Stretch a tightrope supported by poles across a river with rapid currents and deep fords. Stick the poles into the river's bottom. It will make crossing easier for your comrades. You can cross against fast river currents in the following way: stand face to face with your comrade and put the hands on each other shoulders and move across. Water will not knock you down bthold (figure 117).

Figure 117. Crossing fast currents.

If there is no ford, then swim across the river in your clothes and with your weapons. First, take off your boots. Put the boots' tops under your waist belt and wrap them around the belt twice. This will prevent water from pouring into your boots. The heels should up and the toes down. Turn out all your pockets so that they do not take water inside of them and hamper your movements. Unfasten your sleeve and collar buttons and untie the strings of your pants and underpants. Roll your greatcoat into a tight roll and put it across your left shoulder. Pack your kitbag. Put your rifle on the kitbag's top with the butt pointed to your right. Slide the rifle sling over your chest under your armpits.

Use available material to make the crossing easier (figure 118): boards, dry logs, empty barrels, tightly packed bags of hay, straw, dry pine bark. All those things can serve as floats.

Figure 118. Materials that make river crossing easier.

If you have time and suitable materials – boards and poles – make a simple small raft, either rectangular or triangular. Do not secure the joins with nails but tie them together with ropes, wires or bast [inner bark strips]. See figure 119 on how to make rafts. Reinforce the rafts with floats.

Do not let the enemy detect you while crossing the river. Learn how to enter the water silently. Slide from a steep bank into water with your foot forward and your face toward the river. Crawl into the river if the bank is gently sloping. While swimming, do not thrash the water with your feet to reduce splashing sounds.

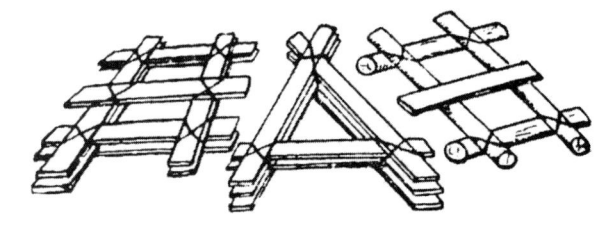

Figure 119. Rafts made out of boards and poles.

After reaching the opposite bank, stay at the edge and wait for a little while. Only after you are sure that the enemy did not detect you, go up to the top and hide in nearby bushes.

CROSSING MARSHES

One needs to exercise caution while crossing marshes to avoid getting caught in a quagmire. Find out if there are any paths used by the locals, what the swamp's depth is and how sturdy its upper layer is. Drop a log onto the swamp's top. If it does not fall into the depth and stays on the top – try to step on the swamp's top layer near the edge. If it holds, stamp your feet several times. And only after making sure that you do not fall into a quagmire, carefully move forward. Use a pole to probe the surface in front of you. Use bushes and hummocks as their roots will provide support for your feet. If the swamp will not support your weight – build a flooring out of brushwood and lay it on the top a layer of poles (gaht' – road of logs laid across a marshy area).

If, for some reason, you cannot build a gaht' – lie down on your stomach and crawl across. It is helpful to have two boards. Put down the first board and move to its end. Then put down another one and pick the first up. Continue shifting the boards until you reach the marsh's opposite side.

When crossing marshes, avoid places covered by bright green vegetation. Those are "windows" you can fall into. If you fell into the "window" – avoid brusque movements. When helping a comrade out of a quagmire, throw some poles, boards or saplings with branches across it to give him support against sinking. Find a safe place for yourself and throw a rope or push a pole to your comrade so you can pull him out.

PARTISAN MARCH RULES

Remember that forests – especially thick evergreen or mixed – are your shield from the enemy's eyes.

But take precautions when moving through forests, look around carefully, especially when coming to forest edges, clearings and roads.

When the detachment is marching, send a three-five man group ahead. They should move in a single file and remain close enough to be visible to the group. Post a similar security patrol behind the detachment.

Avoid making noise while moving in the forest. Do not break branches or deadwood. Do not catch your rifle, mess tin or other gear on trees. Do not talk. While on the move, do not throw away paper, newspaper scraps, cigarette and match boxes, etc. An enemy scout can figure out who crossed the forest from those objects.

If you need to move between inhabited points occupied by the enemy or cross a large field and open spaces – do that at night.

Before moving, conduct a thorough reconnaissance to make sure there is no enemy about.

Before crossing a road, first make sure that there are no enemy patrols about or "cuckoos" [snipers] up in the trees. Also determine how far the forest extends on the other side of the road. Try to cross the road in those areas where trees are close to the road.

If you need to cross a forest glade surrounded by trees, you must determine that the enemy does not occupy the forest edges, especially on the opposite side from you. When crossing the glade, cross it quickly.

HALTS

There are short and long halts. Take a short halt of ten minutes after 40-50 minutes on the march. Take a long halt of two-three hours after four-five hours on the march.

Make the first halt after moving about two kilometers. Check if there are any problems with the adjustment of clothing, weapons and equipment. It could be that a foot wrapping seam is rubbing against a foot or that a kitbag's shoulder strap is disproportionately rubbing one shoulder.

Take off your greatcoat roll and weapons (if conditions permit), unfasten your collar and re-wrap your foot wrappings.

If you are tired – lie on your back and lift up your legs (you can put the kitbag under your feet). That position permits your legs to rest better and quicker.

Make more frequent short halts in the wintertime – after every 30 minutes, but halt no longer than five minutes. If circumstances permit, try to make take long halts inside closed buildings. When stopping on the march, do not lay on the snow. It is better to squat with your back against a tree or haystack. Do not nap during the halts in wintertime. Check the halt area before leaving – some of your comrades may be napping.

Do not make it mandatory to stop every 50 minutes during the march. Sometimes, it is better to move for an extra 10-15 minutes to stop in a secluded, protected area.

During the long halt in the summer, take off your equipment, soldier's blouse, boots and puttees. Shake off the dust. Wash and dry your foot wraps. Wash your face or even better – take a swim. Take turns with your comrades while resting, swimming and undressing.

Stop for your night halt one hour before nightfall. Determine your exact location and make sure that there are no enemy, large roads, forest glades and villages nearby. Then you can stop for the night bivouac. Put out security, especially on the possible enemy routes. The security should be located so that it can quickly warn the detachment of any danger. Put out security even when there are only two or three of you – in this case, you should take turns sleeping.

CAMP FIRES

If you are sure that the enemy is not around, you can light a camp fire, but take precautions so that you are not discovered.

Learn how to start a camp fire quickly and easily and make it "invisible" (figure 120). If bushes and trees do not hide the fire, then make an artificial screen.

After selecting a spot for the fire, clean out the surrounding area to prevent the fire from spreading to nearby trees and bushes. In the summer, dig a small ditch around the fire.

If it is a cooking fire, then pay attention to the wind. If it is calm – place the mess tin above the fire. If there is a wind, then place the tin on the leeward side.

"Star" fire. Place the logs so that they create spokes coming from the fire's center. Such a fire, made of thick logs, burns long and hot. Move the logs toward the center as they burn down.

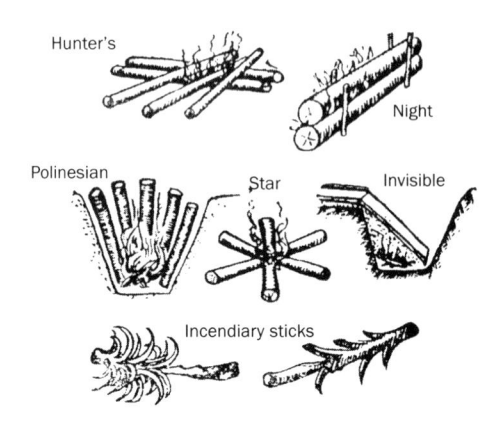

Figure 120. Camp fires and "incendiary sticks".

"Polynesian" fire. This fire is laid in a shallow pit. The logs are in a standing position. This fire does not require much of fuel, but gives off a lot of heat and accumulates a lot of hot coals.

"Hunter's" fire. This fire is made of three logs of any diameter or length. These logs are placed fan-like on the top of two other logs. Start the fire under the upper logs where they cross the support logs. This fire burns slowly and gives off a good heat.

"Night" fire. This is the name for a fire which is invisible even from a short distance away. To make it – take two logs and cut a lengthwise channel in each. Fill the first log's channel with hot coals and cover it with the second log (channel-side down). The coals and logs will burn slowly for long time due to oxygen deficiency. It does not produce bright flames, so it does not show even from a short distance away.

There is another kind of the "invisible" fire. Dig a deep pit and start a fire in it. Place a bark strip or several sticks so that they create a chimney with its end coming out of the pit and lying on the ground. The smoke moves along the "chimney" and the fire is not visible.

HOW TO START A FIRE

Start a fire with fewer matches. To start a fire quickly, find some good kindling – birch bark for instance. It will burn even when it is wet. Dry pine and fir branches and dry lichen also make good fire starters. Make "incendiary" sticks out of dry twigs (figure 120). With a sharp knife, slice some shavings partially off a twig. Surround those sticks with pieces of birch bark, dry grass, and small sticks and light them.

SAVE MATCHES

Matches can get wet during a river crossing or in the rain. Make an emergency reserve of them. Put a few matches, along with the ignition strip, into an empty cartridge case and plug it with a cork.

Rub a wet match in your hair and the match will light when you strike it on the ignition strip.

Remember that a match dipped into melted paraffin is waterproof.

Before the march, matches should be divided among several partisans. If one partisan's matches get wet, another's should still be dry.

WHEN MATCHES ARE NOT AVAILABLE

You can produce a fire using this method. First, prepare kindling out of dry birch bark, paper, etc. Remove a bullet from the cartridge case and pour out some of the gunpowder on the kindling. Loosely plug the cartridge case with a paper wad and fire the cartridge at the kindling. Aim the muzzle slightly above the kindling. The shot flash will ignite the dry kindling.

One can start fire with a flint – striking it with a hard stone or a piece of steel will produce sparks. Cotton is the best material for a homemade wick. Collect and burn some tree fungus growths. Boil the wick in the water-ash mix. Do not remove the burnt part of the wick – it will help start smoldering quicker. Store the wick in a dry place.

DRYING CLOTHES

When you get wet – dry your clothes at the first opportunity. To make it easier, build a drying rack out of long branches by the fire. Figure 121 shows how to build one.

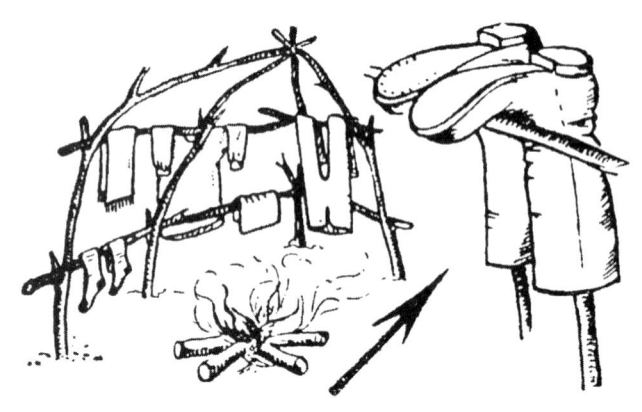

Heat from fire

Figure 121. Rack for drying clothes.

Make sure that the fire does not spread to your items and damage them. Never put wet leather boots near the fire. Overheated leather will curl and crack and make your footwear useless.

OVERNIGHT BIVOUAC

The night bivouac location should be well hidden and if there is a chance – not far from a river or lake. The place should have a dry hard surface – not on sand or on a moist meadow.

If there are tents – lay out a camp. The tents should be erected as shown at figure 122.

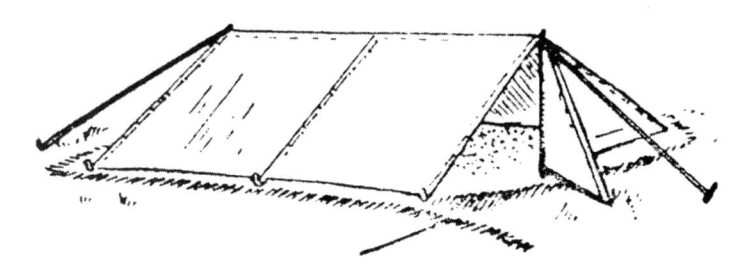

Figure 122. A tent made of six sections.

If you must to sleep on bare ground – do not lie on your left side.

ZASLON (LEAN-TO) AND SHALASH (HUT)

If a tent is not available, then use a lean-to for the night bivouac (figure 123).

The lean-to [zaslon] is a screen that is built at an angle toward the camp fire and located some three-four paces from the fire. The heat from the fire is caught by the lean-to and keeps sleeping people warm. It also protects them from the wind. The lean-to can be used during short halts and one-night bivouacs.

The screen is built out of poles, brushwood and branches. It is quicker and more convenient if you build the lean-to between two trees. If there are no trees, then build the screen using a saw horse or thick poles tied together. A lean-to can be made by using a tent section supported with tent or ski poles.

Make your camp bed slightly tilted toward the fire – it will let you use the heat more efficiently.

When building the lean-to make sure that the wind does not carry the smoke toward you. It is the best if the wind blows parallel to the lean-to.

Figure 123. Lean-to.

Lean-tos may be built facing each other on both sides of the fire.

In heavy woods, you can build a fairly simple hut [*shalash*] from tree branches (figure 124). First clear the site for a night bivouac and make a low horseshoe-shaped earthen wall. Brace two long poles in the wall's banks and tie these together. Insert poles or skis along the wall with their upper ends supported by a frame work of tied poles. Cover the frame with spruce branches. The hut is ready. Build a camp fire in front of the hut's entrance. You should sleep in the hut with your feet toward the fire.

Figure 124. Hut made out of branches.

Before building the hut, determine the wind direction. The hut's entrance should not be on the windward side.

You can make a camp bed out of spruce branches (figure 125).

Bring some dry wood into the hut. Break it into sticks 75-100 centimeters in length and lay them on the ground next to each other. Cover the sticks with spruce branches so that the broken ends face in opposite directions. Use your kitbag as a pillow. Always try to make the entrance of a tent or hut on the leeward side. Build a campfire near the entrance.

Figure 125. Improvised bed made out of spruce branches.

LARGE ROUND HUT – *CHOOM*

A good dwelling for a partisan group is a round hut – choom (figure 126). A choom six meters in diameter can accommodate 20 people.

Use poles seven-ten centimeters thick and four and a half to five meters long to build the frame. First, make a tripod out of three poles tied together at their upper ends with wire or cord. Then put 30-35 poles around the tripod with their upper ends supported by the tripod. The distance between the poles at the base should not be greater than one-half meter.

The completed choom's frame has a conical shape. The pole frame is then interlocked with thick tree branches and covered with coniferous branches. To make the choom retain heat better – throw some snow on the branches. At the choom's top, there is a small opening to let the smoke out like a chimney.

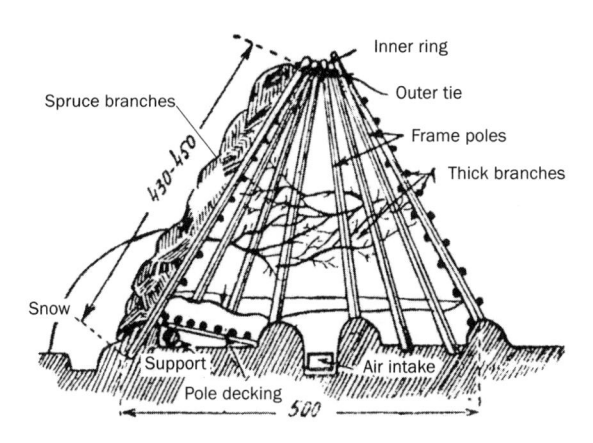

Figure 126. Diagram of a choom.

A fire pit should be made in the choom's center with a small ground wall around it to protect your feet from excessive heat.

To lessen smoke from the fire, dig a small ditch (20 x 20 centimeters in cross section} to conduct air to the fire. Roof the ditch with tree branches and dirt. Inside of the choom, make camp beds made out of coniferous branches.

A good idea is to build the choom out of a ground pit – that makes it warmer.

DUG-OUT [Zemlyanka]

The simplest dug-out is a large pit in the ground with a wooden frame and an overhead cover above it. A layer of dirt is placed on the top. In the wintertime, one needs to find a spot with undisturbed snow, preferably in the forest where the soil is less frozen.

The lower supports are thick logs placed in the pit's sides to support the rafters which create the gable roof. The rafters are covered with layers of brushwood and dirt. A layer of clay will make the roof waterproof. A dug-out for six persons has the following dimensions: height – 1.8 meters; width – 3.2 meters and length – 4 meters (figure 127). The dirt steps lead down to the dug-out's entrance. The entrance itself is covered with a tent section.

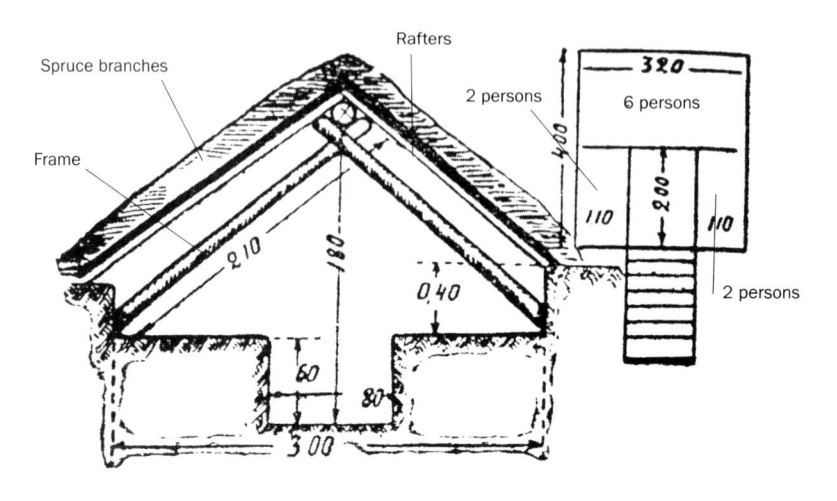

Figure 127. Cross-section and floor plan of the dug-out.

The partisan dug-out must have a spare (emergency) exit in case of unexpected enemy attack. A large window (50 x 50 centimeters) placed opposite to the entrance can serve as the emergency exit. If glass is not available, the window could be covered with greased paper.

The heavier roof can be supported with trestles (sawhorses) which are installed between plank beds and the pit's walls with 1.5 meters between them. The trestles' lower ends are planted firmly against the base logs. The top beam is supported by the trestles. The beam supports the rafters that are laid with 25-30 centimeters between them. To make the roof more durable, the upper ends of the rafters should be extended 15-20 centimeters behind the beam. A layer (5-10 centimeters thick) of brushwood or coniferous tree branches is laid on the rafters. Put a layer of soil (15-20 centimeters) on top of it.

The entrance should be roofed with logs or poles at height of 1.4-1.6 meters and covered with dirt. The side walls are secured with poles braced on the trestles and rafters and supported with soil.

The dug-out is heated with a portable stove. The stove's chimney goes out through the roof with a metal sheet around it. One can also put the chimney through the wall using dirt to isolate the pipe from wooden parts of the dug-out.

WEATHER SIGNS

If fleecy clouds move swiftly from the west – expect bad weather and strong wind in a day or two. If the appearance of the fast fleecy clouds is followed by a sky covered with a thin layer of fleecy-stratus clouds, then rain or snow is coming soon.

If the clouds move in a direction different from the wind near the ground, the weather will turn bad.

Separate, smaller cumulous clouds that move in the same direction as the ground wind indicate that better weather is coming.

If fleecy clouds in whimsical shapes slowly crawl at the high altitudes while below them separate cumulous cloud move swiftly, you can expect prolonged good weather.

The fleecy clouds that look like long stripes radiating from a single point are a promise of rain or snow. The cumulous clouds which do not disappear in the evening indicate coming better weather.

If small flakes separate from large cumulous clouds, becoming transparent and disappear, then quiet warm weather is coming.

Rapidly growing cumulous clouds promise thunderstorm and rain.

Light fleecy clouds in the morning which are replaced by fleecy-stratus clouds in the evening are the sign of an impending night-time thunderstorm.

In the wintertime: if after a fair and windless day, the sky is covered with a low layer of stratus clouds in the evening – the cold weather will stay for a long time.

If during fair weather, the wind blows for awhile in one direction and then suddenly changes direction, expect a sharp change in the weather soon.

If different kinds of clouds – fleecy, stratus, cumulous and light fleecy – are moving in the sky simultaneously – the weather will change. Rain or snow are possible.

But the clouds and wind are not the only signs of the weather. There are some other signs.

Brownish-yellow sunset in the winter tells that the cold weather will stay and the frost possibly will become stronger.

If the night frost eases during the day and becomes stronger in the evening, then the stable fair weather will stay.

A fog bank in the lowlands during evenings and nights, as well as vertical columns of smoke rising from chimneys also indicate that stable weather will stay.

If the moon halo is close to the moon, then the fair weather will turn bad soon.

Stronger-than-usual flickering of the stars also indicates that the weather will get worse.

Evening fog promises better weather.

XIV.

HOW TO STORE FOOD

FOOD PIT (CELLAR)

For the partisans the best way to store meat, potatoes and other food supplies is to keep them underground. Dig out a pit (cellar) as deep as a man's height. The pit should be pitcher-shaped with the top narrower then the bottom. Cover the pit's walls with straw or reeds. Attach them to the walls with horizontal sticks. Now you can put food into the cellar.

Cover the cellar with straw, dry leaves, coniferous tree branches and, finally, with dirt. Build a small brush hut above the cellar. It will prevent water from leaking through during rainy weather. The water could spoil the food.

Potatoes are well protected from the frost during winter in such a cellar.

BERRIES AND MUSHROOMS

Berries and mushrooms can be a big supplement to your diet. Be very careful with mushrooms. You need to separate the edible ones from the poisonous.

Edible Mushrooms[18]

1. **White mushroom** – Boletus. The stem is thick and heavy, white in color. The cap of a young mushroom is light-yellow, later becoming reddish-brown. The cap's underside is spongy, small-porous; initially it is white, becoming yellow later, frequently with a greenish cast to it.

2. **Under-aspen mushroom** – Orange-cap Boletus. It grows near aspens. The cap is red. The cap's underside is initially white, turning grayish later. The stem is white with small striped (dark, almost black) scales. Broken cap flesh first turns blue then purple-black.

3. **Under-birch mushroom** – Brown mushroom. It grows near birch trees. The cap is yellowish-brown. The cap's underside is spongy, light grey in color. The stem is white with some small grey scales. The cap's flesh is white and does not change the color if broken.

4. **Oily mushroom** – Boletus lutens. It grows in coniferous woods. The cap's color is yellow or reddish-brown. Young mushrooms have their edges connected to the stems with a white diaphragm which later stays at the stem as a white ring. The cap's underside is spongy and yellow in color. The stem is also yellow.

5. **Redheaded mushroom** – Saffron milk-cap. The cap and stem are reddish-orange. The cap's underside is gilled. If broken, the mushroom oozes a bright-orange milky liquid. The mushrooms found in coniferous forests have greenish or bluish colors on the caps.

6. **Gruzd'** – Milk-agarics mushroom. The mushroom grows in moist areas of coniferous and deciduous forests. Its cap is white or light yellowish and has a gilled underside. The cap's edge has a fluffy ring around it. The mushroom produces a milky-white acrid juice.

7. **Raw-eaten mushroom** – Russula. It grows everywhere. The cap is brightly colored (yellow, red, green or purple). The cap's underside is always white with fragile widely spaced laminas). The stem is white, short and thick. Some of the Russula mushrooms are edible raw, but not all of them. To run a test – chew a small piece of the mushroom – if it is not edible raw, you will feel a burning sensation in your mouth after five-ten seconds.

8. **Autumn stump mushroom** – Shitake. It grows everywhere on tree stumps in clusters. The cap is grayish-yellow covered with small dark scales. Young mushrooms' edges are linked to the stems by a white filmy pellicle which leaves rings around the stems on older mushrooms. The cap's flesh and lamellas are white.
    Beware of false shitake (see the section following).

9. **Shampinnon** – Field mushroom. The places it grows are meadows, pastures, roadsides and forests. The caps may be white, yellowish or grayish in color. The young mushrooms have the white filmy pellicle

connecting the cap edge with the stem. The pellicle leaves a white ring around the stems on older mushrooms. The cap's top is smooth. The lamellas are light pink initially and meat-red later; Then they become black. Do not confuse the field mushrooms with the pale toadstool – Amanita (see the following section).

10. **Fox-mushroom** – Chanterelle. It is a small mushroom colored as an egg yolk with a cap of inverted cone shape. The lamellas and gills are ingrown into each other. It has a thick stem.

11. **Smorchok** – Morel. It is an early spring mushroom. Its cap has a conical shape with a pointed top. The brown cap's surface is convoluted [brain-like]. The cap's edge is connected with the stem. The stem is white and full.

POISONOUS MUSHROOMS

1. **Red fly killer** – Red fly agaric. The cap is red with raised white shreds. Gills and stem are white. There is a cuff-like ring around the stem in its upper part. The stem base is bulbous, onion-like. The mushroom causes severe poisoning.

2. **Pale toadstool** – Amanita. The cap is greenish or white with few white raised shreds. The gills and stem are white. There is a cuff-like ring around the stem in its upper part. The stem's base has a cup-shaped white enclosure. The mushroom is deadly poisonous.

3. **Lemon-colored fly killer** – Yellow fly agaric. The cap is lemon-yellow with few white raised shreds. Gills and stem are white. It has a ring around the stem in the upper part. The stem's base has an enclosure which is linked to the stem. The mushroom grows in coniferous forests.

4. **Strochok** – False morel. The cap is brown (either light or dark) of extremely irregular shape. It is empty inside and has deep convolutions outside. The cap transforms into the stem by narrowing toward the lower part. The stem is white and hollow inside. But if you boil the false morel and pour off the water – the mushroom looses its poison and can be eaten.

5. **False stump mushroom** – False shitake. It grows everywhere on tree stumps in clusters. The cap and stem are reddish-brown and do not have the scale which is the difference from true shitake. The gills initially are yellow, later – brownish. These mushrooms are quite widespread.

6. **Yellow mushroom** – Oak mushroom. It grows in moist places. The mushroom resembles edible mushrooms – Boletus or Brown mushroom. It differs from them by the pinkish color of the cap's underside and a black net-like pattern on the stem. If broken, the cap's flesh becomes pink.

FROZEN MEAT

The simplest method to preserve meat in the wintertime is to freeze it. Before boiling or grilling frozen meat, it is usually moistened and thawed on a hearth. But if you are in a hurry to cook the meat – cut it into small pieces without defrosting and put these on the bottom of a mess tin. Put few pieces of pork fatback and some salt into the tin. Hang the tin above a cooking fire.

Keep the tin above the fire until the meat pieces have some crunch when you test them by biting.

Meat will thaw and may be spoiled in the spring when the weather becomes warmer. How to preserve it? The meat should be dried, cut into thin strips and put on a metal sheet inside of a heated stove. Then pour some salt on the strips. You get so called "dry meat" It can be kept for quite a while.

STROGANINA – FISH SHAVINGS

During wintertime, a very good food source is frozen fish. One can make a considerable catch of fish cut through holes in ice of rivers and lakes.

All Northern peoples eat *strogina* as a favorite food and even as a delicacy. With a knife, slice fresh frozen fish into very thin strips. It is edible without any further preparation or condiments. It dissolves in the mouth – like ice cream. It is very tasty and keeps its nutritious qualities while frozen.

The thinner the strips – the better the *strogina*. Therefore, shavings are better than strips. Plane the fish with your knife to get shavings.[19]

But good stroganina can only be made from deep-frozen fish.

HOW TO SUBSIST IN EXTREME SITUATIONS

Wood flour. There are times in war when it is necessary to stretch existing food supplies, when each piece of bread or pinch of flour becomes a treasure. At these times, wood flour is a big help.

It is well known that the outer layer of a tree trunk (zabolon' – Á‡·ÓÎÓÌ¸) conducts water and different nutrients from the soil. One can make wood flour from that layer. Pine is the best kind of tree for this purpose. Pick a young tree and carefully cut off the outer layer of bark leaving only the inner layer adjacent to the trunk. Make two complete cuts around the tree with one meter distance between them. Then make several longitudinal cuts. The pieces of the bark should be carefully scratched off with a sharp knife. Then they should be cut into smaller pieces and boiled several times to remove the resinous taste. After the bark has boiled, dry it until it becomes very brittle. Now it can be crushed and ground into flour. A similar flour can be made from birch bark.

The pine flour is light brown. Usually it is mixed with rye flour in proportions 1:3 or even 1:1. It can be used as is without mixing. One can make dough by mixing it with water and sometimes sour milk. Then the dough is thinly rolled, cut into small flatbreads and baked. The flatbreads are quite edible and nutritious.

Take a pine or spruce cone and hold it above a fire. It will open and has edible seeds inside.

There are different kinds of lichens growing on the ground and trees. They are edible, especially the so-called Icelandic and reindeer moss. It is blue-gray in color and tastes bitter. It should be put into a bucket with water mixed with campfire ash for several hours and washed with clean water after. When boiled, it will make a quite edible jelly. If it comes to the worst – you can simply soak the moss in water and eat it raw. Remember, yellow-colored lichens are poisonous.

One can dig out reed roots near rivers and lakes. They are edible raw; they are even better baked or boiled. You can use the roots of swamp grass – *susaka*.[20]

XV.

LIFE IN THE SNOW

HOW TO MAKE SKIES

The best wood for making skis comes from birch trees. If this is not available, use ash, beech, elm (grey or white) or pine wood. Pick only healthy wood that is strong, flexible, with a straight grain and without knots and cracks.

You can make skis from dry wooden boards that are four-six centimeters thick.

You can make skis from a log by splitting the log into planks 15 centimeters wide and three-four centimeters thick (figure 128). It is best to split the log lengthwise to get a couple of equal planks. The planks should be approximately as long as you are tall.

These planks should be tied together at the ends. Insert a spreader-bar that is 10–12 centimeters wide between the planks (figure 129). Dry the planks for five to ten days on a warming stove or above a cooking range, turning them toward the heat source on all sides. Then cut and plane the planks into the shape of skis. Now warm the front ends of the planks over a stove (better yet, use a welding torch or kerosene stove) or keep the front ends in a tub of boiling water for 30-50 minutes. When the wood softens, carefully bend the tips and fix them into a frame (figure 130). Make sure that the tips are bent identically. Dry the skis in a kiln (stove) for three-four days afterwards.

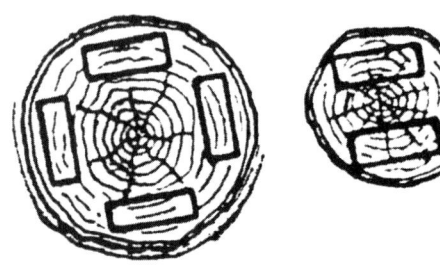

Figure 128. Sawing logs for ski blanks.

Figure 129. Ski planks with the spreader-bar.

Then put the skis into their final form. On the bottom (sliding) surface, cut a half-round groove with a planer or chisel. This should start near the ski's rear end with a graduated finish near the tip's bend. Its width should be 12-15 millimeters with a depth of two millimeters.

Make an opening for a toe belt (four-five millimeters wide and three centimeters long) at the place where the foot platform is supposed to be. Lift the ski by the toe belt – the tip portion should slightly outweigh the rear portion.

Wood is very sensitive to moisture. Smooth it as carefully as possible with sandpaper and glass and then cover it with varnish, resin or tar.

Figure 130. How to bend ski tips.

To make skis to slide better, cover the sliding surface with resin: heat it near a stove, cover this with coniferous resin and heat it again. Make sure the surface does not char. It should be dark brown after the procedure. Before the skis cool down, tie them near the ends and insert a spreader-bar between them. To prevent snow from sticking to the skis, rub the sides and upper surface with wax. Nail a tin sheet, piece of rubber or birch bark to the foot platform – it will prevent snow from sticking.

Good ski poles are made of birch, aspen or pine wood (figure 131). The poles' thickness should be two or two-and-a-half centimeters and they should tall enough to reach your armpits. Make the pole baskets out of flexible reeds, willow or mountain ash branches. They must be wide – 15-18 centimeters in diameter. Fix loops made from a narrow belt or thick canvas strap (one-two centimeters wide) to the poles. This will free your hands to use weapons without dropping the poles.

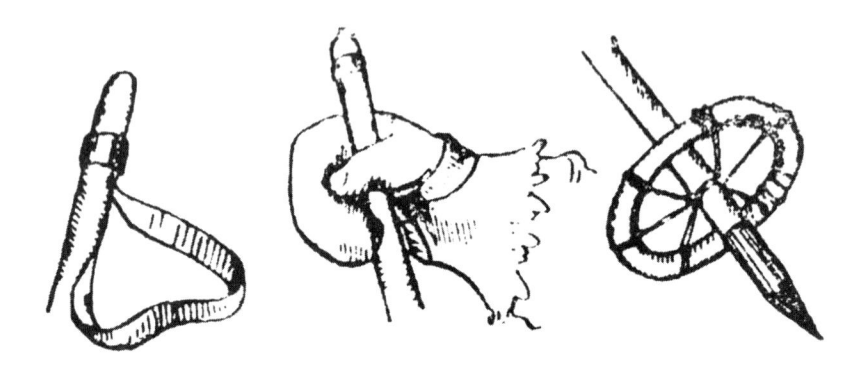

Figure 131. How to make ski poles.

Carry thin tin, thin plywood sheets, small nails or screws and an awl for repairing skis while on the move.

SNOW SHOES (SNEGOSTUPY)

The partisan may not always have skis. In that case, one can use snow shoes.

The simplest snow shows can be made out of thin wooden boards (figure 132). Handy snow shoes could be made out of the seat or back of the Vienna (bent wood) chair. One can use the bottom of a round wicker basket.

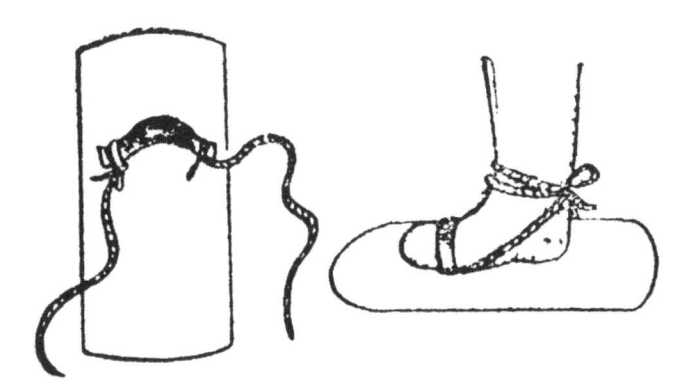

Figure 132. Wooden board snow shoes.

Snow shoes can also be made out of small tree branches (bird cherry or mountain ash are the best). Cut off two branches about 120 centimeters in length and two-three centimeters thick. Bend them into an arc and tie them firmly. Use this as a frame for a woven rope or belt net. The net should have as small openings as possible – it will make moving with snow shoes easier.

If the branches bend easily, then you can use a single one for a snow shoe frame. Join its ends and tie them firmly.

Usually the rope used in weaving the net is pulled through openings drilled in the frame. But it is possible to simply tie the rope net to the frame as shown (figure 133). To prevent the rope from slipping, make small notches in the frame.

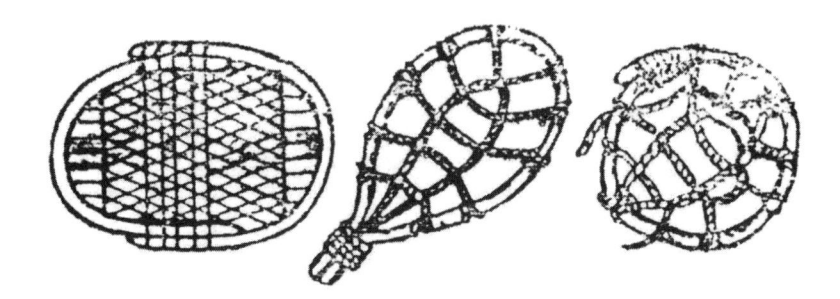

Figure 133. Snow shoes made out of branches. Left – snow shoe made out of two branches; center and right – snow shoes made out of one branch.

The rope net could tear under a person's weight. It most frequently happens under a heel. To reinforce this spot, weave in some thick fabrics or leather. It would be even better to put a heel piece on the frame.

ICE STUDS

Ice studs are a very simple counter to slippery ice. They are easy to make.

Take a belt or a piece of leather and stick it full of 1.5-2 centimeter nails. Put another belt or piece of leather on top of first (it should cover the nail heads to prevent them from getting loose). The result resembles a large currycomb. Then attach the studded belt onto your shoes.

If the partisans have a smithy at their disposal, then they can make their studs more durable and long-lasting. The device is made out of strap iron. It is shaped as a circle or (better) an oval with bent down brackets.

The nails quickly become dull. You need to sharpen them on all sides.

LIGHT SLED

A light sled is very convenient when it comes to carrying loads and the wounded over virgin snow (figure 134).

Make the sled's runners out of bent boards resembling skis (four-five centimeters long). The distance between the sled's runners should be equal to the width of the skier's track (no more than 60 centimeters). The sled should be about 70 centimeters tall. The distance between the runners and the load deck should be about 30 centimeters. The load board is suspended from the sled's upper rails with raw-hide ties. Such a sledge will not get stuck in deep snow.

Figure 134. Light sled.

Add a bow-shaped plank to the sled's front (fixed to the connections of the runners and the upper rails. The bow would protect the sled from striking trees and stumps. The front skier breaks the trail which is used as a trail for the sled.

TOBOGGAN

Use a light wide board that is one-and-a-half to two meters long. Plane its bottom smooth. At the board's sides, drill holes and insert thin strings or ropes to tie down loads. Fix a strap to the board's front to pull the toboggan. The toboggan should have a small bend at its front; otherwise it will sink into snow under the load's weigh. To prevent this, nail a wooden shield to the front of the board. The easiest way to make a bend is to construct the toboggan out of thin plywood nailed to a plank frame (figure 135).

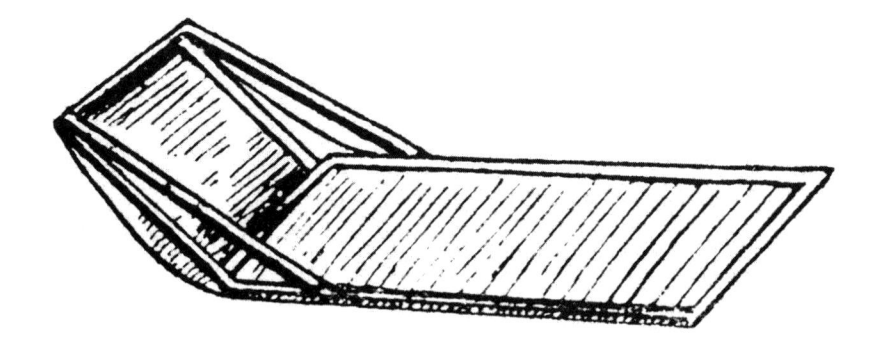

Figure 135. Toboggan.

VOLOKUSHA (TRAVOIS)

Small loads could be carried over soil and snow with the help of **volokusha** – a small travois (figure 136). To make one, tie two thin saplings to the collar of a horse harness, to a saddle or to a dog's collar. Let the other ends slide free over the ground. Fix transverse planking to those ends – it will serve for load support. Using the travois, an animal can carry more weight than on its back.

There is a kind of travois especially useful for transporting wounded. It made out of spruce saplings with their tops left in place.

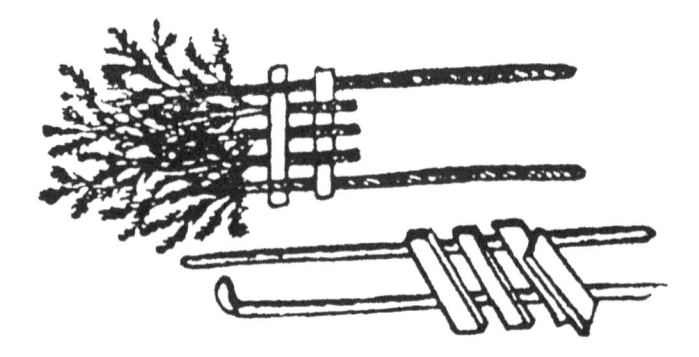

Figure 136. Volokusha (travois).

Transverse planks are fixed to the saplings near the lower ends and several more spruce tops are tied to the planks. This produces a continual soft cushion. This cushion is springy and reduces jolting and bumpiness.

WINTER CAMPFIRE

When making a campfire during wintertime, always shovel snow aside until you get down to the ground – otherwise it will thaw and the fire will sink into a deep snow pit. One needs a good starter to start a fire quickly. Stratified (layered) birch bark will catch fire easily even if it is wet. It is a good idea to use a candle stub to start a fire during snowfall. Its stable flame let you ignite even wet brushwood. Cut ends of small dry branches into broom-like shapes. These are very good starters. Lump sulfur is also very helpful since it burns under rain or snow. A small piece of sulfur is enough to start a fire on wet brushwood. Dry lichen ignites even from a small spark.

Read about the different kinds of campfire on p.321.

SLEEPING BAG

A sleeping bag is your bed on the march. It is a warm envelope sewn out of furs, a quilted cotton blanket, sheepskins, military cloth or down (figure

137). Rolled into a tube it takes very little of space and is easily carried on top of your rucksack.

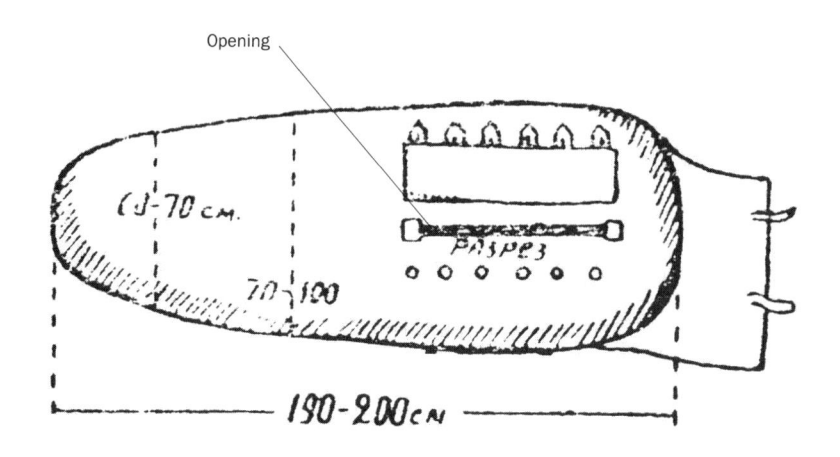

Figure 137. Do-it-yourself sleeping bag.

The sleeping bag's envelope could be made out of percale, ticking, calico or silk. It is recommended making the bottom part of the sleeping bag out of rubberized fabric, light tarpaulin or tent fabric.

The bag's length should be equal to a person's height plus 15-20 centimeters and 100-120 centimeters in circumference. The upper part of the bag has an opening which is covered with two flaps: the inner one is made out of some warm material (cotton padding or down) and the outer is made out of heavy cloth. A piece of heavy cloth is sewn to the bag's bottom near the head of the bag. To roll the bag – start from the narrow part, and then wrap it into the head cloth which serves as a case.

The case is tied up with two strings which could be made out of the same material.

Before sewing the sleeping bag, impregnate the material used in the outer shell with waterproofing.

Make waterproofing solutions using one of the following recipes (depending on which ingredients are easier to find):

Thoroughly saturate the material with warm soapy water solution (500 grams of soap in five liters of water). Then wring it out lightly and submerge it into a saturated alum solution.

Mix 10 parts of good joiner's glue, three parts of essence of vinegar and one part of bi-chrome calcium with 90 parts of water. Impregnate the fabric with the solution and dry it without wringing.

If the bag insulation is made out of down, then it is important to put a cheesecloth layer between the down and the case fabric. The insulation should be spread unevenly: the upper part of the bag should be thinner than the lower. Parts of the bag should have more insulation in those places where the head and thighs will be. After laying out all these layers – cover them with the outer cloth and overstitch the edges. Quilting should be done by hand.

Quilt both the upper and lower parts of the bag, hem the opening's edges, sew on both flaps and the carrying case and then sew the parts together. The insulation layer is sewn very carefully by hand to prevent lumps and empty spots. Several buttons should be sewn on the inside of the bag to fasten the inner flap. Button loops should be made out of thin cord. One can use the wooden frogs instead of buttons. They should be fixed with cord and have notches for the loops.

If the bag gets wet – it should be dried at the first opportunity – preferably in the open air and not near fire or a stove.

SNOW GOGGLES

Reflection from snow during sunny winter days blinds a person. To prevent "snow blindness" make snow goggles (figure 138). Take a piece of birch bark or other bark (18 x 7 centimeters). Trim the edges and make narrow slits for the eyes (two-four millimeters). Make a saddle for the nose and holes for ties at the sides. Glue fabric to the inner side of the "glasses". Paint the bark black (with soot, tar, etc.).

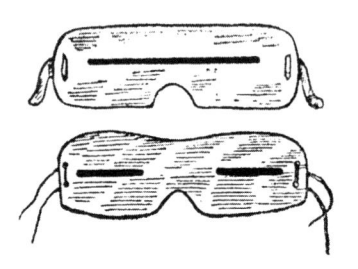

Figure 138. Snow Goggles.

One can also make a blindfold out of a handkerchief or piece of fabric and cut narrow slits for the eyes.

HOW TO PROTECT YOURSELF FROM FROST

Footwear. Protect your feet from frost as they can be frostbitten easily. Harden them with frequent cold baths. Before a march, wash your feet and cut your toenails without fail.

The footwear should not be too tight – it should let you wear extra socks or foot-cloths. It is useful to put improvised soles made of felt or straw inside of the footwear. Also, one can make small fur caps for your toes (they get frostbitten easier than the rest of the foot). Move your toes periodically while out in the very cold weather – it warms them. Do not bind the feet too tightly with shoelaces, puttees, foot-clothes or ski bindings.

Always keep your footwear dry. Damp boots, foot-cloths or socks are the most common reasons for frostbite, even in relatively mild frosts.

Before the march, apply some grease to your leather footwear – fish oil, blubber, beef fat mixed with tar or castor oil. This will make the leather waterproof. Do not dry your leather footwear near a campfire – the leather will "burn" and become brittle. If there is a need to dry footwear quickly – pour some well-heated oats inside your footwear. Its dry shells will absorb moisture from the footwear and make it dry. You can also stuff your boots with dry hay to speed up drying. If you have leather shoes or boots, put cotton socks on your feet first and follow this with one-two pair of wool socks. Put some crushed newspapers between two socks.

It is possible to adapt bast [woven bark] shoes to the frost. Insert some dry hay or straw inside the bast shoes. Wrap your feet with thick layers of warm foot-cloths: first use woolen cloths, then cloths made out of linen or canvas.

The best footwear for strong frost are felt boots (valenki) or boots with fur lining. If you have a chance – make tall boots lined with fur – **unty.** They rise up to the crotch and are tied to the waist belt with loops. The **unty** usually are sewn out of deer, goat or horse skin taken from their lower legs. They are worn with the fur side out.

Clothing. Your clothing should not be too tight or confining. Dry it well before a march. Check the functioning of all your buttons and buckles. It is more effective to have several layers of relatively light clothes rather than one heavy layer. When moving very fast, remove your upper layer and tie it to your rucksack. At the halt, put it on to keep warm.

After spending the night on snow, use any opportunity to dry your clothing. If you are sleeping without a blanket, insert some hay between your underwear and your outer clothing. It will warm you.

Men should put sewn triangles made out of soft cloth on top of their long underpants to prevent frostbite to the genitalia. The cloth of the triangles should be easily washable. As a last resort, put several layers of crushed newspaper inside your underpants.

Women should sew one-two layers of fabric inside of their blouses, sweaters and shirts to protect their breasts from freezing.

Wash your clothing, underwear, socks, foot-cloths and mittens frequently because dirty and sweat-saturated clothing does not provide good protection against frost.

Mittens. The best gloves are those with two fingers – a thumb and an index finger. It makes shooting easier. Leather or canvas mittens are a good idea.

Headgear. Your headgear should fit tightly in the heavy frost to protect you from freezing wind. Pay special attention to your ears. If you do not have a hat with earflaps – make one yourself. Make earflaps out of warm cloth or fur and sew them to your hat.

Make a mask out of soft fabric with eye slits and a mouth opening to protect your face from very heavy frost and cold wind.

Fat – protection from the cold. Before a march during heavy frost and strong wind, put some fat (unsalted) on your most vulnerable body parts: nose, ears, cheeks, chin and fingers.

The appropriate kinds of fat are pork lard, goose fat or butter. Do not use Vaseline. Rub the fat into your skin, leaving some on the surface. It is better to do this immediately before leaving.

SIGNS OF FROSTBITE

In frostbite, the skin becomes pale and loses sensitivity. After warming, the spot swells and becomes red and painful. Later it acquires a bluish-crimson color and gets covered with blisters containing a clouded bloody liquid. Finally, in addition to the blisters, some scabs appear on the body and the flesh becomes necrotic – producing gangrene.

General freezing begins with shivering, a sense of weakness and tiredness. This is followed by irresistible sleepiness. The limbs become numb and breathing slows and cardiac activity weakens. If first aid is not administered in time, the person will die in their sleep.

FIRST AID FOR FROSTBITE

At the first signs of frostbite, immediately begin to rub pale skin with a woolen mitten or coat sleeve. Do it briskly until skin does not retain a red color and sensitivity returns. It is better to do this in a warm place. After this treatment, rub the spot with fat and keep the patient in a warm room.

In a case of heavy frostbite, wipe the injured spot with alcohol and put on a clean bandage. Then elevate the injured to ensure blood drainage.

Do not pierce the blisters as this can produce festering in the wound.

In cases of very heavy frostbite, move the injured to a medical unit.

In a case of general freezing, move the injured into a warm room or covered space, undress him and rub his body with mittens and pieces of woolen cloth. If the patient shows no signs of life, give him artificial respiration (see figure 302).

After the injured regains consciousness, cover him warmly and give some hot drink.

Chapter notes

1 **Объединение государственных книжно-журнальных издательст**, [United government book-journal publishing house], the publishing monopoly established in the Soviet Union in 1930.
2 Stalin is referring to the Russian proverb, **За двумя зайцами погонишься – ни одного не поймаеш**, if you chase two rabbits, you won't catch either.
3 Mikhail Ivanovich Kalinin was the President of the Supreme Soviet of the Soviet Union from 1938 to 1946.
4 This is a very dangerous hand grenade—to the user. The grenade must be primed immediately before use—not very convenient in combat and the grenade is activated by holding the safety retainer left with the right thumb. Once the grenade is thrown or the thumb slips off the retainer, the grenade fuse is ignited. Soviet soldiers avoided using this grenade and preferred to use captured German "potato masher" grenades.
5 There were two types of DEGTYAREV – the DT for tanks and the DP – for infantry; the infantry model had a stock.
6 This drops the magazine to the ground so that the weapon runs out of ammunition. It does nothing to fix the main problem which is probably a broken sear.
7 Other sources state that the light-weight bullet cartridge primer seat is green and the heavy-weight bullet cartridge primer seat is black. The light-weight bullet was 154 grains while the heavy-weight bullet was 196 grains.
8 Once the MG-34 is fitted for magazine fire, it cannot fire belts until the lid is removed.
9 This is actually a Czechoslovak machine gun that had been produced at the Brno Arms plant since 1923. The Germans took over the plant when they took over Czechoslovakia. The British produced the weapon under license as the famous Bren gun.
10 Most Soviet grenades required last-minute priming and arming before employment. This was done by the combat soldier just before use.
11 The Soviet and Russian Army has long attacked with the war cry of "ura".
12 "Molotov cocktail" is a Western term which was first used by the Finn's during the Soviet-Finnish Winter War of 1939-1940. It was derisively named after the Soviet People's Commissar for Foreign Affairs, Vyacheslav Molotov. Such devices had been used earlier in the 1936-1939 Spanish Civil War.
13 KS is a Russian acronym for Kachygin Solodovnikov, the last names of the two

inventors. The Red Army issued two types of incendiary bottles. The self-igniting liquid KS, which is a blend of phosphorus and sulfur and has a very low melting point. Pure KS is yellow-green. KS bottles were plugged with rubber corks and their necks were reinforced with wire and tape. The other type of incendiary bottle had to be ignited. There were two incendiary blends for this type of bottle—#1 and #3. These blends were a mixture of gasoline and powders or fuel thickeners to turn the gasoline into a sticking gel similar to napalm or sterno. These blends are dark brown in color.

1 **Объединение государственных книжно-журнальных издательст**, [United government book-journal publishing house], the publishing monopoly established in the Soviet Union in 1930.

2 Stalin is referring to the Russian proverb, **За двумя зайцами погонишься – ни одного не поймаеш**, if you chase two rabbits, you won't catch either.

Zippo" by tank crews. The Soviets who received Lend-Lease Sherman tanks were also leery of them.

15 The book is giving sight range selections for various types of Soviet weapons. They range from 250 -600 meters, a function of the bullet's trajectory for each system.

16 Burning the material seems like a sure way of contaminating the area.

17 The handbook is referring to the short entrenching tool which is about two feet long. Red Army soldiers often filed its edge to a knife edge for close combat.

18 Europeans are accustomed to mushroom hunting in the woods and the Russians are among the most avid Europeans in pursuit of these edible fungi. While most Americans are hard pressed to identify any edible wild mushrooms beyond the morel, most Russians have at least a nodding acquaintance with various types of edible wild mushrooms. Wild mushrooms have long been a part of Russian farmer's markets and a staple in many Russian menus.

19 Stroganina comes from the Russian **строгат** – to plane. Sushi isn't just Japanese.

20 This is the local name for ocoka-sedge. Reprinted from "Molodaya Gvardia" edition, 1942.

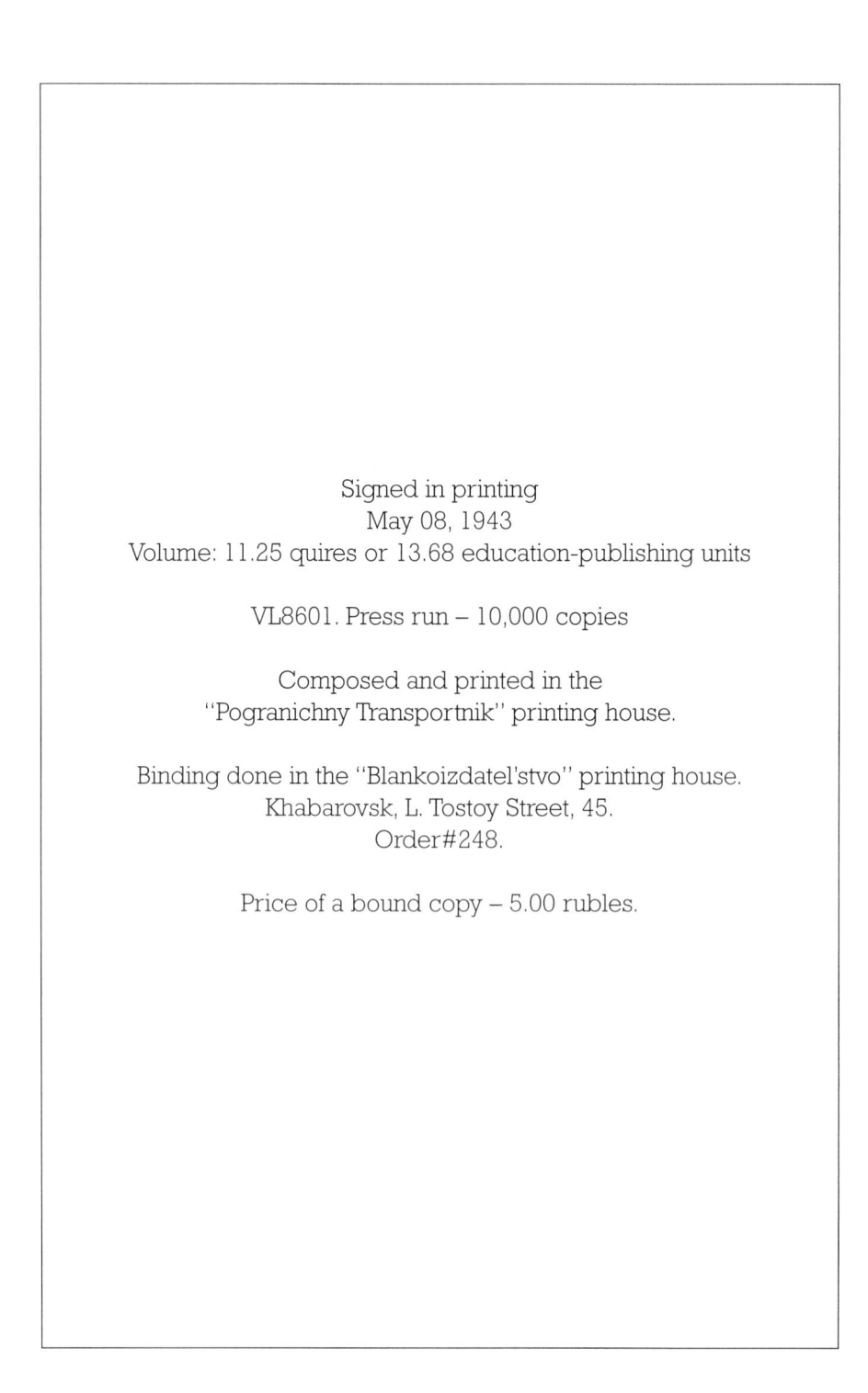

Signed in printing
May 08, 1943
Volume: 11.25 quires or 13.68 education-publishing units

VL8601. Press run – 10,000 copies

Composed and printed in the
"Pogranichny Transportnik" printing house.

Binding done in the "Blankoizdatel'stvo" printing house.
Khabarovsk, L. Tostoy Street, 45.
Order#248.

Price of a bound copy – 5.00 rubles.